Four Trines in Vedic Astrology

(A comprehensive Book on Vedic Astrology)

By

Jyotish Bhushan

Lakshmi Narayan Sharma

M.A. (Geography), B.Ed., S.R.

UNICORN BOOKS

Publishers
UNICORN BOOKS

F-2/16, Ansari Road, Daryaganj, New Delhi-110002
☎ 23275434, 23262683, 23262783 • Fax: 011-23257790
E-mail: info@unicornbooks.in • Website: www.unicornbooks.in

Distributors
Pustak Mahal®
J-3/16, Daryaganj, New Delhi-110002
☎ 23276539, 23272783, 23272784 • Fax: 011-23260518
E-mail: info@pustakmahal.com • Website: www.pustakmahal.com

Sales Centres
• 10-B, Netaji Subhash Marg, Daryaganj, New Delhi-110002
  ☎ 23268292, 23268293, 23279900 • Fax: 011-23280567
  E-mail: salespmahal@airtelmail.in, rapidexdelhi@indiatimes.com
• 6686, Khari Baoli, Delhi-110006
  ☎ 23944314, 23911979
• **Bengaluru:** ☎ 080-22234025 • Telefax: 080-22240209
  E-mail: pustak@airtelmail.in • pustak@sancharnet.in
• **Mumbai:** ☎ 022-22010941, 022-22053387
  E-mail: rapidex@bom5.vsnl.net.in
• **Patna:** ☎ 0612-3294193 • Telefax: 0612-2302719
  E-mail: rapidexptn@rediffmail.com
• **Hyderabad:** Telefax: 040-24737290
  E-mail: pustakmahalhyd@yahoo.co.in

ISBN 978-81-7806-197-9

Edition: July, 2010

Printed at : Param Offsetters, Okhla, New Delhi-110020

!! Shri Ganeshay Namah !!

Om Gajananam Bhutganadi Sevitam Jambuphal charu Bhakshanam
Uma Sutam Shokvinashkarkam Navami Vighneshwar Padpankjam

Om   Vakratund   Mahakay   Suryakoti   Samprabha
Nirvighanam   Kuru   Me   Deva   Sarva   Karyeshu   Sarvda

FOREWORD

Astrology is indeed a great human guide, which can give a fair idea of the possibilities in human life. The events in the life of an individual can be accurately predicted, which can help one to meet the ups and downs of life with equanimity to take full advantage of one's auspicious periods. Life on this planet as well as human behaviour is greatly influenced by planetary configurations and the transits, which highly influence the lives of natives in all spheres of human activity particularly health, happiness, marital bliss, financial gains, prestige, business acumen and most important of all is personal relations. One must have the right type of astro guidance to acquire the best of these virtues and for solving many vexing and intricate problems with timely effective remedial measures.

The main object of Astrology is to enable an individual to achieve the ideals, implied in the four fold Purusharthas i.e. Dharma (to follow the right path), Artha (to earn money), Kama (fulfilment of desires) and Moksha (liberation and emancipation). In order to attain Moksha, release from worldly bondage is a primary condition. To achieve this it is necessary to develop calmness of mind and leave (destroy) all human desires. Astrology helps one to note the pitfalls in one's progress through various phases of life and helps get over them with least mental disturbance and thus providing perfect mental equilibrium.

Past few decades have witnessed a phenomenal upsurge in the field of astrology and the intelligentia has become wilfully receptive towards its genuinity by appreciating its sound principles and unchallenging efficacy in a manner more cordial than ever before. There was a time in not very distant past that the savants considered this ancient Indian Wisdom as an admixture of dogmas and superstitions, but the veteran author of this book, Sh. Lakashmi Narayan Sharma has been constantly making efforts in writing to remove the cobwebs of ignorance that have come to cluster round this divine science of astrology.

Lakshmi Narayan Sharmaji with his matchless analytical acumen and superb scientific temperament inculcated under the rigorous discipline of research work of several decades has completed an unparalleled treatise for the students of Astrology. He has another masterpiece to his credit named "Jyotish Pradeep" in Hindi, which was very well received in the market and has gone in to second edition soon after.

"Four Trines In Vedic Astrology" is a comprehensive description of Vedic Astrology and presents this difficult subject in a simple, practical and lucid way. Topics mainly included are the prediction of houses (Bhavas) in the form of four Trines i.e. Dharma, Artha, Kama and Moksha Houses, Star Constellations, Signs of Zodiac, Planets, Significance of Yogas and Life Related Important Aspects. It also outlines the remedial measures of Vedic Astrology including Mantras, Yantras, and Gemstones etc.

The basic tenets and principles explained in the several chapters of the book have been tested and tried and I sincerely hope that the general guidelines contained in the book would be found useful and helpful by one and all. An attempt has been made in this book to bring to you in a capsule, the wider influences and impact of ancient Hindu Astrology in a fairly exhaustive manner, including the significance of planetary configuration and their impact on human life.

I heartily congratulate Lakshmi Narayan Sharma for his highly useful contribution in authoring the treatise, which constitutes a most helpful and elucidative addition to the existing literature on the subject, which is highly useful to every professional as also to the beginners in this field.

Dr. Shukdev Chaturvedi
M.A.,Phd.
Awardee Hon'ble Presidend of India.
Former Dean Ved & Astrology Department,
Shri Lal Bhadur Rashtriya Sanskrit Vidyapeeth, Delhi

PREFACE

Indian Astrology is Vedic Astrology. It is a vast subject. It is the science or knowledge of time. It is the mother of Astronomy, Cosmo-mathematics and Metaphysics. So there are many type of books on the different aspects of Astrology such as Star Constellations, Signs of Zodiac , Houses and Planets. Casting a Birth Chart, Judging a birth chart, Twelve Houses and their predictions, Vimshotri dasha results etc.

Vedic Hindu Culture lays stress on four primary goals of an ideal life i.e. Dharma, Artha, Kama and Moksha. One should perform one's duties according to tenets of one's Dharma and earn one's livlihood. From such righteous earnings, one should spend on one's legitimate desires i.e. pleasures and physiological necessities. At the same time, the person should practise virtue and spare something for the deprived, who don't have basic facilities to live.

This book aims the right place of Dharma, Artha, Kama and Moksha houses in one's birth chart in the form of Trines. To the best of my knowledge no such book is avilable at the moment, which has been written from this angle. Dharma (religion) means duty, Artha (wealth) means prosperity, Kama (desires) means fun and pleasures, and Moksha (salvation) means union with God, the essence of Hindu way of life.

This book is written in simple language, which could easily be understood by a common man. Several astrological terms used in Hindi are given in parenthesis. They are also given in a glossary at the end of the book.

This book is of its own kind to relate predictions of houses (Bhavas) in the form of four trines. Each trine has three houses of similar parameters. There are twelve houses in a birth chart and these are classified in four trines as:

First trine (Purush Trine) of Dharma relates to first, fifth and ninth houses.

Second trine (Aishwarya Trine) of Artha relates to second, sixth and tenth houses.

Third trine (Prakrati Trine) of Kama relates to third, seventh and eleventh houses.

Fourth trine (Vairagya Trine) of Moksha relates to fourth, eighth and twelfth houses.

The book has nine chapters. The **first chapter** describes as to why Indian astrology is Vedic astrology, which is the most accurate and the oldest.

The **second chapter** indicates constellations and their effects, signs of zodiac with their characteristics and planets with their Vedic qualities and mottos.

The **Third chapter** deals with the casting of all types of birth charts; either in Indian or in Western style easily, with the help of almanacs or ephemeris with examples of each style. All the points regarding overall effects of each house with their significations and significators, principles and rules that judge them, are described.

From **fourth to seventh chapters** contain the significations of all the 12 houses and their effects as per placements, aspects and combinations of planets in houses. The **fourth chapter** describes first trine Dharma houses. **Fifth chapter** describes second trine Artha houses. **Sixth chapter** describes third trine Kama houses. **Seventh chapter** describes fourth trine Moksha houses. Each chapter is explained with examples. In all 36 Kundlis of various dignitaries and famous persons of India and abroad along with the planetary positions in their charts are given.

Different type of Combinations of the planets in the houses and signs produce varioursYogas. Their effects have been explair.ed in **chapter Eighth**.

The **Ninth chapter** deals with important questions relating longevity, education, profession, marriage, children, financess foreign travels, various male/female diseases and their remedial measures. All these aspects of life are explained with examples more than 24 kundlis (Birth Charts) and their astrological observations.

I am thankful to Dr. Shukdev Chaturvedi M.A., Ph.D., Awardee by the Hon'ble President of India and Former Dean, Ved and Astrology Deptt.Shri Lal Bahadur Rastriya Sanskrit Vidhyapeeth, Delhi, who went through the typescript of this book and encouraged me getting it printed.

Lakshmi Narayan Sharma
E mail : lakshmi_parwati@yahoo.com

ACKNOWLEDGEMENTS

I sincerely express my thanks and gratitude to my wife **Smt. Parwati Devi** and my eldest son **Rajesh Bharti** to encourage me to write this book.

I am thankful to my youngest son **Tarun Bharti** and daughter in law **Sunita Sharma** for helping me in typing, editing the typescript, tables and birth charts.

I feel obliged to my friend Professor **Ajeet Singh** for his valuable suggestions to present the text in a more explicit and systematic form.

Thanks are due to **Shri S. P. Gaur**, Director, Nakshatra Niketan, Gurgaon an astrologer for his advice on the contents of the book.

Lastly, I am thankful to **Dr. Ashok Gupta**, M. D. Unicorn books, for making this book available to the readers and astrologers.

Lakshmi Narayan Sharma

CONTENTS

৪০৪৪

Indian Astrology is Vedic Astrology

On the basis of Ancient Hindu Vedas / Puranas (Vedic Scriptures), three Yugas in the history of mankind namely Satyuga (Golden Age), Tretayuga (Silver Age) and Dwaparyuga (Bronze Age) have passed thousand centuries earlier. Presently, we are living in Kaliyuga, the last and fourth Yuga called Iron Age. Kaliyuga machines and devices minimize the distance between the countries. Now the world has become one. We can communicate with someone in another corner of the world at a moment's notice and go around the world in a day. Our life is faster. International brotherhood is coming closer. But we have become more power hungry, more money oriented and more materialistic. Consequently we have lost the path of the truth and abandoned most social values. As a result, malpractices, corruptions, crimes and wars of terrorism are expanding day by day all over the world. Our researchers have been trying their best to control everything in nature but Birth and Death are still in the hands of the Omnipresent, Omniscient and Omnipotent, the Almighty God. The Vedic astrology helps us to understand all this.

1.1 Vedic Astrology and ancient Vedas

Ancient Vedas (Vedic Scriptures) are six thousand years old sacred texts in the Sanskrit literature. They are the first and foremost in authority, importance and ideal life for the development of Hindu Culture and Civilization. About great teachings of ancient Hindu Vedas, Purans and Upanishads (Sacred books of Hindus) some philosophers, logicians, mathematicians, astrophysicist and historians express their opinion as under :

1. **Henry David Thoreau**, an American philosopher and writer wrote," Whenever I read any part of Vedas, I have felt that some unearthly and unknown light illuminated me. In the great teachings of Vedas, there is no touch of sectarianism. It is, of all ages, climes and nationalities and is the royal road to the attainment of great knowledge. When I am at it, I feel that I am under the spangled heavens of summer night."

2. **Arthur Schopenhauer**, a German philosopher and author wrote, "In the whole world there is no study so beneficial and so elevating as that of Upanishads. It has been the solace of my life and it will be solace of my death."

3. British mathematician, a logician, philosopher and author **Alfred North Whitehead** wrote," Vedanta is the most impressive Metaphysics, the human mind is conceived."

4. **Dr. Carl Sagan**, an astrophysicist and author in his book 'Cosmos' wrote," The Hindu religion is the only one of the world's great faiths dedicated to the idea that the Cosmos itself undergoes an immense, indeed an infinite number of deaths and rebirths. It is the only religion, in which the time scales correspond to those of modern scientific Cosmology. Its cycles run from our ordinary day and night to a day and night of Brahma 8.64 billions years long, longer than the age of Earth and Sun and about half the time since The Big Bang. And there are much longer time scales still."

5. **Romain Rolland**, a French professor of History told," Religious faith in case of the Hindus had never been allowed to run counter to scientific laws."

1.2 Jyotish Vedang – A Segment of Vedas

As per our great seer Maharishi Lagadh "Jyotish Vedang" is the fourth segment out of six segments of Vedas. It is the world's oldest Sanskrit text of Indian astrology. It is one of the most important gifts of Hindu Vedas to the mankind. Therefore Indian astrology is known as Vedic Astrology. In Sanskrit language, it is called "Jyotish". Regarding Jyotish, its place and position in the Vedas here is a famous *Shlok*:

" *Yatha Shikha Mayuranam Naganam Manyo Yatha,*

Tavadvedangshastranam Jyotisham Murdhani Sthitam. "

This *shlok* indicates that "Jyotish" (Vedic Astrology) is the best segment of the Hindu Vedas. "Jyotish" shines like Mayursikha and Nagmani. "Jyotish" controls the seed stores of the Vedas and nourishes the seeds to make them fruitful and beneficial to the mankind. Therefore those, who have its deep knowledge, get salvation along with timely Dharma, Artha and Kama locations in life. Here is a Shlok-

"Jyotishchakre Tu Lokasya Sarvshyoktam Shubhashubham,

Jyotirgyanam Tu Yo Ved Sa Yaati Parmam Gatim."

It tells that Jyotish Chakra (chart) defines auspicious and inauspicious facts of life. Therefore the people, who care and study Jyotish, the science or knowledge of time, follow dharma (Religion), earn artha (Wealth), enjoy kama activities (Desires) i.e. all the fun and pleasures of life, lastly obtain *Moksha* (salvation) in life.

Three words of Sanskrit "Jyotisham Vedanam Chakshu" are remarkable. Indeed "Jyotish" is the eyes of the ancient Vedic scriptures. "Jyotish" is a science or knowledge of time. It looks into the human's past, present, and future. It reminds us of our past Karmas (actions) done before coming in to the existence and now our present Karmas (actions) after being born. It works to identify our actions when and why what to do and what not to do and how to perform Karmas (actions) best in time, so that we can be healthier and happier keeping our future life more comfortable, peaceful, respectable, honourable and over all an ideal life? Therefore Indian astrology is called Vedic Astrology.

1.3 Vedic Astrology and Karmas

In a fundamental way, Vedic astrology is based on Karmas (actions), which decide the destiny (fortune) of every human being. Good deeds result in an ideal life and a path to *Moksha* (salvation). *Moksha* means relief from the stresses of the formal events of worldly life. People, who have done good deeds, are always found enlightened. They meditate and unite with nature. They balance themselves and do traditional rites and rituals to appease Almighty God leaving all things on Him. Bad deeds (Dushkarmas) lead them to 84000 *yonis* (births) and life in every birth towards sins and sorrows.

So those, who never think of doing good deeds and are rolling in *Mayamoh* i.e. are always busy in earning wealth and fulfilling various Kama activities, are always found passing through miseries and misfortunes. Their life becomes hell. Dharma is a gateway to know the destiny of life. It is the first step of fourfold goals of human existence to make life prosperous and happy.

1.4 Fourfold goals of human existence

Dharma, Artha, Kama and Moksha are the fourfold goals of human existence. These are the essence of Hindu way of life. The great Hindu Seers and Sages of epic age namely Parashar, Varahmihir, Garga, Jaimini and many others clearly laid down the theory and details of these goals thinking, that the real purpose of human life lies in them. They are defined as below:

1. Dharma (Religion) means duty, righteousness and virtue.
2. Artha (Wealth) means success, prosperity and fame.
3. Kama (Desires) means fun, pleasures and sensual delight.
4. Moksha (Salvation) means liberation, spiritual performances and union with God.

The first three out of these constitute the path of an active life called 'Pravrati' the nature and temperament. This Pravrati is to be gained in domestic life being a member of the society. He is to discharge his duties as a householder and a citizen. He is to acquire wealth, gratify his legitimate desires and at the same time practice virtue. The first stage of life, for which his whole career has been a preparation, is one of 'Nivrati' the complete surrender and union with God and hence the *Moksha* (Salvation). Thus, this formula Dharma, Artha, Kama, Moksha, that indicates the ideal of a complete life taking into account of all facts of human nature without doing violence either to the flesh or to the spirit, is the base of Vedic astrology.

1.5 Fourfold goals place in a Birth chart

In Vedic Astrology these goals are given the right place in a birth chart, therefore 1st, 5th, 9th, houses are called Dharma houses, 2nd, 6th, 10th houses Artha houses, 3rd, 7th, 11th houses Kama houses and 4th, 8th, 12th houses *Moksha* houses. Kama sense gratification, is the lowest state of existence for the living entity. Artha means economics development. It becomes helpful for the human being to achieve and maintain sense gratification and Dharma turning away from animal life and accepting / adopting godliness, the path to *Moksha*. The following chart representing all the four goals, Dharma, Artha, Kama & Moksha, is presented for the reader's benefit.

Dharma, Artha, Kama, Moksha Houses

Figure1.5 (F-1)

Indian astrology acts and directs the human beings, how to lead an ideal life? The Western astrology differs with the Vedic or Indian astrology mainly because of that. The main differences are givevn have under:

1.6 Differences between Vedic & Western astrology

1. Vedic astrology deals with both inner and outer life of a person, whereas Western astrology deals with only outer realm of a person.

2. Vedic astrology refers ascendant's position in the sky, while Western astrology refers only Sun's position. Ascendant changes its position after about every two hours, while Sun changes its position after every month.

3. Vedic astrology uses sidereal zodiac of constellations (Nakshatras), while Western astrology uses tropical zodiac of signs (Rashis). Western astrology focuses primarily on analysis and psychological matters, while Vedic astrology focuses both on analysis and therapies to remove problems.

4. Vedic astrology uses Sun, Moon, Mars, Mercury, Jupiter, Venus and Saturn as planets along with two shadowy planets north node and south node of Moon namely Rahu and Ketu,

while Western astrology uses all the ten star planets. Out of these Uranus, Neptune and Pluto three slower moving planets are totally unseen by naked eye. They are of no use and don't seem to have much effect. Moreover predictions are overall in general.

5.   Vedic astrology adopts the equal house system of 30* Degree each, looks into qualitative and quantitative influence of aspects, degree of power of yogas (special combination of planets), time of event through Vimshotri and Yogini dashas and prepare Shodasvarga divisional charts for better results. Western astrology does not have such interpretive techniques. This is the reason, that many people in India educated or illiterate, such as priests, officers, executives, employees, workers, shopkeepers believe in Vedic astrology and take the benefit of remedial measures (spiritual performances) from time to time.

1.7 Vedic Astrology is oldest and most accurate

Vedic astrology is considered to be one of the oldest, most accurate and consistent form of astrology all over the world. Though some people may argue yet there is no place for arguments as per the following *shlok*:

" Apratyakshani   Shastrani   Vivadasteshu   Kevalam,
Pratyaksham Jyotisham Shastram Chandrarkayu yatra Sakshino."

It means that "Jyotish" is the practical science of time, where the Sun and the Moon witness the mankind on earth. The daily changes in weather and timely eclipses of Sun and Moon affect and create problems in the way of man's daily life. Hence it is very much the true science. It is generally regarded predictive in nature and essential to the conduct of any of the events of life since early birth such as child's name, his/her early education, his/her admission to school, his/her timely marriage, applying for a post or a job, starting a new business, joining a service, buying / building a new house, participating in politics / elections, traveling abroad and so on. To millions of Hindus the birth chart called "Janam Kundli" is an invaluable possession for a man or woman from the time of his/her birth to know the course of life.

ॐ

Chapter

2

Constellations, Signs of Zodiac, Planets

2.1 Constellations (Nakshatras) - What is a constellation?

First we take Constellations. Our learned seers and sages have divided the 360^0 degrees of Zodiac in 27 sub divisions for astrological considerations. One sub division consisting of several stars or a group of stars having special shape and size like horse, dog, snake, deer, elephant etc. is called the area of one constellation. It is further divided in four segments / quadrants. They are named after the bigger stars of the groups such as Krittika for Pleiades, Rohini for Aldebaran, Mrigshira for Lambda Orionis, Ardra for Betel Geuse, Punarvasu for Pollux, and so on.

Actually these constellations are used as imaginary milestones or sky rail stations to know the angular distance of the planets, which they come in the way of the Moon's revolution around earth. One full day travel distance of the Moon makes one *tithi* (lunar date). Indian Almanacs (Panchangs) show these *tithis* (lunar dates) along with calendar dates (solar dates). *Tithi* and day starts from one sunrise and ends at next sunrise, while calendar date and day starts from one midnight and ends at next midnight. One constellation in degrees is $360^. \div 27 = 13^.\text{-}20'$ and its one segment / quadrant in degrees is $13^.\text{-}20' \div 4 = 3^.\text{-}20'$. Nine segments or 2 ¼ constellations totalling $30^.$ degrees confirm a *sign* (Rashi). It indicates, that some of the constellations are not fully confined to a sign. They overlap the signs. For this purpose, please see natural characteristics of 27 constellations with 12 signs table 2 .1 (T-1) given on next page.

Natural Characteristics of 27 Constellations with 12 Signs Table-2.1(T-1)

Sr. No	English Name	Vedic Name	Diety	Sex	Element	Segment	Segment Owner	Dasha Years	Nakshtra Paya	Moon's motion D. M. S.	Signs
1	Beta Arietis	Ashwini	Ashwini	M	Fire	1,2,3,4	Ketu	07	Gold	00°-13'-20"	Aries (Mesh)
2	Gama Arietis	Bharni	Yamraj	F	Fire	1,2,3,4	Venus	20	Gold	00°-26'-40"	Aries (Mesh)
3	Pleiades	Krittika	Agni	F	Fire	1	Sun	06	Gold	01°-10'-00"	Aries (Mesh)
	Pleiades	Krittika	Agni	F.	Earth	2,3,4	Sun	06	Gold	01°-10'-00"	Taurus (Vrishabh)
4	Aldebaran	Rohini	Brahma	F.	Earth	1,2,3,4	Moon	10	Gold	01°-23'-20"	Taurus (Vrishabh)
5	Lambda Orionis	Mrigshira	Chandra	N.	Earth	1,2	Mars	07	Gold	02°-06'-40"	Taurus (Vrishabh)
	Lambda Orionis	Mrigshira	Chandra	N	Air	3,4	Mars	07	Gold	02°-06'-40"	Gemini (Mithun)
6	Betel Geuse	Ardra	Rudra	F	Air	1,2,3,4	Rahu	18	Silver	02°-20'-00"	Gemini (Mithun)
7	Pollux	Punarvasu	Aditi	M	Air	1,2,3	Jupiter	16	Silver	03°-03'-20"	Gemini (Mithun)
	Pollux	Punarvasu	Aditi	M	Water	4	Jupiter	16	Silver	03°-03'-20"	Cancer (Kark)
8	Delta Caneri	Pushya	Guru	M	Water	1,2,3,4	Saturn	19	Silver	03°-16'-40"	Cancer (Kark)
9	Hydrae	Ashlesha	Sarpa	M	Water	1,2,3,4	Mercury	17	Silver	04°-00'-00"	Cancer (Kark)
10	Regulas	Magha	Pitara	F	Fire	1,2,3,4	Ketu	07	Silver	04°-13'-20"	Leo (Simha)
11	Delta Leonis	Poorva Phalguni	Bhaga	F.	Fire	1,2,3,4	Venus	20	Silver	04°-26'-40"	Leo (Simha)
12	Beta Leonis	Uttra Phalguni	Aryama	F.	Fire	1	Sun	06	Silver	05°-10'-00"	Leo (Simha)
	Beta Leonis	Uttra Phalguni	Aryama	F.	Earth	2,3,4	Sun	06	Silver	05°-10'-00"	Virgo (Kanya)
13	Delta Corvi	Hasta	Surya	M.	Earth	1,2,3,4	Moon	10	Silver	05°-23'-20"	Virgo (Kanya)
14	Spica	Chitra	Vishwa.	F.	Earth	1,2	Mars	07	Silver	06°-06'-40"	Virgo (Kanya)

#	Star	Nakshatra	Deity	Gender	Element	Pada	Lord	No.	Metal	Degrees	Sign
15	Spica	Chitra	Vishwa.	F.	Air	3,4	Mars	07	Silver	06°-06'-40"	Libra (Tula)
16	Arcturus	Swati	Vayu	F.	Air	1,2,3,4	Rahu	18	Silver	06°-20'-00"	Libra (Tula)
16	Alpha Librae	Vishakha	Indragini	F.	Air	1,2,3	Jupiter	16	Iron	07°-03'-20"	Scorpio (Vrishchik)
	Alpha Librae	Vishakha	Indragini	F.	Water	4	Jupiter	16	Iron	07°-03'-20"	Scorpio (Vrishchik)
17	Delta Scorpii	Anuradha	Mitra	M.	Water	1,2,3,4	Saturn	19	Iron	07°-16'-40"	Scorpio (Vrishchik)
18	Antares	Jyeshtha	Indra	F.	Water	1,2,3,4	Mercury	17	Iron	08°-00'-00"	Scorpio (Vrishchik)
19	Lambda Scorpii	Moola	Raksha	N.	Fire	1,2,3,4	Ketu	07	Iron	08°-13'-20"	Sagittarius (Dhanu)
20	DeltaSagittarii	Poorva Ashadha	Jal	F.	Fire	1,2,3,4	Venus	20	Copper	08°-26'-40"	Sagittarius (Dhanu)
21	Sigma Sagittarii	Uttar Ashadha	Vishve.	F.	Fire	1	Sun	06	Copper	09°-10'-00"	Sagittarius (Dhanu)
	Sigma Sagittarii	Uttar Ashadha	Vishve.	F.	Earth	2,3,4	Sun	06	Copper	09°-10'-00"	Sagittarius (Dhanu)
22	Altair	Shravan	Vishnu	M.	Earth	1,2,3,4	Moon	10	Copper	09°-23'-20"	Capricorn (Makar)
23	BetaDelphini	Dhanishtha	Vasu	F.	Earth	1,2	Mars	07	Copper	10°-06'-40"	Capricorn (Makar)
	BetaDelphini	Dhanishtha	Vasu	F.	Air	3,4	Mars	07	Copper	10°-06'-40"	Capricorn (Makar)
24	Lambda Aquarii	Shatbhisha	Varuna	N.	Air	1,2,3,4	Rahu	18	Copper	10°-20'-00"	Aquarius (Kumbh)
25	Alpha Pegasi	Poorva Bhadrapad	Surya	M.	Air	1,2,3	Jupiter	16	Copper	11°-03'-20	Aquarius (Kumbh)
	Alpha Pegasi	Poorva Bhadrapad	Surya	M.	Water	4	Jupiter	16	Copper	11°-03'-20"	Pisces (Meen)
26	Gama Pegasi	Uttra Bhadrapad	Ahirbu.	M.	Water	1,2,3,4	Saturn	19	Copper	11°-16'-40"	Pisces (Meen)
27	Zeta Piscium	Revti	Pusha	F.	Water	1,2,3,4	Mercury	17	Gold	12°-00'-00"	Pisces (Meen)

2. 2 Classification of constellations

After many decades, now the position of each constellation is seen a little bit backward in the sky. It is because of the motions of our earth, but there is no ill effect of that. Favourables are positive and beneficial as usual. Adverse are always adverse and harmful. Constellations on the basis of their nature and temperament can be classified as below:

1. Favourable-1, 3, 4, 5, 7, 8, 12, 13, 14, 15, 16, 17, 21, 22, 23, 24, 26, 27.
2. Cruel-2, 9,10,11, 20,25.
3. Violent-6, 9,18,19.

Note: Out of the above classification, five are Panchak sangyak No.23, 24, 25, 26, 27, six are Mool sangyak No.1, 9, 10, 18, 19, 27 and six are Gand nakshatras - first two ghatis (48 minutes) of No.1, 9, 10 constellations and last two ghatis (48 minutes) of No. 18,19,27 constellations. Here one thing is also notable that out of the above listed 27 constellations except favourables No. 9 is overlapping in cruel and violent classification. So nature of nakshatra No. 9 may also be kept in mind while predicting a birth chart.

If we count further from the birth constellation, their nature and temperament may change and disfavour the person. Please see column "Result" in the table 2.2 (T-2) given below.

Constellations and their Nature Table-2.2 (T-2)
(Counted from Birth Constellation)

Sr. No	NakshtraStar	Constellations from Birth			Result
1	Janam	1	10	19	Favourable
2	Sampat	2	11	20	Favourable
3	Vipat	3	12	21	Adverse
4	Kshem	4	13	22	Favourable
5	Pratyari	5	14	23	Adverse
6	Sadhak	6	15	24	Favourable
7	Vadh	7	16	25	Adverse
8	Mitra	8	17	26	Favourable
9	Atimitra	9	18	27	Favourable

The table of rulers of each segment / quadrant called "Charans" in Sanskrit is also given below for the very purpose, that you can easily know the birth constellation with its segment ruler-table 2.2 (T-3) given below.

Rulers of Constellations Segments (Charans) Table-2.2 (T-3)

Constellations(Numbers)	Charan	Charan	Charan	Charan
	I	II	III	IV
1,4,7,10,13,16,19,22,25	Mars	Venus	Mercury	Moon
2,5,8,11,14,17,20,23,26	Sun	Mercury	Venus	Mars
3,6,9,12,15,18,21,24,27	Jupiter	Saturn	Saturn	Jupiter

2.3 Effects of Constellations at birth

1. Ashwini-Beautiful, healthy, happy, simple living, high thinking, intelligent, clever, successful, wealthy, popular, liked by all.
2. Bharni-Healthy, truthful, balanced, learned, wealthy, fatalist, selfish, violent, always gloomy and unhappy.
3. Krittika-Handsome, bold, brave, strong, knowledgeable, good connections in high circles, famous, fond of rich food, lustful, hopeful, miser, deceitful.
4. Rohini-Tall and thin, balanced mind, good eyesight, soft-spoken, truthful, charitable, evil-minded, sarcastic nature.
5. Mrigshira-Good natured, good talker, easygoing, happy, wealthy, proud, feeling inferiority complex and sickly.
6. Ardra-Healthy, gentle, religious, powerful, selfish, mean, ungrateful, short tempered, wicked, foolish, becomes poor.
7. Punarvasu-Well behaved, devotee to parents, gentle, tactful, clever, cunning, harsh tongue, living abroad, may be drunkard.
8. Pushya-Good natured, virtuous, learned, righteous, dutiful, wealthy, famous, honourable, loves family, ethist.
9. Ashlesha-Strong, joyful, learned, multitongued, aggressive, non-vegetarian, ungrateful, deceitful, win over enemies.
10. Magha-Studious, courageous, wealthy, loving flowers, God fearing, ethist, many servants, proud, sexy.

11. Poorva Phalguni-Sweet spoken, far-sighted, successful, charitable, capable pandit (priest), honourable, happy, but worried.

12. Uttara Phalguni-Healthy, balanced, intelligent, knowledgeable, truthful, popular, have children, like a saint, short tempered.

13. Hasta-Learned, bold, courageous, grateful, wealthy, influential, merciless, shameless, potential thief.

14. Chitra-Good constitution, Smiling figure, good natured, wealthy, writer, dull, idle, miserly, deliberate, fond of ornaments and jewellery.

15. Swati-Well behaved, knowledgeable, administrative post, dutiful, sweet spoken, god-fearing, theist, have sons, charitable.

16. Vishakha-Good orator, serviceman, God-fearing, religious, short-tempered, jealous, greedy, miserly, proud.

17. Anuradha-Handsome, dutiful, wealthy, honourable, happy, facility of vehicles, flare for sex, always journey abroad, loves pan (betel leaf).

18. Jyeshtha-Joyful, religious, charitable, becomes poor, few friends, harsh tongue, cruel, juggler and liar.

19. Moola-Good talker, disciplined, balanced mind, ease loving, short-tempered, harsh tongue, have proud, jealous, hates relatives.

20. Poorva Ashadha-Tall, peace-loving, far-seeing, fortunate, kind to mother, loves wife, truthful, journey abroad, wealthy, many friends.

21. Uttara Ashadha-Bold, brave, energetic, humble, knowledgeable, god-fearing, grateful, popular, loves parents and relatives, good understanding.

22. Shravana-Enthusiastic, intelligent, learned, gentle, humble, high post, loves opposite sex, cautious, loves perfume.

23. Dhanishtha-Noble, valiant, fearless, high thinking, independent, esteemed, wealthy, book business, loves music.

24. Shatabhisha-Brave, courageous, uncompromising, tactful, truthful, capable, loved by high-ups, a good astrologer.

25. Poorva Bhadrapad- Always sad, unhappy, atheist, easily win over women, inherit money from them, avaricious, jealous, desperate.

26. Uttara Bhadrapad-Talkative, tactful, virtuous, fond of arguing, charitable, prolific in procreation, aptitude for learning.

27. Revti-Healthy, heroic, tactful, good speaker, most popular, weakness for women, scorns other's money, blameless, easily swayed.

Note: As stated above some segments of a few constellations called Moola sangyak are considered to be harmful for the person and his family. First segment of Ashwini, Magha and Moola nakshatras and fourth segment of Ashlesha and Jyeshtha nakshatras are said to be dangerous to the parents and the child. It is possible that child may not survive, and if it survives due to some good combinations, then he may be halo of glory in old age. If Moon is in first or second segment of Jyeshtha at birth, it may cause danger to the life of elder brother / younger brother. He may be sickly or die.

2.4 Signs of Zodiac (Rashis)-What is a Sign and Rising signs?

The zodiac, an imaginary circle of 360* degrees, is a broad belt in the heavens extending about 9* degrees on each side of the path of the Sun. This path of the Sun is called ecliptic and it passes through the centre of the zodiac. Our learned seers divided this zodiac in 12 groups of bigger stars having different shapes and sizes of living / non living things such as humans (a male or a female), animals (a lion or a bull), watery creatures (an alligator or a fish), non livings (a balance or a water pot), each sign of 30* degrees and thus twelve signs are known as Signs of zodiac (Rashis). The Sun takes about one month to cross one sign of zodiac to reach to the next, while Moon takes only 2.25 days to cross the area of a sign. All the 12 signs rise in the east every day after almost every two hours.

Now the question arises what is the rising sign (ascendant sign)? Rising sign is the base value and face value of a birth chart. Rising sign means the ascendant (lagna). Our Zodiac is constantly moving and all the twelve signs get an opportunity to rise to be an ascendant till the 24 hours comprising a day. Generally the duration of one ascendant sign is of two hours. Ascendant sign can also be Moon sign (Janam Rashi), if Moon occupies ascendant sign (lagna rashi).

Moon sign (Janma Rashi) means the sign, in which Moon is posited at the time of birth. In Vedic astrology Moon sign is called "Chandra lagna" and it is as important as lagna (Ascendant) in a birth chart. The effects of the signs, in which lagna and Chandra lagna falls, will almost be the same. Both should be taken together, while analyzing and predicting a birth chart.

2.5 Twelve Rising signs (Aries to Pisces)- Their characteristics

When a person takes birth and one of the signs of zodiac appears in the east as an ascendant (lagna), the following specific and essential features of lagna, individual's appearance and his/her personality traits emerge in the mind and body. An astrologer may describe properties / features of each sign as given below -

 1. Rising sign Aries (Mesh lagna)

It is the first sign of zodiac. It consists of Ashwini, Bharni and Krittika nakshatras. It is the sign of action and initiative of leadership and innovation. Its specific features with physical appearance and personality traits are as under-

i) Specific features

1. Owner of Mesh lagna- Mars

2. Benefics in Mesh lagna- Jupiter, Mars, Sun

3. Malefics in Mesh lagna-Mercury, Saturn, Venus

4. Marak planets in Mesh lagna- Mercury, Saturn

ii) Physical appearance

Persons born under Aries rising sign (Mesh lagna) are of middle stature. They possess a lean and muscular body. They are neither stout nor thick. They have ruddy complexion, broad head and narrow chin, fair long face and neck, curly rough hair, round eyebrows and a sharp eyesight. They may have a mark or scar on their head or forehead.

iii) Personality traits

As Mars, the planet of passions and anger rules this sign Aries, the persons are active and ambitious, bold and impulsive. If there is a bad influence, they might become rash and aggressive. If there are good influences on lagna they may feel confident, courageous, enterprising with high aims, most sympathetic, generous and sensitive.

Aries lagna persons desire to be the head of all the affairs according to their own independent thinking and judgement. They can guide, control and govern themselves and others. Aries, the positive sign of Mars gives determination and force of character, they act with self-confidence and interest. They have much executive ability and uncompromising spirit. Aries is a movable sign, hence they are capable of making changes quite often. Being a fiery sign, they are aggressive and their desire is always to implement their ideas as quickly as possible. Bad influences make the person somewhat quarrelsome and obstinate.

Aries lagna persons are over optimistic and they like to take up fresh ventures without completing the one already in hand. It is not good on their part. Sometimes they lose their credit being the previous work lying pending. Generally their impulsive and changeable moods are not capable of amassing wealth. Ups and downs may ever be seen in their life. They are good lovers and have a charming personality that attracts the opposite sex. If there are bad influences on the lagna, the persons may become jealous, passionate and they go astray.

Aries lagna persons shine in profession of martial nature as high officers in army or police. They can be good surgeons, chemists, law officers, civil, mechanical and electrical engineers, wrestlers, sportsmen or athlete. They may also be good artists, singers, actors and astrologers.

iv) Famous names

Alexender-the Great, King Prithviraj Chauhan, Netaji Subhash Chandra Bose,C.M. Dr. Sampurnanand, Sardar Ballabhbhai Patel, Actor Ashok kumar, Actress Smita patil,C.M. Haridev Joshi, Astrologer R.P. Gaur, C.M. Chandrababu Naidu, Gurudeva Ravi Shankar, Retd. Police Officer K.P.S.Gill.

2. Rising sign Taurus (Vrishabh Lagna)

It is the second sign of zodiac. It consists of Krittika, Rohini and Mrigshira nakshatras. It is the sign of energy, strength and endurance. Its specific features and other points related to physical appearance and personality traits are as under-

i) Specific Features

1. Owner of Vrishabh lagna-Venus
2. Benefics in Vrishabh lagna- Saturn, Mercury, Mars, Sun
3. Malefics in Vrishabh lagna - Jupiter, Moon
4. Marak planets in Vrishabh lagna - Jupiter, Mars

ii) Physical appearance

Taurus (Vrishabh) lagna persons are of medium stature and plumpy. But they have square build solid body with broad forehead, neck thick and stout, eyes and ears bright and large, hair dark, short and broad plumpy hands. Their complexion is very clear. They have strong stoop shoulders and muscles well developed.

iii) Personality traits

Taurus is a fixed and earthy sign, therefore this lagna people have great endurance and much patience. But when provoked, they become angry and vicious like a bull. They are slow and steady, plodding and persevering, patient and persistent. They are conservative and a man of strong will. They can be good administrator. They do not waste their energy. They do not act in an impulsive manner. They wait for the opportunity to come and then take full advantage of it.

If there are bad influences on lagna, they become lazy and self-indulgent. The persons of this lagna are fond of good food and are very much after money and other worldly possessions. They are ambitious and cheerful. Venus being the owner makes them fond of fun and pleasures, delights and enjoyments. Venus gives wealth. So they are fortunate and are favourites of Goddess Lakshmi. They worship Goddess Lakshmi.

They are sexy and steadfast in their love. Bad influences may make them interested in women other than their own wives. They are fond of music, arts, cinema, drama etc. because of Venus, the owner of the sign. They generally enjoy good health. If they fall ill, recovery in their case is slow. They accumulate and hoard money and are very cautious in spending. They never take risks in money matters. They are good husbands or wives and their domestic life is stable and happy.

They are generally attached to their birthplace. They take up trade of luxury goods such ৎ৵ cosmetics, scents, jewellery and gems. Being earthy sign, they can also be agriculturists and farmers. They can be actors or actresses, musicians, singers, dancers, film produc-ers, theatre owners etc.

iv) Famous names

Lord Krishna, Saint Gyaneshwar, Surya Narayan Rao, Lata mangeshkar, Manisha Koirala, George Bernardshaw, Jagdish Chandra Basu, Queen Victoria, Maharaja Sawai Jaisingh. Industrialist Rahul Bajaj, Actor turned politician Shatrughan Sinha

3.Rising sign Gemini (Mithun lagna)

It is the third sign of Zodiac. It consists of Mrigshira, Ardra and Punarvasu nakshatras. Its realm is that of communication and information. Its specific features with physical appearance and personality traits are as below-

i) Specific features

1.Owner of Mithun lagna- Mercury

2.Benifics in Mithun lagna-Venus

3.Malefics in Mithun lagna- Mars, Jupiter, Sun

4.Marak planets in Mithun lagna- Mars, Jupiter

ii) Physical appearance

Persons born in Gemini (Mithun) lagna are tall, upright, straight body. They have long face, long nose, long chin, long arms and fingers. Their complexion is moderate. They have dark hair, gray and sharp eyes. They look active. Actually they are weak and thin but bold, brave and energetic.

iii) Personality traits

Gemini is an airy sign. So persons of this lagna fly in the air. They are carefree and joyous. Their minds are positive and strong. They are versatile, restless and like changes. Very often, even if they do not like changes, they still get changes. Mercury being the owner of this sign, they are good readers, fond of writing and capable of acquiring good education. They have the capacity to adapt themselves to any circumstances.

Gemini is a dual sign. This makes the persons to travel frequently. They are always of dual minded and are, therefore, not able to take decisions quickly. They follow more than one occupation at a time. Their faults are mainly because of the duality in their nature that makes them fickle minded and unable to finish their work in time. In spite of these faults, they have intellectual qualities. They can understand, grasp and analyze things quickly. They have good retentive power and reproduction ability.

However, they do well when they work under some officer. They are not successful, when they are the heads or bosses. They are good husbands and wives, but they do not tolerate, if their married partners come in their way for love of variety and change. They are curious to know new things.

They can be good detectives, research scholars, computer wizards, chip makers, publishers, editors, journalists, commercials, travellers, accountants, mathematicians, lecturers, solicitors, professors, businessmen, secretaries, personal assistants, brokers and advertisers.

iv) Famous names

Great Poet Kalidass, Ex. P.M. Morarji Desai, President Dr. Jakir Hussain, Minister Arjun Singh, Deen Dayal Upadhyaya, Nathu Ram Godsey, Ram Krishna Dalmia, Pak. P.M. Julfikharali Bhutto, Poet Kaka Hathrasi, Actor Rajesh Khanna, Actress turned Politician J. Jaya Lalitha, Rahul Gandhi, Albert Einstien, Bill Gates, Vijay Raje Scindhia, President Pratibha Patil

 ## 4.Rising sign Cancer (Kark lagna)

It is the fourth sign of zodiac. It consists of Punarvasu, Pushya and Ashlesha nakshatras. It opens the hidden treasure of emotions lying within the protective outer shell. Its specific features with physical appearance and personality traits are as below:

i) Specific features

1.Owner of Kark lagna- Moon.

2.Benefics in Kark lagna- Jupiter, Mars

3.Malefics in Kark lagna- Venus, Mercury

4.Marak planets in Kark lagna- Venus, Mercury.

ii) Physical appearance

Persons with Cancer (Kark) lagna are of above average height, heavy body, slender limbs and tight claws. They have long face, wide chest. So the upper portion of body is generally large. They have light blue eyes. Their hands & feet are small. In later age, they get a fat abdomen and a pale complexion. They can only walk with a rolling gait.

iii) Personality traits

The owner of this sign Moon sometimes waning and sometimes waxing makes the persons life a remarkable and changeable especially when Saturn influences. If Moon is placed in a fixed sign 2nd, 5th, 8th and 11th, their nature becomes Moonlike full of tides and ebbs (ups and downs). Their imagination is fertile, but they are often seen emotional and over-sensitive but sympathetic. Because of sensitivity, there is a high degree of nervous irritability in their nature. They are timid at one time and courageous at other time.

In public life, they are generally successful and are able to achieve honours and wealth. They get angry suddenly but their anger disappears soon. They are fond of home and family comforts. They have a very good memory. When they get into old age, they take pleasure in telling to their grand children, the minute details of some good events, they passed in their life. Ladies with this lagna are discreet and independent in many ways. Often they are not easy to cope with the family because of their changing ideas and moods. They generally prosper in the later part of their life. They also get inheritances but after difficulties or obstructions.

Persons of this sign are fond of traveling. Cancer is a movable sign, so they are steadfast in their life. If Saturn is in 7th house, they generally have to face an unhappy married life. Benefic planets aspect the 7th house or the owner of 7th house then chances of happiness are possible. They take a long time in coming to a decision. They love money and like to hoard money. Many of them are of a miserly nature. They are all prone to digestive and lung troubles and also hysteria, nervous debility etc.

The professions suited for these persons are government service, commercial career, business in liquids, sea products, jewellery and gems, running restaurants. They can be good sailors, sea captains and explorers. If Jupiter is in this sign, they can also become leader or founder of an organization, jury judges or cabinet ministers.

iv) Famous names

Lord Shri Ram, Maharaja Veer Vikramaditaya, Gautam Budha, Prime-Minister Pt.Jawahar Lal Nehru and Indira Gandhi, Swami Aurobindo Ghosh, Prince Charles, Lokmanya Bal Gangadhar Tilak, Changez Khan, Mirza Ismail Beg, Dr. M. Chenna Reddy, Pakistan Ex. President Parvez Mussharaf. C.M. Mayawati, Ex. President USA Bill Clinton.

5.Rising sign Leo (Simha lagna)

It is the fifth sign of zodiac. It consists of Magha, Poorva Phalguni and Uttra Phalguni nakshatras. It illustrates the qualities of courage, leadership and pride. It has specific features, different physical appearance and personality traits of the person born in Leo lagna. They are as under-

i) Specific features

1. Owner of Simha lagna - Sun

2. Benefics in Simha lagna-Mars, Sun

3. Malefics in Simha lagna- Mercury, Venus

4. Marak Planets in Simha lagna-Mercury, Venus

ii) Physical appearance

Persons born in Leo ascendant whose owner is the Sun, are of well-developed bones and broad forehead. They have well built, moderate and muscular body. Their appearance is dignified, rather imposing and commanding. The significator of royalty and kingly the Sun with pictorial symbol of a lion make them bold and courageous. The above features will naturally be striking, if Sun is also situated in the sign Leo in the birth chart.

iii) Personality traits

They are generally sympathetic, generous and helpful to the mankind. They have great faith in friends and relatives. They may be head of some community or connected organizations. If they are in government service or in any commercial organisation, they attain high position there. They do not talk much. They are fair in their views and want to be treated as they deal or treat others.

Leo is a fiery sign. It gives authority, brilliance, high ambition and a boasting nature. They get honours and respect. They are kind and royal and like pomp and show. Leo is a fixed sign. There fore, a person born in this sign may be obstinate and firm in thinking and attitudes. One gets angry soon, but anger is short lived. He/she has a splendid constitution and recovers early from illness.

Leonines are generally extravagant, but if their financial position is not good, they have the capacity to face difficulties. They like gambling. They indulge in speculations. Leo lagna persons try to dominate their households. There may be peace at home, if all the members accept their authority. Very often their married life is unhappy. If his/ her life partner's lagna owner is an enemy as Saturn or Rahu, the married life becomes hell. They have often only one capable son in life.

Profession most suited to them is to be a leader of political party, president, prime minister, minister in the cabinet, army officers, higher post in government, business in jewellery, dealership in precious metals, actors, preachers.

iv) Famous names

Chhatrapati Shivaji, President Dr. Shankardayal, P.M. Rajeev Gandhi, Fieldmarshal Manekshah, President Johnson and Nixon, Ghanshyam Dass Birla, C.M. Bansi Lal, Actor Shahrukh Khan and Krishna Kant.

6.Rising sign Virgo (Kanya lagna)

It is the sixth sign of zodiac. It consists of Uttra Phalguni, Hasta and Chitra nakshatras. It symbolizes the harvesting of experiences and further their discrimination. The specific features, physical appearance and personality traits of the person, born in Virgo sign, are as below:

i) Specific features

1.Owner of Kanya lagna-Venus

2.Benefics in Kanya lagna-Venus

3.Malefics in Kanya lagna-Moon, Mars, Jupiter

4.Marak planets in Kanya lagna- Mars, Jupiter

ii) Physical appearance

Virgo (Kanya) lagna persons are tall with a slender body. They are moderately plumpy with oval face and dark hair. Their eyebrows are curved with hair growth. Their voice is very often thin and sometimes even shrill. They walk quickly and they seldom have a potbelly. They are very active and energetic. They often appear younger than their actual age.

iii) Personality traits

Virgo (Kanya) sign is ruled by Mercury, which is an inconstant planet, so such lagna persons are fond of quick changes. However, they are very conscientious and very capable of handling work even in unfavourable situations. They are fast moving. They are thorough and methodical, practical and discriminative but they lack will power. Virgo is an earthy sign, so they have desire to save money. They have sound commercial instinct and want to grow rich as quickly as possible.

In spite of the fact that Virgo lagna persons are changeable in nature, their married life is happy. It is noticed that they take a long time in taking a decision about their marriage. Some of them remain bachelors for a long time and some remain unmarried for the whole life.

Virgo lagna life parteners wants to treat their married life as a legal partnership. They do not find the sexlife very attractive and like to respect each other. Our own experience has shown that both Virgo lagna husband and wife are not so critical or dominating in their homes. Virgo lagna wives criticise their husbands, sometimes to such an extent that their discussions take the shape of a quarrel. It does, when lagna gets evil influence of Saturn, Mars, Rahu or ketu.

The professions most suited to them are to become leaders, doctors, officers, auditors, journalists, teachers, players, commercial agents, accountants, lawyers, statisticians and so on.

iv) Famous names

Emperor Shahjahan, Sheikh Mujiburrehman, President John F. Kennedy, Singer Malika Surraia, Napolean Bonapart, P.M. Narsimharao, Minister K.C. Pant. Sachin Tendulkar, Leander Paes, Retd. Police Officer Kiran Bedi.

♎ 7.Rising sign Libra (Tula lagna)

It is the seventh sign of zodiac. It consists of Chitra, Swati and Vishakha nakshatras. It is the sign of scales of justice and balance. Its specific features and physical appearance along with personality traits are as under:

i) Specific features

1.Owner of Tula lagna-Venus

2.Benefics in Tula lagna- Saturn, Mercury, Venus

3.Malefics in Tula lagna-Sun, Jupiter, Moon

4.Marak planets in Tula lagna-Jupiter

ii) Physical appearance

Persons born in Libra (Tula) lagna generally possess middle stature. They are fair, handsome and attractive. They have broad face and nose like a parrot. Their eyes are fine and attractive. They have broad chest but their constitution is seen phlegmatic. They are balanced.

iii) Personality traits

They are levelheaded persons. They weigh the merits and demerits of a subject and then express their opinion. They are constructive critics. The pictorial symbol of this sign is 'balance'. Hence they are, therefore, reasonable and just. They are also modest and gentle. They love happy and harmonious life. They want peace even if they are losers in transactions. If they lose their temper, they soon subside. Libra is a movable sign. Therefore such persons like changes in their lives and environments. They are popular and have a spirit of sacrifice.

Libra is an airy sign. All airy signs make the native intellectual. So they have fertile imagination, correct intuition, brilliance, intellect, refinement and pleasant nature, and humanitarian instincts. They lean more to the spiritual side than to the pure physical one. Many illustrious saints of the world were born in Tula lagna. They love peace. They cannot be bullied. You will not get anything out from them by threatening or by force. On their side they are against such things.

They are fond of good dress and other comforts as Venus being the owner of this sign. As Tula lagna people love peace, their domestic and married life is generally happy. They love their home, family and their property. Tula lagna girls are tactful, intelligent and wise. They love and adore their partners.

Libra lagna persons are most suited for business but they may also join service. They can become famous leaders, party heads, orators, good actors, musicians, writers, architects, salespersons etc.

iv) Famous names

Emperor Jahangir, Queen Lakshmibai of Jhansi, Gopal Krishna Gokhle, Mahatama Gandhi, Actor N.T. Ramarao, Ex. P.M. Atal Behari Bajpai, C.M. Narendra Modi, Musician O.P.Nayyar, Adolf Hitler Germany, Josef Stalin Russia. President Barrac Obama,

8. Rising sign Scorpio (Vrishchik lagna)

It is the eighth sign of zodiac. It consists of Vishakha, Anuradha and Jyeshtha nakshatras. It is a very calm and quite sign, but when it is threatened, it stings. Its specific features with physical appearance and personality traits are below:

i) Specific features
1. Owner of Vrishchik lagna-Mars
2. Benefics in Vrishchik lagna-Moon, Jupiter, Sun
3. Malefics in Vrishchik lagna-Mercury, Venus
4. Marak planets in Vrishchik lagna-Mercury, Venus, Saturn

ii) Physical appearancs

Scorpio (Vrishchik) is the negative sign (rashi) of Mars and therefore, such persons will manifest the different qualities from those of Aries (Mesh) the positive rashi. This is one of the bad signs of the zodiac. Its pictorial symbol is a venomous Scorpio. Persons born in Scorpio lagna are well built. The stature is above average. Face is broad with commanding appearance, thick dark hair, long nose, long hands and feet. They have dusky complexion and a good personality.

iii) Personality traits

Scorpio is a fixed sign. So the person is particularly determined individual. He crushes and removes the obstacles and moves forward. He fights up to the end of the problems; even if he is not winning. It is also a watery sign, which gives fertile imagination and sharp intelligence. He is emotional and has remarkable intuitive powers. In case of a doctor, it helps him to diagnose correctly. The person has self-assertion, impulsiveness, courage, energy, resolution, independence, excitement and forcefulness. He has his own likes and dislikes. He is totally an extremist. He has either practical business ability or quite reckless thinking. Life is unyielding. He is a self-made man.

Our experiences after examining several horoscopes of Scorpio lagna indicates that people having scorpio lagna are sexually mad.

A good Scorpio lagna person evinces great interest in occult sciences and spiritual experiments. They are good research scholars. They have a very harsh tongue. They are selfish to the core. They do not hesitate in passing sarcastic remarks. They have something hidden up in their sleeves with which they beat or disgrace others. They are revengeful by nature. If they are at any time troubled by some body, they remember it and wait for an opportunity to take revenge. They take pleasure in criticizing others to prove their own superiority. If bad influences from planets like Jupiter, they lose control and can go to the farthest limit of depravity.

The domestic life of these people become happy only, if every member of the family is submissive to them and their say in all matters is counted. They are extravagant. They spend most of money on their own comforts and pleasures, thus creating at times difficult situations in the family.

The professions most suited to them are concerned with leaders, administrators, chemistry, medicine, insurance, surgery, army, police, games, butchery, dacoity and naval services. They can become very successful detectives, research scholars and astrologers. These are general features of this lagna persons, hence they should not be interpreted as bad as usual

iv) Famous names

Colonel Nasir, Ayub Khan, Hennry Ford, Palmist Keero, Daku Mansingh, Ex. Home Minister L.K.Adwani, Bhairo Singh Shekhavat, Madhav Rao Scindhia, Cricketer Imran Khan, Princess Diana, Ex. P.M.Lal Bahadur Shastri.

9. Rising sign Sagittarius (Dhanu lagna)

It is the ninth sign of zodiac. It consists of Moola, Poorva Ashadha and Uttra Ashadha nakshatras. It aims at the pursuit of knowledge. Its specific features with physical appearance and personality traits are as under:

i) Specific features

    1. Owner of Dhanu lagna-Jupiter

    2. Benefics in Dhanu lagna-Mars, Sun

    3. Malefics in Dhanu lagna-Venus, Saturn, Mercury

    4. Marak Planets in Dhanu lagna-Venus, Saturn

ii) Physical appearance

Sagittarius (Dhanu) is one of the positive signs of zodiac and Jupiter is the owner. The persons of this lagna have a developed stout body. They are generally tall with a large forehead and long oval face. They have bushy eyebrows, bright eyes, long nose and long ears. They have a gracy look and fair complexion. They overall look like a handsome figure.

iii) Personality traits

Sagittarius is a fiery sign. The persons are, therefore, bold, courageous and pushing. They are ambitious, greedy and have high aspirations. They are not timid. They face adverse situations with fortitude. They have self-confidence. They are at their best when they have difficulties and obstacles before them. The fiery sign gives them energy, enthusiasm, vigour and vitality.

Sagittarius is a dual sign. Sagittarians are, therefore, unable to take quick decisions. They, for quite sometime consider the pros and cons of the problems that may come in the way. As Jupiter is the owner of this sign, the persons are Godfearing and truth loving. They stick to their principles, Even though their action is likely to bring unfavourable results for them.

They go in for higher education and are fond of traveling. The owner of the sign Jupiter gives them a broad mind, confidence, truth and spiritual uplift. They are very intuitive and their intuition generally proves correct. They are always for justice.If the lagna is afflicted by evil influences of Saturn, Mars, Rahu or Ketu, the person become deceptive. They exaggerate their own qualities. They try to show themselves as great men, but they know they are not. They make promises with no intention of keeping them. They enjoy outdoor sports regularly.

Sagittarius lagna persons can get success in government service, as teachers, professors, principals, preachers, judges, lawyers, bank officers, writers, models, actors, orators, players, industrialists, politicians, ministers, astrologers and heads of religious institutions.

iv) Famous names

Ishwar Chand Vidhyasagar, Ex-President Rajendra Prasad and Neelam Sanjeeva Reddy, A.P.J. Abdul Kalam, P.M. Chaudhary Charan Singh, Man Mohan Singh, Dr. K. B. Hedgewar, Pak P.M. Benazir Bhutto, Film Director V. Shanta Ram, Roman King Nero, Vinoba Bhave, Actor Manoj Kumar, Industrialist Dhirubhai Ambani, Rattan Tata, CEC.T. N. Shesan, Mahendra Singh Dhoni, British P.M. Margrat Thacher, Mother Teresa.

10.Rising sign Capricorn (Makar lagna)

It is the tenth sign of zodiac. It consists of Uttra Shadha, Shravan and Dhanishtha nakshatras. It reminds your ability to keep your feet on the ground and your sight on the goal. Its specific features with physical appearance and personality traits are as below-

i) Specific features

1.Owner of Makar lagna-Saturn

2.Benefics in Makar lagna-Venus, Mercury, Saturn

3.Malefics in Makar lagna- Mars, Jupiter, Moon

4.Marak planets in Makar lagna-Mars, Jupiter

ii) Physical appearance

The persons born in Capricorn ascendant (Makar lagna) are generally weak. They grow slowly and become tall in young age. Their body will not be plumpy or muscular but slender. Their constitution improves with age. They have long nose, thin neck and long chin. Their eyes are deep. They have dark and coarse hair.

iii) Personality traits

Capricorn is an earthy sign. So the Capricorn lagna persons are economical. They are prudent, reasonable, thinker and practical minded. They are most methodical, but slow and steady and have patience. They are calculative and businessminded. Capricorn is also a movable sign. This indicates that they always come to a quick decision. They will have push and confidence. They have special organising capacity and a lot of tolerance. They are generally passimistic but very cautious and calculating. They accept the reality of a thing on its practical outcome .The owner of this sign is Saturn. If this lagna has no evileffect, the native will be honest, sincere and reliable. If the lagna is afflicted, he will be dishonest, miserly and may even become a criminal. Further with good influences on lagna the native will never be idle. On the other hand, he will be very hard-working always keep himself busy. With bad influences on lagna the native will become lazy and a pessimist to the extreme.

Capricorn lagna persons are conservative by nature. They will not care for difficulties, handicaps and hindrances, which will always be there in the way. They will continue to work until they bring their work or task entrusted to them to a successful conclusion. They are hard workers and are able to consolidate their position sooner or later.

Capricorn lagna people generally marry late. They are good husbands / wives and parents of many good children, but they do not make a show of their affection. On the other hand, they would enforce discipline in the house as they do in the place of their work.

Professions most suitable to Capricorn lagna people are service in business concerns, limited companies, institutions, municipalities, corporations and government offices. They are also very well suited to work in metal mines and oil and gas concerns. They can also become research scholars, scientists, engineers, professors, singers, actors and religious healers.

iv) Famous names

Maharana Pratap, Maotese Tung, Swami Vivekanand, Sanjay Gandhi, H.G. Wells, Queen Elizabeth II, Actress Aishvarya Rai Bachchan, Singer Anuradha Paudwal.

11. Rising sign Aquarius (Kumbh lagna)

It is the eleventh sign of zodiac. It consists of Dhanishtha, Shatbhisha and Poora Bhadrapad nakshatras. It represents your desire to use your way of life in order to differentiate humanity. Its specific features with physical appearance and personality traits are as under-

i) Specific features

1. Owner of Kumbh lagna-Saturn

2. Benefics in kumbh lagna –Venus, Sun, Mars.

3. Malefics in kumbh lagna-Jupiter, Moon

4. Marak planets in Kumbh lagna-Mars

ii) Physical appearance

Aquarius ascendant persons are generally tall and lean with square built figure. They are strong and stout. They have clear complexion. They are handsome and elegant. They have bright hairs, long fleshy face, fleshy lips & broad cheeks. They are always friendly.

iii) Personality traits

Aquarius is an airy sign, so such lagna persons are intelligent and learned. They have good memory and are capable in dealing with the facts. They are not carried away by flattery. They act carefully after considering the pros and cons of everything. They are slow in understanding things, but once they get at them, they can handle them with ease and confidence. They have a broad outlook and human understanding. They move in a select society or a group of persons. They are reserved in nature and are great moralists. They have wonderful intuitional capacity.

Aquarius is a fixed sign, the persons born in Aquarius stick to their principles. They work persistently in all their undertakings. They are very strong in their likes and dislikes. They have inclination towards learning psychic subjects. They develop intuition and inspiration. They prefer secluded places and go in deep meditation. Many of the saints of our times and great men, who have or had sacrificed their lives for the good of humanity, were born in Aquarius lagna.

Their married life may be happy only if their partners are as intelligent as they are. They are steadfast in their affection but they do not like to display it. They are liable to suffer colic troubles, chest pain and lungs-problems.

Aquarius lagna persons are at home in every profession. They are good in government service as head of the state/country and army officers, in commercial institutions as engineers, research scholars. On account of their intuitional capacity, they become very proficient astrologers, poets and writers. They shine best as heads of religious or charitable institutions. They may be good sportsmen or athletes,

iv) Famous names

Ram Krishna Param Hans, Carl Marx, Poet Jai Shankar Prasad, Novel writer Acharya Chatursen, Emperor Aurangzeb, Pak P.M. Mohammad Ali Jinnah, Actress Rekha, General B. M. Kaul, U.S.President Abraham Lincoln. Actor Amitabh Bachchan, Athelete/Runner P.T. Usha.

12.Rising sign Pisces (Meen lagna)

It is the twelfth and last sign of zodiac. It consists of Poorva Bhadrapad, Uttra Bhadrapad and Revti nakshatras. It reveals your tendency constantly pulled by the tides of emotions and signifies your ability to connect them strongly. Its specific features with physical appearance and personality traits are as under-

i) Specific features

1. Owner of Meen lagna-Jupiter

2. Benefics in Meen lagna-Moon, Mars

3. Malefics in Meen lagna- Saturn, Sun, Venus, Mercury

4. Marak planets in Meen lagna-Mercury, Saturn, Venus

ii) Physical appearance

Pisces (Meen) lagna persons are generally short in stature and short limbs. They are plumpy with short hands and feet. They have dark hair. They have fleshy face and wide mouth. Their eyes are good looking. Their complexion is seen pale, sad and tired. They may be fat in later years.

iii) Personality traits

Pisces is a watery sign ruled by Jupiter. The persons are, therefore by nature easy going, quick understanding, philosophical, restless, imaginative, trustful and fond of romantic life. They are modest and timid and hesitate putting themselves forward. They are honest, humane and helpful. They are idealistic and always believe in "forget and forgive" spirit in life. Sometimes they are inclined to be over anxious and become disheartened, indecisive and lacking in energy. On account of their being over liberal and overgenerous, they often hamper their own progress. They are very happy when they spend their money to help others and on charitable causes.

The married life of Pisces lagna persons is generally happy, but they have a jealous nature. They are always double minded. Their life partners are therefore to be more careful and try to adjust themselves with their changing moods, tastes and fancies, if they want a peaceful and happy domestic life.

Pisces is a dual sign, so the persons are not steady. They are imaginative in nature. They may easily change from one profession to another. They can be good poets, writers and occultists. They can be successful traders dealing in liquids or import and export business. They are best suited for charitable institutions. They can become good actors and musicians, as Venus is exalted in this sign. They can also be physicians. They are also successful in naval services, in shipping organisations, hospitals or sanatoriums. They can go in politics and become ministers.

iv)Famous names

Swami Ram Tirtha, Ravindranath Tagore, Dy. P.M. Jagjeevan Ram, Ex C.M, Jagannath Mishra, Arvind Mafat Lal, US President.Eisenhower, Upendranath Ashk.

Solar System and Signs of Zodiac

Following is the figure 2.5 (F-2) of the solar system and the signs of zodiac. You can well think of the position of the Earth with Moon and other planets and also12 signs of zodiac in different shapes & sizes.

Solar System and Signs of Zodiac

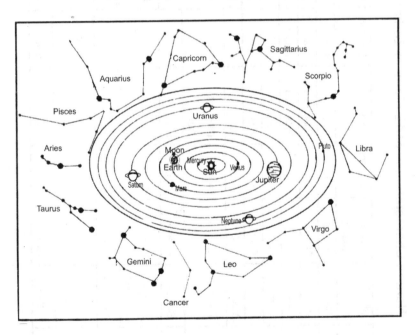

Figure 2.5 (F-2)

Note: Natural characteristics of 12 signs of zodiac table is given on the next page. Please See the table 2.5 (T-4) for those characteristics

Natural Characteristice of 12 Signs of Zodiac Table-2.5 (T-4)

Sr. No	English Name	Vedic Name	Shape	Typical Qualities	Element	Consti-tution	Direction	Benefic/ Malefic	Mutual Aspects	Owner Planets
1	Aries	Mesh	Ram	Movable	Fire	Pitta	East	Malefic	5,8,11	Mars (Mangal)
2	Taurus	Vrishabh	Bull	Fixed	Earth	Vata Kapha	South	Benefic	6,9,12	Venus (Shukra)
3	Gemini	Mithun	Twins	Dual	Air	Pitta, Vata,	West	Benefic	8,11,2	Mercury (Budh)
4	Cancer	Kark	Crab	Movable	Water	Kapha	North	Benefic		Moon (Chandra)
5	Leo	Simha	Lion	Fixed	Fire	Pitta	East	Malefic	7,10,1	Sun (Surya)
6	Virgo	Kanya	Virgin	Dual	Earth	Vatta	South	Benefic	9,12,3	Mercury (Budh)
7	Libra	Tula	Balance	Movable	Air	Pitta, Vata, Kapha	West	Benefic	11,2,5	Venus (Shukra)
8	Scorpio	Vrishchik	Scorpion	Fixed	Water	Kapha	North	Malefic	10,1,4	Mars (Mangal)
9	Sagittarius	Dhanu	Centaur Bowman	Dual	Fire	Pitta	East	Benefic	12,3,6	Jupiter (Guru)
10	Capricorn	Makar	Crocodile	Movable	Earth	Vata	South	Malefic	2,5,8	Saturn (Shani)
11	Aquarius	Kumbh	Water Carrier	Fixed	Air	Pitta, Vata, Kapha	West	Malefic	1,4,7	Saturn (Shani)
12	Pisces	Meen	Fishes	Dual	Water	Kapha	North	Benefic	3,6,9	Jupiter (Guru)

2.6 Planets (Grahas)-Used in Vedic astrology

In Vedic astrology seven of the heavenly bodies and two nodes of Moon total nine planets are considered because of their size, proximity, and influence on the earth and also living and non living kingdoms. For various reasons, it is more convenient to speak of the Sun as transiting the zodiac instead of earth. It is very simple to imagine the earth as the centre of observation and all planets revolving around it. Although in astronomy Sun is the epicentre of the Universe and father of all the planets and they revolve around the Sun, yet in astrology earth and its inhabitants living and nonliving are more important, who are always being affected by the Sun. The same way, Moon being a satellite of the earth and revolving around earth is given the position of a planet. Moon appears to be going through one sign (rashi) after another making a circuit of about 28 days.

Moreover nodes of Moon, Rahu and Ketu are also given the position of planets, though they are not the physical bodies. They are the points of intersection of the apparent lunar and solar orbital path. Rahu is north node (ascending) and ketu south node (descending). Indeed they are shadowy planets but more effective and influential. Thus total nine planets are given places in Vedic astrology. Natural characteristics of the planets are given in the table 2.6 (T-5).

2.7 Planets-Their Vedic qualities and mottos

 1.Sun

Sun is the father and king of all planets. It is 3rd malefic. Its images at one time early in the morning look like Brahamdev, the creator of the world, next time after morning like Vishnudev, the sustainer and third time at sunset like Mahadev, the destroyer. Though it is a positive, generous, self-confident, high thinking planet, yet it is power hungry, vain, arrogant and egotistical. Its anger is momentary. It wants to be an independent and an authoritative. It has a bilious (Pitta) temperament. Its motto is how we act and direct? It favours our fortune and blesses with prosperity and riches at the age of 22 years. It looks after soul, father and children. It produces presidents, governors and leaders. It governs eyes, heart and upper part of abdomen.

Natural Characteristice of Nine Planets Table-2.6 (T-5)

Sr.	English	Vedic	Sex	Colour	Nature	Element	Direction	Time in a sign	House Karak	Benefic/ Malefic	Own Sign	Owner of Individual's
1	Sun	Surya	M	Pink	Pitt	Fire	East	1 month	1,9,10	Malefic	Leo	Soul
2	Moon	Chandra	F	White	Vatt	Water	North West	2 ¼ days	4	Benefic	Cancer	Mind
3	Mars	Mangal	M	Red	Pitt	Fire	South	1 ½ months	3,6	Malefic	Aries Scorpio	Boldness
4	Mercury	Budh	MN	Green	Pitt VattKaph	Earth	North	21 days	4,10	Benefic	Gemini Virgo	Speech
5	Jupiter	Guru	M	Yellow	PittVatt Kaph	Sky	North East	13 months	2,5,9,10,11	Benefic	Sagittarius Pisces	Knowledge
6	Venus	Shukra	F	Grey	VattKaph	Water	South East	21 days	7	Benefic	Taurus Libra	Pleasures
7	Saturn	Shani	FN	Black	Vatt	Air	West	2 ½ years	6,8,10,12	Malefic	Capricorn Aquarius	Struggle
8	North Node	Rahu	F	Blue	Vatt	Air	South West	1 ½ year	3,6,11,12	Malefic	-	Pride
9	South Node	Ketu	N	Smoky	Vatt	Air	South West	1 ½ year	3,6,11,12	Malefic	-	Troubles

2.Moon

Moon is treated as a royal queen. It is 3rd in benefics. It is cold, calm and quite and has motherly qualities such as love, understanding and care. For first two weeks, it wanes and gives light and second two weeks, waxes and brings darkness. It is a continuous process. Though it is well behaved, sweet spoken, humanitarian, social planet, yet it is sensitive, emotional, imaginative and passive. It has a phlegmatic (Kapha) and windy (Vatta) temperament. Its motto is how we feel and respond? It brings good luck and success at the age of 24 years. It governs external identity of the person. It produces harbour controllers, ship builders, psychologists and naturopathists. It governs lungs and influences our mind.

 3.Mars

Mars is the Army Chief. It is called Bhumiputtra. When the mother earth was submerged in celestial water, Vishnudev, the sustainer lifted her and Mars was born. It is 2nd malefic. Though it is bold, courageous, firm, freedom fighter, yet self-seeking, impulsive, adamant, cruel and burglar. It wants to be a conqueror. It has a bilious (Pitta) temperament. Its motto is how we execute and take action? It makes the person daring and enthusiastic and fulfils all desires and comforts of life in the age of 28 years. It produces policemen, army men, mechanical engineers, players and athletes. It governs skull, blood and testicles.

 4.Mercury

Mercury is known as prince being nearest to Sun. It is 4th in benefics. It is intelligent, wise and inventive. It brings droughts, floods, earthquakes etc. Though it is a diplomatic, skillful, communicative, versatile, humorous planet, yet it is much talkative, critical, sarcastic, restless and nervous. It gives learning and knowledge. It is in nature phlegmatic (Kapha), bilious (Pitta) and windy (Vatta). Its motto is how we think and speak? Mercury makes intelligent and improves the status of the person at the age of 34 years. It looks after sense, memory, brain, throat, skin and arms. It produces publishers, editors, speakers and transporters.

5.Jupiter

Jupiter is known as the teacher (Guru) of devtas (suras). It is the largest planet next to Sun and 1st in benefics. It is intelligent and learned in shastras. It makes the person capable in many fields. It is religious and devotee of God. Though it is just, virtuous, fair, optimistic, caring, good advisor, yet overindulgent, overestimate, too leisurely and much extravagant. It has a phlegmatic (kapha) constitution. Its motto is how we know or grow? It extends our education and brings good luck, wisdom and success from the early age of 16 to 20 years. It looks after courts, administration, public ceremonies and foreign tours. It produces teachers, principals, judges, scientist, writers and priests. It governs back, hip and feet.

 6.Venus

Venus is known as the teacher (Guru) of rakshas (asuras). It is nearest to Mercury and 2nd in benefics. It is charming and splendid. It is called lord of wealth and comforts of life. It causes obstructions to rain. It knows 'Mritsanjeevani Vidhya' by which it can bring back a dead person to life. Though it is well-mannered, courteous, balanced, soothing, artistic, social, yet indolent, indulgent, pleasure seeking, manipulator and unproductive. It has a phlegmatic and bilious (Kapha and Pitta) constitution. Its motto is how we enjoy, love and relate? Venus favours fortune with all the pleasures and luxuries at the age of 25 years. It looks after dancing, singing, love, sex, beauty, cleanliness and character. It produces poets, actors, singers, dancers, astrologers, doctors and automobile engineers. It governs human's face, kidney and urinary organs.

 7.Saturn

Saturn is the son of the King Sun. It keeps enemity to its father. It is most malefic among all other malefics i.e. first in the series. It is assumed to be Yama, the God of Death and a sustainer of spiritual life like a sage (sanyasi). If well placed, it gives success in life. Though it is dependable, preserving, structured, yet boring, dry, leads to hard working and restrictions. It has a windy (Vatta) temperament. Its motto is how we focus, take responsibility and regulate our life? It helps in favouring fortune and prosperity at the age of 36 years. It governs longevity, death, enemies, politics, rank in government and all gaseous and electronic products. It produces farmers, leaders, lawyers, ministers and electronic engineers. It governs legs, knees and portion up to feet.

8.Rahu

Rahu is north node of Moon. It is a bodiless head and smoky-blue in appearance. It treats like Saturn and reflects the results of the owner of sign, in which it falls. It brings eclipses. It is 4th in the series of malefics. Although it is innovative, investigative, gives material success, carry abroad, yet confused, treacherous, deceptive and brings losses. Some times it gives hidden treasure (unexpected wealth). It has a windy (Vatta) constitution. Its motto is how we unveil or shadow our character? It encourages in progress and accumulating riches at the age of 42 years. Its good and bad effects are sudden such as benefits, receiving money through lottery and losses by accidents, heart attack, paralysis and so on. Its benefic houses are 3rd, 6th and 11th houses but powerful and favourable in 4th, 9th and 10th houses.

9.Ketu

Ketu is south node of Moon. It is headless body. It has smoky-blue appearance. It is 3rd in malefics. Its vehicle, on which it travels, is a vulture. It treats like Mars but it results as per the owner of the house, it occupies. Though it is highly adaptable, very intuitive, spiritual in nature, helps to recognize others, yet it is chaotic, ungrounded, unstable and undependable. It shows the way of Moksha. It has a windy (Vatta) constitution. Its motto is how we recognize or enlighten our ideals? It gives peaceful and comfortable life at the age of 48 years. Sometimes it makes the person quarrelsome, moody, mentally disturbed but other way detached with the people and devotee of almighty God leading towards Moksha (Salvation). Ketu is benefic in 3rd, 6th and 11th houses and malefic in remaining houses of a birth chart.

Note: The positions of all the planets in Signs and Houses, where they crop up to be exalted and debilitated, friendly and inimical, in mool-trikon sign and in neutral signs are given on next page. See table 2.7 (T-6) and know about them.

Position of Nine Planets in Signs and Houses Table-2.7 (T-6)

Sr. No	English Name	Vedic Name	Own Sign	Exalted Sign	Debilitated Sign	Mool-Trikon Sign	Friendly Sign	Inimical Sign	Neutral Sign	Houses Aspect	Favours Houses
1	Sun	Surya	Leo 21°-31°	Aries 01°-10°	Libra 01°-10°	Leo 01°-20°	Cancer Scorpio Sagittarius Pisces	Taurus Capricorn Aquarius	Gemini Virgo	7th	3,6,10,11
2	Moon	Chandra	Cancer 01°-30°	Taurus 01°-03°	Scorpio 01°-03°	Taurus 04°-30°	Gemini Leo Virgo Capricorn Pisces		Aries Libra Sagittarius Aquarius	7th	3
3	Mars	Mangal	Aries 19°-31° Scorpio 01°-30°	Capricorn 01°-28°	Cancer 01°-28°	Aries 01°-18°	Leo Sagittarius	Gemini Virgo Pisces	Taurus Libra Aquarius	4th, 7th, 8th	3,6,10,11
4	Mercury	Budh	Gemini 01°-30° Virgo 21°-30°	Virgo 01°-15°	Pisces 01°-15°	Virgo 16°-20°	Taurus Libra Leo	Cancer	Aries Scorpio Sagittarius Capricorn Aquarius	7th	2,3,6,8,10
5	Jupiter	Guru	Sagittarius 14°-30° Pisces 01°-30°	Cancer 01°-05°	Capricorn 01°-05°	Sagittarius 01°-13°	Aries Scorpio Leo	Taurus Libra Gemini Virgo	Aquarius	5th, 7th, 9th	7,9,11
6	Venus	Shukra	Taurus 01°-30° Libra 11°-30°	Pisces 01°-27°	Virgo 01°-27°	Libra 01°-10°	Gemini Aquarius Capricorn	Cancer Leo	Aries Sagittarius Scorpio	7th	1,3,4,7,8,9, 11,12
7	Saturn	Shani	Capricorn 01°-30° Aquarius 21°-30°	Libra 01°-20°	Aries 01°-20°	Aquarius 01°-20°	Taurus Gemini Virgo	Cancer Leo Scorpio	Sagittarius Pisces	3rd, 7th, 10th	3,6,11
8	Moon's North Node (Ascending)	Rahu	Virgo 01°-30°	Gemini 01°-15°	Sagittarius 01°-15°	Aquarius 01°-30°	Taurus Libra Capricorn	Aries Cancer, Leo Scorpio	Aries Sagittarius Aquarius	5th, 7th, 9th	3,6,10,11
9	Moon's South Node (Descending)	Ketu	Pisces 01°-30°	Sagittarius 01°-15°	Gemini 01°-15°	Leo 01°-30° Scorpio	Aries Cancer Aquarius	Taurus, Libra Capricorn	Virgo	5th, 7th, 9th	3,6,10,11

Chapter

3

Birth Chart (Janam Kundli) and Houses (Bhavas)

3.1 What is a Birth Chart and its Ascendant (Lagna)?

Birth chart (Janam kundli) is a sky map (space chart) showing positions of planets at the time of an Individual's birth in a square / triangular / circular shape chart with 12 columns called houses (bhavas). It is prepared on the basis of rising sign of zodiac in the east putting in the first house. The first house is known as its ascendant (lagna). In northern India rising sign is fixed in the middle top coloumn of a square or rectangular shape birth chart. Other signs are written anti clockwise continuously. Similarly these are written in the western astrology, but in a circular shape chart. In southern India, though square shape chart is used, yet the signs are always put in the fixed houses clock-wise and the ascendant (lagna) in ascendant sign and then all other planets in the houses of signs, where they exist at birth. The same style is adopted in eastern India, but the signs are fixed anti clock-wise. They also write ascendant (lagna) in ascendant sign, where it is and then the remaining planets in the respective houses.

3.2 What we need for casting a Birth Chart

For casting a Birth chart (Janam kundli) of an individual, first we need the following information:

1. Exact date of birth - Either of English Calendar date, i.e. solar date or Indian Panchang's (Almanac's) Tithi, i.e. lunar date.

2. Exact time of birth - When the child is severed from umbilical chord of mother and becomes a separate entity. Time in A.M./ P.M.

3.   Exact place of birth - Latitude N. or S. and longitude E. or W.
        Please note that the I.S.T. was advanced by one hour from
        01/09/1942 to 15/10/1945 almost 3 years. Deduct one hour
        for casting the birth chart of this period.

3.3 Birth Time adjustment

Sometimes in a few cases, it is possible that the person is confident
about date and place of birth such as September 21st, 1960 Delhi (India)
but he / she is not confident regarding his / her exact birth time. He / she
may say it is between 06-30 to 08-30 AM, then there may be a problem
to determine the accuracy of the rising sign, which sets the tone of entire
birth chart in analyzing and predicting the facts of life. Since the rising
sign changes roughly after every two hours, therefore easiest method to
reach to the correct time birth chart is to cast three lagna charts together.
The first chart of mid hours of above quoted time 06-30 to 08-30 AM that
is 07-30 AM and other two a few hours or one hour ahead of 08-30 AM
and one hour back of 06-30 AM. Thus there will be three different charts
of rising signs. After it, read the following table of rising signs
characteristics and compare his / her nature and habits. Accordingly
finalise the correct rising sign (lagna rashi).

For more accuracy astrologer can ask some incident / accident of
the period of his / her short span of life that is up to the age of 32 years.
It will help you in knowing / connecting his / her nature and habits with
one of three lagnas and you can be sure regarding correct rising sign. In
such a chart, there may come a slight or little difference of degrees /
angles of planets and a few days difference in dasha period of a planet
but predictions will be somehow positive and reasonable.

The second easiest method is to cast Chandra kundli birth chart.
Here starting sign will be the Moon occupied sign, where Moon exists
on that day and date. From Moon occupied sign called Chandra lagna,
we can fix other signs anti-clock-wise in the houses and also all the
planets in the signs. It will be quite enough to analyze and predict the
facts of a birth chart of a person. Results will almost be the same as
one gets from the rising sign (ascendant).

Please see features of the person born in rising signs given in the
table 3.3 (T-7).

Features of the person Born in Risings Signs Table-3.3 (T-7)

Sr. No.	Rising Signs	Characteristics – Habits of Rising Signs
1	Aries	Stature more than average, healthy, handsome, bold, rash, passionate, selfish
2	Taurus	Broad forehead, thick neck, easy-going, has patience, materialistic, regular, & dutiful
3	Gemini	Curious, truthful, flexible, communicative, good racer, easy to let others go policy
4	Cancer	Wide face and chest, fat, homely, family oriented, emotional, let others not go policy
5	Leo	Strong, bold, medium stature, Leader type, likes attention of others, dramatic, vain
6	Virgo	Tall stature, healthy, perfect, critic, communicative, weak nervous system, ENT patient
7	Libra	Tall stature, artistic, driven, tactful, diplomatic, indecisive, sweet spoken, fast walking
8	Scorpio	Wide head, attractive face, intuitive, penetrating, emotional, secretive, magnetic
9	Sagittarius	Big ears, long nose, philosophical, fanatical, outspoken, impatient, balanced, blunt
10	Capricorn	Tall stature, healthy, handsome. Cautious, business minded, conservative, isolated
11	Aquarius	Tall stature, wide shoulders, wise, clever, humanitarian, strong views, independent
12	Pisces	Short stature, sacrificing, mystical, emotional, escapist philosopher, dreamer,

3.4 How to cast a birth chart in North Indian, South Indian and Western style?

Now a days, it is most easy to prepare a Birth chart (Janam Kundli). In India many Almanacs (Panchangs) based on certain Latitudes and Longitudes of cities such as Delhi, Jullundur, Neemach, Varansi etc are available. In these Panchangs month wise Tables of ascendants (Dainik Lagna Sarinis) for the year are given. Tables of Latitudes and Longitude of the important cities of India and other countries of the world are also given. Latitudes differ in time of Dainik lagna; therefore, for correction in time, other tables such as a table of change in time of ascendants Dainik Lagan Parivartan Sarini (Lagna Sanskar Sarini) is also given. As per date, time and latitude of place of birth, one can find out the correct time of lagna from Dainik Lagna Sarini after doing plus or minus for the difference of time, if it needs.

And then cast a Birth Chart (Janam kundli) and also put planets in the signs already exist date wise in the Panchang showing degrees of morning time 05-30 AM. One can easily work out birth time degrees of all the planets in a short while and note them on the sheet of the birth chart. For this purpose, we can also take help from the book "Annual Ephemeries" by N.C.Lahiri. Positions of the planets in the constellations may also be noted. Three examples of birth charts are prepared with the help of Delhi based Panchang Individual (A) North Indian style, Individual (B) South Indian style and Individual (C) Western style follows:

3.5 Example Kundlis Individual A, B and C

1. North Indian style-

Individual(A). Date of Birth 15-07-1967,Time of Birth 17-55PM (IST),
Place of Birth-Palwal, Lat.$27^0/09'$ N., Long.$77^0/20'$E.

On July 15th, 1967 according to the *Dainik* lagna sarini Sagittarius lagna begins at 17-13 PM. and ends at 19-18 PM. Difference of latitudes from Delhi to Palwal is 28^0-38', minus 27^0-09', almost 01^0-29' degrees=3minutes as per *Lagna Parivatan* Table. After deducting 3 minutes, the correct time of Sagittarius lagna in Palwal will be from 17-10 PM. to 19-15 PM.

Now we can prepare a birth chart starting from sagittarius as the ascendant sign. In that case the time of birth of the Individual- (A) is 17-55 PM., comes between 17-10 PM. and 19-15 PM., All the planets with their signs and degress will be placed in the chart accordingly. See the kundli (birth chart) given below based on North Indian Style.

BIRTH CHART

NAVANSH CHART

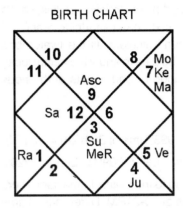
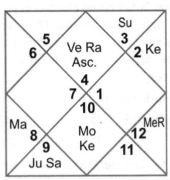

Kundli No. 3.5 (K-1)

After casting a birth chart (Janam Kundli), it is necessary to prepare a Cuspal Chart (Bhava Kundli). For the preparation of Cuspal Chart, we have to take the longitude of ascendant (Lagna Spashtha). In this case Lagna Spashtha is 08 / 09 / 12 / 59. This is called centre (middle point) of first house (bhava). If we want to know all the longitudes house-wise (bhava spashtha), we have to add 30° degrees (1 rashi) further in each bhava. Now for 2nd bhava spashtha see below:

Longitude of ascendant (Lagna spashtha)   = 08* / 09⁰ / 12'/ 59"

Addition   + 01* / 00⁰ / 00' / 00"

Longitude of 2nd house (2nd bhava spashtha)= 09* / 09⁰ / 12' / 59"

Therefore 09* / 09⁰ / 12' / 59" will be 2nd bhava. For third house (bhava), we can add 30° degrees (1rashi) in 2nd bhava. In this way for next other bhavas continue to add 30° degrees (1 rashi) in each to reach the remaining bhavas. Sometimes it does that more than one cusp fall in one sign (rashi). As a result, the owner of one sign (rashi) becomes the owners of both the cusps. For this, we have to carry out Bhava Sandhi, the point between two houses (bhavas). For first bhava sandhi, we have to add 15° Degrees in longitude of lagna (lagna spashtha). For example:

Longitude of ascendant (Lagna spashtha)   = 08* / 09⁰ / 12' / 59"

Addition   + 00* / 15⁰/ 00' / 00"

For First house mid-point (bhava sandhi)   = 08* / 24⁰ / 12' / 59"

But for the 2nd house mid-point (bhava sandhi), we have to add 30° degrees (1rashi) in 1st bhava sandhi, then 2nd bhava sandhi will be

09* / 24⁰ / 12' / 59". For other houses mid-points (bhava sandhis) continue adding 30⁰ degrees (1rashi) in each next bhava sandhi to reach to the last 12th bhava sandhi. Thus we can calculate all the twelve bhava spashthas and Bhava Sandhis. It will help us to know the actual location of the planet in the house and the good or bad results of the houses (bhavas).

2. South Indian style

Individual(B).   Date of Birth 30-10-1993,Time of Birth -19-45pm.(IST),

Place of Birth - Palwal, Lat.27⁰/09' N., Long.77⁰/20'E.

On October 30th, 1993 according to the Dainik lagna sarini-begins at Taurus lagna 18-27 PM. and ends at 20-21PM. Difference of time is 3minutes. After deducting difference of time the correct time of Taurus lagna at Palwal will be from 18-24 to 20-18 PM. Birth time of individual (B) is 19-45 PM. and it is between 18-24 PM.to 20-18 PM. therefore, his birth chart lagna or ascendant is Taurus.

On the basis of Taurus lagna, we can prepare Individual (B) birth chart and cuspal chart as per above method. See Janam kundli (birth chart) 3.5 (K-2) of the Individual (B) given below in the South Indian Style.

BIRTH CHART

12	1 Mo	Asc 2 Ke	3
11			4
10 Sa			5
9	8 Ra	Su Ma 7 MeR Ju	6 Ve

NAVANSH CHART

Ke 12	1	2	MeR Ma 3
Su 11			Asc 4
10			Ve 5 Mo
9	8 Ju	7	6 Ra Sa

Kundli No. 3.5 (K-2)

3. Western style

Individual(C) Date of Birth .15-01-2007,Time of Birth.04 42AM(UST),

POB. San Jose (Ca-USA) Lat.30⁰/20' N. Long.121⁰/53' W

On January 15th, 2007 Individual (C) birth time 04-42 AM comes in between the beginning of Scorpio lagna 02-52 AM to the end of Scorpio lagna 05-11 AM. Therefore the ascendant will be Scorpio (Vrishchik). Now we can cast his birth chart, cuspal chart and other charts as per our specifications and needs. First we have to put all the signs and planets in the houses and then prepare a table of longitude degrees of planets, bhava spashthas and bhava sandhis etc. Please note that San Jose city is in western longitudes and comes in 08-00 hours time zone. See below the circular type kundli (birth chart) 3.5 (K-3) in the Western Style:

BIRTH CHART

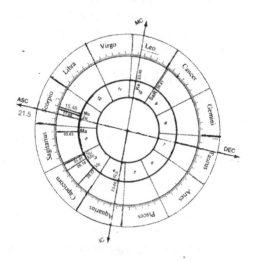

Kundli No. 3.5 (K-3)

In Western style there is no place for Navansh Chart or any other chart as already stated in first chapter under the heading Differences Between Vedic and Western Astrology. Western astrologers, while predicting a birth chart, first they see the position of the Sun and then other planets. Secondly they note their angular distance from the house they occupy, treating it as zero house. From there, they see other houses and location of planets at 60^0 and 120^0 angles. At these angles, the planets give best and most favourable results. At 72^0 and 144^0 angles planets also produce good results but at 45^0, 90^0, 135^0, 150^0, and 180^0 angles, they bring unfavourable and harmful results.

Therefore in the above case, we can predict that this is a Scorpio ascendant birth chart. Scorpion individuals are mysterious and materialistic. They are committed and determined. They are intelligent, generous, loyal and dutiful. They are hungry of affection and love. They do not like flattery. They are calm and quiet. But when they lose temper, they start roaring. If someone attacks them, they sting to protect themselves. Thus they are diplomatic and revengeful.

Note: Thus we can prepare birth charts in any style, which we prefer. In this book the author has used the North Indian Style Birth Charts with Navansh Chart for quoting examples prepared on single time zone used in our country. In case of India the Time Zone is 05-30 hours. However Glossary of some special Vedic words is also given for your relevance at the end of the book.

3.6 Example birth chart- Individual (A) An astrological observations

For astrological observations, the author is using three-point simple procedure everywhere, as it is in the case of Individual (A). See below.

Astrological observations

Individual (A) birth chart ascendant (lagna) is Sagittarius. Sagittarians are always bold, courageous, pushing, ambitious, enterprising and have high aspirations. They are very confident, open minded, sincere and honest. Individual (A) is such a man, who raised his status from low paid salary job to a Manager's post. At present he is having his own house to live in, vehicle for conveyance and other things of comforts to maintain happy and peaceful life. He has a missionary zeal and sacrificing nature.

1. Lagna considerations

Lagnesh Jupiter is placed in its exalted sign in the 8th house of longevity and aspects 12th house and its own 4th house which deals with the motherly love and comforts of life. Chandra lagnesh Venus is situated in the 9th house of fortune and religion. Mercury aspects the lagna from the 7th house. In Navansh chart, owner of lagna Moon is placed in 7th house and aspects lagna. Therefore lagna is fortified. Being born in Swati constellation, he is well-behaved, knowledgeable, sweet spoken, dutiful and hard working.

2. Planets placements, aspects and combinations

Saturn is placed in the 4th house, Rahu in 5th house and Sun in 7th house, all aspects lagna. Rahu aspects 9th house, while Mars from 11th house of aspects 5th house and 6th houses of debts, diseases and enemies owned by Venus. Saturn aspects 6th house also. Because of these aspects, the individual fell a prey to a painful disease in the dasha period of Saturn-Sun. It prolonged up to almost one year. Now he is cured and healthy. From Moon, Jupiter is in Kendra. It is forming Gajkesri yoga, Amalkirti yoga and Hans yoga. Because of these favourable yogas, he is now holding a good post and is popular among friends and relatives.

3. Conclusions

We may conclude that he is intelligent, virtuous, prosperous, benevolent and religious having a loving and caring wife and two children. It is because of the position of exalted Jupiter in Kendra from the Moon producing yogas, sitting in the 8th house and aspects its own 4th house which deals with comforts and luxuries. Mars from 11th house (of profits) also aspects 2nd house (of wealth) and its own 5th house (of education and children). Saturn from 4th house and Sun and Mercury from 7th house also aspect lagna, strengthening the native's status. This time Saturn-Mars dasha is operating, which is better and beneficial. Further, anterdasha of Rahu and Jupiter may also be positive and favourable. His future looks bright and he may shine for a long time. His domestic life may also be happy and peaceful.

3.7 Houses (Bhavas) classification in a birth chart

Birth Chart (Janam kundli) consisting of twelve houses (bhavas) describes an individual's full image of the body, behaviour, personality, his stature, health, character, finances, family, courage, paternal love, home, conveyance, education, union or partnership, children, span of life, fortune, religion, profession, occupation, ambition, income, pleasures of life and overall demeanour.

Houses of trine (1st, 5th, 9th) houses of angles (4th, 7th, 10th) and houses of gains (2nd, 11th) are the benefic houses? If the owners, significators (karaks), occupying, conjoining, aspecting planets in the above houses are powerful and strong being benefics, they always provide good results in their mahadasha / anterdasha and the person enjoys all the pleasures in life such as name, fame, love, status, dignity, honour and reputation. If weak, debilitated and combust being malefics and owners of 6th, 8th, 12th (bad houses) are occupying or aspecting these above houses, the person loses all kinds of gains and profits in life. His / her life becomes miserable, painful and sinful. He / she may feel perturbed and disturbed. It is all ascertained by the principles and rules of Vedic mathematics, the astronomy and astrology both.

Now casting a birth chart is an easy job described earlier but how to predict it is a hard task. Defining the word "Astrology" Delhi based famous cosmo-theorist Dr. Raj Baldev wrote—

"Astrology " is the mother of astronomy, cosmo-mathematics and metaphysics and unless the astrologer is well versed in all these branches of science, he never will be considered a qualified astrologer. The real knowledge of astronomy cum astrology does not live in the books but stays in the minds of genius people. Firstly it takes about 25 years of time to accomplish the whole course theory and practical. Now with the present advancement, it may take at least seven years".

The author agrees with the above lines that it takes years of time and experience to define and predict an individual's birth chart.

3.8 Long time study of practical birth charts

Over and above this fact, to a capable astrologer, for a long time study of practical birth charts is quite necessary to grasp the true knowledge of the subject of astrology and to prove it an exact science and no superstition. Now it is true and beyond doubts that it is a science or knowledge of time of the motions of planets and their effects on human life. An astrologer must not forget to use the principles, rules and techniques properly and carefully, while predicting a birth chart and forecasting about each and every event in one's life.

Millions of people in India and in many other countries are always curious to know about their future. It is but natural. Vedic astrology is one the time tested science or knowledge, which can throw light on one's past and predict on the future events of life. It can also help the person to face the future in a better way evading misfortunes and obstacles that might come in the way of success, status, dignity and honour.

3.9 Twelve houses and other Factors

Although constellations, signs, planets and houses (bhavas) are all important factors for casting and predicting a birth chart, yet houses (bhavas) are said to be more important to analyze its worth. Houses represent the entire history of life from 1st house of Ascendant (Beginning of life) to 12th house of Moksha (End of life). So houses (bhavas) can be classified in to three groups (sets).

1.Kendras (Angles)-1st, 4th, 7th, 10th houses

2.Panpharas (Cadent)- 2nd, 5th, 8th, 11th houses

3.Apoklims (Succedent)-3rd, 6th, 9th, 12th houses

3.10 Four trines (Trikonas)

Due to specific reasons, their importance and strength, four kendras (1st, 4th, 7th and 10th houses) and two trikonas (5th and 9th houses) of a birth chart are known as beneficial and favourable. If we count 5th and 9th houses from above mentioned four kendras, they indicate four separate trines (triangles) consisting of the houses as First trine-1, 5, 9 houses, Second trine-10, 2, 6 houses, Third trine-7, 11, 3 houses and Fourth trine- 4, 8, 12 houses. They all come in one and the same category. These four separate Trines (Trikonas) have their four different entities in Vedic astrology. Therefore above three groups are further placed / fixed in four trines (four triangles). In Vedic astrology they are called Dharma, Artha, Kama and Moksha houses.

These houses decide the actual status of the native Sun, Moon, Mars, Mercury, Jupiter, Venus and Saturn are the owners of these houses. Rahu and Ketu shadowy planets have been left out here. Read the following Shlok -

"Mesha VrishchikayorBhaumah Shukro VrishTuladhipah
Budh KanyaMithuno Karkadhishastu Chandrama
DhanurMeenadhipo Jeevah   ShanirMakaraKumbhyo
Singhasyadhipati Suryo Rashyadhisha ime smrata"

The 1st bhava (lagna bhava), 5th bhava (putra bhava) and 9th bhava (bhagya bhava) become visible in the category of first trine (trikona). It is the main trine known as "Purush Trine". They give 'Paurush' that is power and energy to the person. These are most important houses (bhavas) of a birth chart. These houses are the houses of religious sentiments, truth, morality, consciousness, spiritual knowledge, worshiping, mediation, charity, sacrifice and lastly faith in God. Hence are also called Houses of Dharma (religion). These should not be treated as kendras, panpharas and apoklims.

The 2nd, 6th, 10th houses (bhavas) are related to financial matters, wealth, gains and losses, occupation and profession, dignity and status, name and fame. It is the second trine namely "Aishwarya Trine". They provide wealth and riches in life from many sources. Although each of these houses are the identity of different groups as 2nd cadent, 6th succedent and 10th angles yet they are called Houses of Artha (wealth).

The 3rd, 7th, 11th houses (bhavas) respectively known as succedent, angles and cadent, represent desires, passions, sensual delights, marital happiness and all other comforts of life. They are connected with the nature, temperament, mentality and behaviour of a person, so it is the third trine namaly "Prakrati Trine". Good behavirour or bad habits whatever it may be, indicate the prakrati (nature) of a person. Therefore, they are also called Houses of Kama (Fun and Pleasures).

The remaining 4th, 8th, 12th houses (bhavas) show motherly love, care and understanding, personal conveyance, residential house, span of life, divine knowledge, and devotion to The God. It is the fourth and last trine namely "Vairagya Trine". They lead towards 'Vairagya' that is to know and understand the ideals of life. Therefore, they are also called the Houses of Moksha (Salvation).

With the help of above Trines, we can reach to the exact outcomes (results) of a birth chart (Janam kundli). A set of another four 3rd, 6th, 10th, 11th bhavas is called upachayas (Houses of Growth). It is believed that all the planets show good results, when they are situated in upachyas. One more set of four 3rd, 6th, 8th, 12th bhavas is treated as bad houses (Dustha bhavas). Two houses (bhavas) 3rd and 6th are common in both the sets, hence required more attention, while predicting a birth chart. They may give good results, if posited in their own houses. If not and they are placed in other than own, as per placements, aspects and combinations, they try to destroy the significations of those houses (bhavas), in which they are posited.

3.11 Points describing over all effects of each House

While describing houses (bhavas) following four headings have been taken to clarify and understand all the facts of life related to the houses of one's birth chart. We can easily judge the overall effects of each house (bhava) as illustrated in 4, 5, 6, 7 chapters of the book.

1.   **Owner of the house (bhava) in various houses-**
     (i) Powerful
     (ii) Weak

Powerful planets means strong (shadbali) / in exalted / in Own sign in benefic houses or signs in a birth chart. Weak planets are those, which are debilitated, combust and occupy malefic houses or signs.

What will be the effects (results) if the owner is powerful or weak ? Effects are shown separately. Powerful planets always produce beneficial and favourable results, while weak planets prove worst, harmful and painful results especially in their dasha period.

2.   **Planets occupying the house (bhava)-**
     (i) Positive
     (ii) Negative.

Regarding planets in houses (bhavas), both the natures best and worst are described separately in headings as positive and negative. Positive planets are those, which are always beneficial and improve the status of the person, while negative planets put him/her into all types of losses. If the planet is positive in nature and occupy positive sign or house in a birth chart, results will be better and beneficial in comparison to the effects of those planets, which are negative in nature and are posited in the malefic signs or houses. Their results will be reverse, say worse and melancholy.

3.   **Planets placements, aspects and combinations-**
     Miscellaneous yogas

It is the third separate heading, in which effects of different planets as per placements; aspects and combinations in the houses / signs are accorded. Thus a reader can easily well understand the effects and results of concerned house (bhava). Chapter 8, Significance of Yogas (combinations) is also given separately for the referenc of the reader. How are they formed and what are their effects in life is clearly mentioned?

4.   **Events affecting during dasha Sign in houses**

     (i) Favourable

     (ii) Unfavourable

Maharishi Parashar held that most believable Vimshotri dasha is the base for the events affecting one's life. We have to find out the position of the house (bhava) owner, if it exists in its own house / sign and whether its dasha is advancing. If not, notice the planets of which Mahadasha and Anterdasha are operating. What will be the dasha effects? favourable or unfavourable? The planets, which are exalted either in birth chart or in navansh chart, or in mool trikon or in own or in friendly sign or in arohi location, are called strong benefics. They prove favourable. The planets, which are debilitated or weak in situation or in avrohi location or in pap kartari yoga, bring miseries and misfortunes, debts, diseases and enmity.

So everything is made easy to know the effects of planets in above headings. The planet position in houses / signs, where they appear exalted / debilitated and benefics / malefics with star constellation, is given in the table 3.11 (T-8) on the next page. If Sun is exalted in the 1st house, it will be treated same in 5th and 9th houses being houses of one trine i.e. Purush Trine. If Jupiter is debilitated in 10th house, it will be treated debilitated in 2nd and 6th houses also being of one trine Aishwarya Trine. This is to be noted for astrological observations.

Lastly in every chapter of a trine of each three houses , some example kundlis (birth charts) are also given in all the four trine chapters analyzing the facts after casting birth charts of Individual (A) (B) and (C) with " Astrological Observations " of Individual (A)

1. Lagna considerations.
2. Placements, aspects and combinations
3. Conclusion.

Positions of planets Exalted / debilitated Table-3.11 (T-8)

Sr. No.	Planets	Exalted in Signs Powerful & Favourable)	Debilitated in Signs (Weak & Unfavorable	Benefics Malefics	Stars Constellations
1	Sun	1, 5, 9 Dharma houses	7, 11, 3 Kama houses	M-5	3, 12, 21
2	Moon	2, 6, 10 Artha houses	4, 8, 12, Moksha houses	B-3	4, 13, 22
3	Mars	10, 2, 6 Artha houses	4, 8, 12 Moksha houses	M −2	5, 14, 23
4	Mercury	11, 3, 7 Kama houses	12, 4, 8 Moksha houses	B - 4	9,18, 27
5	Jupiter	4, 8, 12 Moksha houses	10, 2, 6 Artha houses	B - 1	7, 16, 25
6	Venus	12, 4, 8 Moksha houses	6, 10, 2 Artha houses	B - 2	2, 11, 20
7	Saturn	7, 11, 3 Kama houses	1, 5, 9 Dharma houses	M -1,	8, 17, 26
8	Rahu	3, 6, 11 Benefic houses	Remaining houses	M - 3	1, 10 19
9	Ketu	3, 6, 11 Benefic houses	Remaining houses	M - 4	6, 15, 24

3.12 Planets relations and Matters with significators (Karaks)

Planets, those are owners and occupy, conjoin, aspect the houses and confirm special yogas (combinations) in the houses, are friendly or inimical or neutral. What are the matters, pertaining to the significators (Karaks) of the houses? Please see table 3.12 (T-9) given on next page to understand all this.

Planet's Natural Relations and Matter pertaining to Significators of Houses Table-3.12 (T-9)

Sr. No	Name	Friendly	Inimical	Neutral	Matter pertains to the Significators of Houses
1	Sun	Moon, Mars, Jupiter	Venus, Saturn	Mercury	Body, Head-1, Right eye Male –2, Left eye Female –12, Heart –4, Stomach-5, Fire-6, Father-9, Rank/Status, Fame-10, Place of worship –12
2	Moon	Sun, Mercury (But not in Cancer)	Mercury, Venus, Saturn (Only in Cancer)	Mars, Jupiter, Venus, Saturn (But not in cancer)	Childhood, Birthplace-1, Face, Mouth-2, Lungs-3/4, Breast, Mind, Mother, Home-4, Emotion-5, Ovaries/Uterus/Bladder, Pregnancy, Residence-7, Sea-Voyages-8, Left eye Male/ Right eye Female-12/2, Sound sleep-12
3	Mars	Sun, Moon (But not in Scorpio), Jupiter	Moon (Only in Cancer), Mercury, Venus (Only in Scorpio)	Venus (But not in Scorpio), Saturn	Blood relations-12, Courage, Younger Siblings –3, I mov able Property-4, Enemies/Disputes/Litigation, Accidents, Competition, Injury-6, Male sexual organs-7, Major accidents-8, Blood-9
4	Mercury	Sun, Moon (But not in Gemini), Mars	Sun, Moon, Jupiter (Only in Gemini)	Mars, Jupiter (But not in Gemini) Saturn	Early Childhood, Smell/Nose, Speech-2, Communication, Short Journey, Writings-3, Education, Family/Caste, Friends, relatives-4, Intelligence-5, Intestine, Maternal Uncle-6, Business/Trade-7

5	Jupiter	Sun, Moon, Mars (But not in Pisces)	Mars (Only in Pisces), (Only in Sagittarius)	Saturn (But not in Sagittarius)	Wealth, Bank balance-2, Hearing/Sense-3/11, Happiness-4, Liver-4/5, Divine love, Gall/Bladder-5, Pancreas-6, band, Hus Famous in society-7, Pilgrimage/Long Journey/ Religious inclination-9, Elder Siblings, Income-11
6	Venus	Mercury, Saturn	Sun, Moon Mars (Only in Libra)	Mars (But non in Libra Jupitar	Jewellery, Poetry-2, Throat, Neck, Music/Dance-3, Vehicle-4, Romance-5, Kidney-6, Partnership, sexuality, Wife-7, Female sexual organs –8, Sexual Pleasures-12
7	Saturn	Mercury (But not in Aquarius), Venus	Sun, Moon, Mars, Mercury (Only in Aquarius)	Jupiter	Hair-1, Teeth-2, Agriculture, Public, Discomforts-4, Debts, Diseases/obstacles, Intestines, Servants/Subordinates, Bodily exertion, worries-6, Danger, Longevity, Return, sorrow-8, Joints/Profession/Livelihood-10, Feet-12
8	Rahu	Venus, Saturn	Sun, Mars, Jupiter	Moon, Mercury	Riots-4, Diplomacy, Paternal Grandfather-5, Friend, outsiders-6, Maternal Grandmother-7, Long time disease, Vice/Sin-8, Journey Abroad –9, Imprisonment-12
9	Ketu	Sun, Moon, Mars	Mercury, Venus	Jupiter, Saturn	Paternal Grandmother, Maternal Grandfather, Spiritual pursuits, Occult Power-12

3.13 Twelve houses (bhavas) and their main significations

There are twelve bhavas in a birth chart. First is the lagna bhava or tanu bhava. It deals with the person's birth, childhood, body, health and personality. Second bhava is dhanu bhava and kutumb bhava indicates financial matters and joint family. Third bhava is bhratra bhava and parakram bhava represents siblings, intelligence and courage. Fourth bhava is matra bhava and sukha bhava. It expresses motherly love, home, conveyance and peace of mind. Fifth bhava is putra bhava and vidhya bhava, which represents children and education. Sixth bhava is ripu bhava and roga bhava, which creates enemies, brings debts and diseases. Seventh bhava is jeewansathi bhava and marak bhava. It represents marital happiness and death. Eighth bhava is aayu bhava and mratue bhava. It signifies span of life and end of life. Ninth bhava is bhagya bhava and dharam bhava, which rules over father, fortune, religion and higher education. Tenth bhava is karma bhava and pitra bhava and indicates occupation, action and prestige. Eleventh bhava is labha bhava and aaya bhava, which deals with means of gains, success and elder brother. Twelfth bhava is vyaya bhava and moksha bhava, which indicates miseries, misfortunes and divinity, the state of death.

Describing the facts regarding any bhava (house) of a birth chart, bhavas (houses) are more important than Constellations (Nakshatras), Signs of Zodiac (Rashis) and also Planets (Grahas). Houses (bhavas) have their own separate entity. They indicate and represent many aspects of life about a human being from the beginning of life to the end of life as stated above. Janam Lagna (ascendant), Chandra Lagna (Moon sign), Surya lagna (Sun sign) and Navansh Lagna, all should be given due importance along with Birth Constellation (Janam Nakshatra) and other constellations associated with signs and planets in predicting a birth chart to reach the accuracy.

3.14 Principles and Rules judging house (bhavas)

While judging and predicting about a bhava (house) or bhavas (houses) of a birth chart following important principles, rules and their scientific values may kindly be kept in mind.

1.   Lagna kundli, Chandra kundli, Surya kundli and Navansh kundli all should be taken for analyzing the facts of the houses of a birth chart.

2.   The placement, conjunction, combination, aspect and overall strength of the owner of the bhava should be taken into account.

3.   With overall strength, natural qualities of the bhava itself may also be studied and noted.

4.   The position of the natural owner (significator) of the bhava should also be considered carefully.

5.   Planets, which are natural benefics, always give good results, while natural malefics spoil the progress of the bhava. Natural benefics and malefics should be carefully observed.

6.   If a natural benefic occupies a bhava in its exalted or own or friendly sign and is in association with or aspected by significator, it is always favourable.

7.   If a bhava significator (karak) is aspected by a malefic planet or planets or an owner or owners of 6th, 8th and 12th bhavas, it leads to destruction (extinction) of the house.

8.   If both sides of a bhava are placed malefic planets and they occupy 4th or 8th bhava and 5th or 9th bhava from the specific bhava, they lessen the better results.

9.   If a bhava is occupied or aspected by its owner, it becomes stronger and gives good and beneficial results.

10. First house owner (Lagnesh) is always treated as good as a benefic as karak. May it be a malefic? It provides good and beneficial results.

11. If a bhava is conjoined or aspected by owner of 1st house, whether it is in trines or kendras, i.e. 5, 9, 1, 4, 7, 10 houses, it is always taken as an auspicious and beneficial for the native.

12. If a bhava is conjoined or aspected by the owners of 6th, 8th 12th bad bhavas, result will be inauspicious and troublesome.The owner of 6th brings debts and diseases and creates enemies, the owner of 8th risk to life or death and owner of 12th poverty and disgrace.

13. If planets occupy such a bhava, which is in conjunction with or aspect by the owners of 3rd, 6th, 8th and 12th bhava, they provide bad results.

14. If the owner and karak of a bhava both are placed in 8th house in Navansh chart, they will be unfavourable, even if they be located in an exalted, own, or friendly sign?

15. If owners of the evil houses i.e. 6th, 8th and 12th houses are in their own houses, they give auspicious results and sometimes form Vipreet Rajyoga, that awards most beneficial results.

16. Each sign (rashi) consists of certain planets well placed, such as Sun in Aries (Mesh) being friendly and certain planets if ill placed such as Saturn in Leo being in enemy sign. So this point should not be overlooked and proper consideration be given. In both the situations results will be different.

17. There may be some special yogas (combinations) and if it is such, their influence on the house (bhava) must be considered carefully.

18. If planets are inclined to favourable nakshatras, they give good results and if they are in cruel or in violent nakshatras,, they give adverse effects. Therefore nakshatras may also be kept in mind.

19. If the owner of the bhava in a birth chart is in the same sign (rashi) in the Navansh chart then it is in a very good position, called 'Vargottam' and it provides favourable results. Exalted planets also give good results but debilitated and weak planets reduce the good effect.

20. If owner of a bhava occupies or aspects its own bhava, it is assumed to give excellent results. May it be a malefic?

21. Weak planet tends to give more adverse results in its major periods or sub periods of Vimshotri dasha (mahadasha / anterdasha). Unhappy developments may arise. One should keep in mind the dasha period of planets.

3.15 Vimshotri Dasha-Planetary Years

Great seer Parashar's views on the Vimshotri dasha should be taken into account to know the span of life of a person. On the basis of triangular method of the Zodiac of 360* degrees, consisting each angle of 120* degrees and also after recording the total period of rotation and revolution of all the nine planets on their path of 120 years, the maximum span of life of a person is considered 120 years. It is further divided among 27 constellations and 9 planets. Please see Vimshotri Dasha Planetary Years in a series below:

Sun	Moon	Mars	Rahu	Jupiter	Saturn	Mercury	Ketu	Venus	Total Years
06	10	07	18	16	19	17	07	20	120

The table 3.15 (T-10) on next page consists of the main and sub priods of Vimshotri Dasha of all the nine planets.

Planetary Years Mahadasha and Anterdasha Table-3.15 (T-10)

Sun Mahadasha 06 years — Krittika, U.Phalguni, U.Ashadha

PL	M	D
SU	03	18
MO	06	00
MA	04	06
RA	10	24
JU	09	18
SA	11	12
ME	10	06
KE	04	06
VE	12	00

Moon Mahadasha 10 years — Rohini, Hasta, Shravan

PL	M	D
MO	10	00
MA	07	00
RA	18	00
JU	16	00
SA	19	00
ME	17	00
KE	07	00
VE	20	00
SU	06	00

Mars Mahadasha 07 years — Mrigshira, Chitra, Dhanishtha

PL	M	D
MA	04	27
RA	12	18
JU	11	06
SA	13	09
ME	11	27
KE	04	27
VE	14	00
SU	04	06
MO	07	00

Rahu Mahadasha 18 years — Ardra, Swati, Shatbhisha

PL	M	D
RA	32	12
JU	28	24
SA	34	06
ME	30	18
KE	12	18
VE	36	00
SU	10	24
MO	18	00
MA	12	18

Jupiter Mahadasha 16 years — Punervasu, Vishaksha, P. Bhadrapad

PL	M	D
JU	25	18
SA	30	12
ME	27	06
KE	11	06
VE	32	00
SU	09	18
MO	16	00
MA	11	06
RA	28	24

Saturn Mahadasha 19 years — Pushya, Anuradha, U. Bhadrapad

PL	M	D
SA	36	03
ME	32	09
KE	13	09
VE	38	00
SU	11	12
MO	19	00
MA	13	09
RA	34	06
JU	30	12

Mercury Mahadasha 17 years — Ashlesha, Jyestha, Revti

PL	M	D
ME	28	27
KE	11	27
VE	34	00
SU	10	06
MO	17	00
MA	11	27
RA	30	18
JU	27	06
SA	32	09

Ketu Mahadasha 07 years — Magha, Moola, Ashwini

PL	M	D
KE	04	27
VE	14	00
SU	04	06
MO	07	00
MA	04	27
RA	12	18
JU	11	06
SA	13	09
ME	11	27

Venus Mahadasha 20 years — P.Phalguni, P.Ashadha, Bharni

PL	M	D
VE	40	00
SU	12	00
MO	20	00
MA	14	00
RA	36	00
JU	32	00
SA	38	00
ME	34	00
KE	14	00

Abbreviations:
PL (Planets) M (Months) D (Days)
SU (Sun) MO (Moon) MA (Mars)
RA (Rahu) JU (Jupiter) SA (Saturn)
ME (Mercury) KE (Ketu) VE (Venus)

3.16 Effects of planets during Mahadahsa / Anterdasha

While analyzing effects of dasha period, we must keep in mind all the three lagnas 1.Janam lagna 2.Chandra lagna 3.Surya lagna called Sudarshan lagans. They may be favourable and friendly or unfavourable and inimical. For Vimshotri dasha results considerations for favourable,benefic and influential lagna signs are noticed as Leo, Cancer, Aries, Scorpio, Sagittarius, Pisces and so their owners Sun, Moon, Mars and Jupiter. The unfavourable, malefic and harmful lagna signs are the remaining signs, Capricorn, Aquarius, Gemini, Virgo, Taurus, Libra and so their owners Saturn, Mercury and Venus also. In a natural way Mercury and Venus are benefics, while in dasha period their results are treated unfavourable. Favourables and benefics produce beneficial , and unfavourables and malefics give unwholesome and unhealthy results during their dasha period. Regarding results and effects of powerful and wellplaced or weak and afflicted during dasa years please see table 3.16 (T-11) below-

Results and effects of planets during dasa Table-3.16 (T-11)

Sr.No.	Planets	If Powerful & wellplaced	If Weak & afflicted
1	Sun	Fame, good for father	Lack of confidence and
2	Moon	Sympathetic, good for	Confused and difficult
3	Mars	Passion, power,	Accidents, arguments
4	Rahu	Worldly success	Losses, downfall
5	Jupiter	Prosperity, good for	Unlucky, difficult for
6	Saturn	Wealthy, honour	Poverty, delay,
7	Mercury	Reading, writing,	Nervousness,
8	Ketu	Mystical, spiritual	Cheat, hypersensitive
9	Venus	Love, money,	Love challenges, loss

3.17 More aspects regarding effects

Please note that anterdasha of a planet is more effective in results either good or bad than mahadasha. More aspects are below:

1. If a planet is powerful and benefic and placed in 1st, 10th, 11th houses always bestows good results.It brings prosperity, dignity and wealth.

2. If a planet is weak and malefic and placed In 1st, 4th, 7th, 10th houses always spoils one's health, wealth and popularity.

૪૦૦૨

Chapter

4

First Trine Purush Trine (Dharma Houses)

4.1 What is Purush Trine? Related Houses

We have already mentioned about constellations with the tables of their characteristics, their nature, classification and effects, signs of zodiac and rising signs at birth with their specific features and description along with the table of characteristics, planets used in Vedic astrology and the table of their characteristics, their qualities and mottos and also the table of planet position in signs / houses and lastly the Birth Chart (Janam kundli) and method of casting a birth chart in three styles (1) North Indian style (2) South Indian style and (3) Western style with examples.

Now we will take 1st, 5th, 9th first trine houses of Purush Trine also called Dharma houses describing their significations, their influencing results on the basis of their placements, aspects and combinations, their owners - benefics or malefics, significators (karaks), planets occupying these houses and also events affecting during their Vimshotri mahadasha and anterdasha period running on as per their birth charts. Purush Trine indicates the 'Paurush' (the power and energy) of a person, which provides him/her a good body stature, health, behaviour, soul, character, knowledge, wisdom, ambition, sentiments, pious deedes and religion. Please see Figure 4.1 (F-3) at the end of chapter.

4.2 First House (Lagna Bhava)

First house is well known as Lagan bhava / Tanu bhava (House of lagna and Individual's body). This bhava deals with the person's birth and childhood. It indicates body, its shape, size, constitution, complexion, vitality, vigour, mind, character, behaviour, personality, honour, dignity, environment, prosperity and longevity. A planet owning or occupying this house tends to produce religious sentiments, truth and morality in a person's life at the time of its mahadasha / anterdasha. So this house is also called the first house of Dharma houses pertaining to religion. The planets Sun and Moon are closely related to it.

It is the centre point of the birth chart. Every activity of life of a native is manifested through this house and sign is called lagna (ascendant). It defines the person's physical appearance and personality traits especially his/her health and behaviour. Lagnesh (1st house owner) and significator (karak) both determine it. Significator of the 1st house is always Sun, while lagnesh (owner of ascendant sign) may vary and differ on the basis of lagna rashi , if it is Aries or Scorpio - Mars, if Taurus or Libra - Venus, if Gemini or Virgo - Mercury, if Sagittarius or Pisces - Jupiter, if Capricorn or Aquarius - Saturn, if Cancer - Moon and if Leo - Sun will be the owner of ascendant (lagnesh).

Features and mentality of the person is also known or verified from Navansh Kundli through the owner of Navansh lagna or planet occupying Navansh lagna. Apart from Navansh lagnesh or occupied planet, if Sun and Moon are placed in their own signs in Navansh, the person may have king like health, habits and complexion and if they are in Saturn and Mars signs, he will be lean and thin having different types of habits.

4.3 Owner of first house in various houses

Powerful and strong owner of 1st house (lagnesh), if it is in favourable nakshatra, in exalted or own or friendly sign, in the houses of Purush trine i.e.1, 5, 9 houses, in angles i.e.1, 4, 7, 10 houses, and in houses of gains - 2,11 houses, (but not in conjunction with or aspected by malefics) always produces good results. The person may be bold, handsome, healthy, wealthy, successful and respectable .If the owner of 1st house occupies 9th or 10th house or owner of 9th or 10th house aspects it, person may rise and improve his/her status. Similarly if lagnesh occupies 4th, 7th, 5th, 11th houses respectively, the person may get all comforts in life such as mother's love, a good house to live in, personal transport, loving and caring life partner, good children, higher education, top level job and a lot of wealth. Weak and afflicted lagnesh results in diseases, litigation, loss of money, debts etc. Person may not progress much. He may always be unhealthy, mentally disturbed and bodily troubled. However house wise effects of 1st house owner are given below:

In first house

(i) **Powerful** - The person will be healthy, happy and prosperous and act according to his own thinking and understanding independently to gain name and fame in his own country. He may be hard working and popular. He may inspire, help and direct others. He may be long lived. He may marry second time and first-born child become a son.

(ii) **Weak** - He may any time be angry and irritable. People may not like his personal views and this position may hurt his mental peace and happiness. His health and longevity may also suffer.

In second house

(i) **Powerful** - He will be generous, sympathetic, a man of good character and high ambitions. He may work for the family welfare and acquire good financial gains, happiness and comforts in life. He may have forethoughts and foresights for better future to be a great man.

(ii) **Weak** - His secret enemies may harm him creating problems and obstructions in the way of his progress. He may go in darkness losing all his riches.

In third house

(i) **Powerful** - He will be bold, brave, courageous, energetic, firm, determined, intelligent, fortunate, religious and respectable. He may be popular in the community. He may head an organization. His younger brothers may also rise in his good time and become prosperous and happy. He may be a good mathematician or a writer or a musician.

(ii) **Weak** - His younger brothers may not progress and go against him. This is also possible, that he may not have younger brother or brothers. His vitality and vigour may suffer.

In fourth house

(i) **Powerful** - The person will be obedient to his parents and get love and happiness from them. He may acquire landed property, a big house, personal transport and a lot of wealth. He may continue his education to be more qualified and knowledgeable. He may have domestic peace and happiness. He may improve his status. He may be sympathetic and generous.

(ii) **Weak** - He may lose his property and wealth. This situation may disturb his family happiness. He may become poor and bereft of motherly love.

In fifth house

(i) **Powerful** - The person will be an efficient leader in his field. He may be religious and get good reputation in the community. He may be genius. People may like and admire him.

(ii) **Weak** - His children may not be able to give him a good support for leading a comfortable life. He may be short tempered and lose his control. He may be busy in helping others.

In sixth house

(i) **Powerful** -The person will take up risky and courageous occupations, legal and medical professions. He may be fortunate and respectable.

(ii) **Weak** - He may be a victim of enemies and run in debts. He may have skin diseases. His health may suffer. He may be anxious and worried.

In seventh house

(i) **Powerful** - He will be fully devoted to his life partner and travel to distant places in country or abroad. He may probably live abroad and lead a good, happy and respectable life.

(ii) **Weak** - He may marry second time. But this marriage may disturb his personal life. He may feel unlucky and unhappy.

In eighth house

(i) **Powerful** - He will be intellectual, learned, religious and contented always helping the poor. He may be a good astrologer having so many friends and followers. He may be long lived.

(ii) Weak - He may be selfish and greedy. He may suffer diseases in secret organs. He may adopt gambling like bad habits. Sudden but peaceful death may occur.

In ninth house

(i) Powerful - The person will be proud but daring, courageous, fortunate, religious and charitable. He may be healthy and wealthy. Life partner and children may also be well educated. He may earn popularity. His father may also be rich and prosperous.

(ii) Weak - He may be unlucky in sharing paternal property. His brothers and friends may go against him. This situation may shape and change him to be an atheist, pessimist and unhappy.

In tenth house

(i) Powerful - He will professionally be successful in earning a lot of wealth and improving his status. He will be intelligent, learned and a man of character. He may be popular among friends and foes. He may obtain honour and dignity. He will be self-made man and long lived.

(ii) Weak - He may lose his chances of research, health, wealth, status, dignity and popularity.

In eleventh house

(i) Powerful - The person will be hard working and a man of character. He may discharge his duties well .He may gain more profits from his occupation or service. He may be virtuous for his elderly brothers and uncles.

(ii) Weak - His occupation or service status may go down. This may lessen his income and popularity.

In twelfth house

(i) Powerful - He will be well educated, religious and wealthy having many friends. He may settle abroad. He may have better connections with the foreigners and buy a big property (estate) there.

(ii) Weak - He may lose his health and heritage, riches and property. He may travel to holy places. He may suffer at the hands of foreigners in his business endeavours and become poor.

4.4 Planets occupying the first house

Almost all the planets are better and beneficial in 1st house (lagna bhava), if they are placed in favourable nakshatras and in exalted or own or friendly signs with good conjunctions, combinations and aspects as already stated. Malefics, especially owners of 6th, 8th, 12th houses are harmful and troublesome. Thus planets occupying the house (bhava) determine the ways, manners and area of rise of the person. Planet wise merits and demerits (benefits and losses) may turn up either in positive or negative situations as under:

1.Sun

    (i) **Positive -** Sun is the significator (karak) of first house. If Sun is in first house in favourable nakshatra, in exalted or own or friendly sign and in conjunction with or aspect by benefics, the person will be healthy, happy, optimist, cheerful, ambitious, righteous and powerful. He may procure respect and popularity in government, also favour of authority and income. His father may also be healthy, happy and prosperous. God may grant him a son, if Sun is attached with the owner of 5th house. Combination with 2nd and 4th house owners may provide him all kinds of comforts in life. He may prosper to be wealthy.

    (ii) **Negative -** If Sun in first house is in debilitated sign and weak or in conjunction with Saturn or Mars or Rahu or Ketu, he may be wretched (pitiable) and lose his dignity and grace .He may suffer from stomach problems, eye disease, tooth pain, impurity in blood, hot constitution and scars or itches all over the skin on body.

2.Moon

    (i) **Positive -** Moon is the planet of individual's mind and moods. It gives an attractive, handsome and romantic appearance and an easy-going life. If it is in first house in conjunction with Jupiter, the person may be learned and respected in society. He may be seen untiring, traveling, thinking and exploring new ideas. It may magnify his fortune and fame. He may choose public related occupations or jobs to come into direct contact with common men and to be popular in public sector.

(ii) Negative - Moon in first house in conjunction with Saturn may cause him anxieties and worries, with Mars in case of men - the feelings of anger and blood pressure or in case of women - menstrual disorder and with Rahu disease of hysteria.

3.Mars

(i) **Positive** - The positive location of Mars in 1st house will make the person bold, courageous, energetic, independent, self-confident and firm. He may be handsome, pleasing, capable, studious and hardworking. He may be aggressive too. He will not tolerate, if someone interferes in his work.

(ii) **Negative** - If Mars is negative in first house, he may be prone to accidents. Scars may be seen on his body. It may cause bad health. His domestic life may also be disturbed.

4.Mercury

(i) **Positive** - He may be learned and intellectual, if Mercury is in first house. He may be inclined to occult sciences and become a good astrologer. It may bestow him beautiful appearance and humorous nature. This nature may make him to be loveable and popular everywhere. He may excel in literary and communicative activities. He may be a good orator. If it is in conjunction with Venus, he may be a talented artist, a musician or a singer.

(ii) **Negative** - The conjunction of Rahu or Ketu may bring break down in his nervous system, causing unhealthy conditions with long time illness.

5.Jupiter

(i) **Positive** - Jupiter in first house (lagna) provides a person a magnetic personality. He may be highly ambitious, optimistic, good mannered, happy and joyful getting respect everywhere. He may be fond of sweet delicious food. He may be a good teacher, lecturer, professor, writer, speaker, lawyer, financial adviser and political leader. He will be religious and God fearing. If 5th house is powerful, he may have capable sons.

(ii) **Negative** - The habit of taking sweet delicious food in much quantity may make him a prone to diseases such as impurity of blood and skin problems. If Jupiter is in conjunction with Rahu, it may lead him to commit sins creating many troubles in life.

6.Venus

(i) **Positive** - If Venus is placed in lagna in its exalted or own or Capricorn or Aquarius sign, the person may join high-level post. He may be happy and cheerful enjoying music and dance. He may be admired by opposite sex. He may go abroad and earn a lot of wealth. He may be fortunate enjoying luxurious life. He may marry at an early age with a beautiful and devoted lady.

(ii) **Negative** - If Venus is negative; he may be inclined to excessive sexual activities. This may affect his health, wealth and character.

7.Saturn

(i) **Positive** - If Saturn is in lagna, the person may be lean and thin but serious in his duties. He may be busy in work patiently with self-confidence. He may do good deeds helping others in many ways .He may be wealthy and turn to be religious. He may be conservative.

(ii) **Negative** - If Saturn is negative and afflicted; he may appear to be inactive and anxious. Sorrows and misfortunes may affect his routine life. He may feel lonely and suffer from depression.

8.Rahu

(i) **Positive** - If Rahu is in lagna, he may be studious and hard working in earning money. He may have landed property, conveyance and enough bank balance. He may have a few children. He may go abroad and capture authority and status there.

(ii) **Negative** - Rahu is like Saturn in nature. If negative, it is not good in lagna. It creates long-term diseases and the person may be weak and sickly always under treatment. He may be obstinate and stubborn. If lagna sign is Sagittarius, where Rahu is debilitated and weak, he may lose his property and reputation and feel confused and perturbed. His marriage may also be delayed.

9.Ketu

(i) **Positive** - If it is in Sagittarius sign, it may encourage long journeys. He may earn lot of wealth and manage all comforts to lead a better and peaceful life.

(ii) **Negative** - Ketu gives weak health. It works like Mars. If it is debilitated and negative in nature, the person may turn to be angry and aggressive. He may have strange food habits. He may be deceitful in nature. He may become mentally instable. His married life may also be unhappy.

4.5 Planets placements, aspects and combinations 1st house

The following placements, aspects and combinations are given regarding lagnesh and its effects especially to know the significations to the first bhava.

1. If 1st house owner (lagnesh) is in Vargottam, it is a very good position. Here Vargottam means 1st house owner is in the same sign in Navansh chart as that in the Birth chart. It is most favourable. The person will be healthy and happy.

2. If movable signs 1,4,7,10 are in lagna, the person will be healthy, wealthy and prosperous.

3. If Jupiter is in lagna or in one of 4th, 7th, 10th, 5th, 9th houses, person will be handsome, healthy intelligent, knowledgeable, influential, popular and fortunate.

4. If all the planets aspect lagna, the person will be healthy, wealthy, long-lived and happy.

5. If lagnesh aspects lagna, he will be healthy, wealthy and happy like a king..

6. If lagnesh is in any one of 1st, 4th, 7th, 10th, 9th, 5th houses and aspects lagna, the person becomes well known.

7. If Lagnesh and owner of 8th house occupy lagna, the person will be healthy and long-lived.

8. If owner of lagna is Venus or Moon and Jupiter aspects, the person will be strong, bold and courageous.

9. If lagnesh is placed in 9th house, the person will be happier and healthier after the teenage and if lagnesh is in 10th house, he will be daring and energetic till long life.

10. If lagnesh is in 9th house and owner of 9th house is in lagna or vice versa, the person travels to abroad and becomes well known.

11. If lagna is Taurus or Libra and lagnesh Venus and Jupiter are in kendras, The person will be a great singer. He / she will be wealthy and well known.

12. If lagnesh is in conjunction with or aspected by owners of 6th, 8th, 12th houses, his health will suffer. He will surely be sickly.

13. If lagnesh is in 8th house, the person will have weak constitution and if lagnesh and 8th house owner both are in lagna, he will be healthy and happy.

14. If Sun, Mars and Saturn all are in lagna with lagnesh, the person will be very weak and lean.

15. If Rahu, Mars, Saturn occupy lagna, person may have trouble in sexual organs.

16. If Cancer or Scorpio or Pisces sign is in lagna, the person will be fat or corpulent.

17. If there are more malefics in lagna, the person will always be miserable.

18. If Mars or Saturn is lagnesh and Rahu occupies Lagna, person may get head injury due to some accident.

19. If lagnesh is in 2nd house and Rahu aspects or in 12th house and Saturn aspects, in both the situations, person will lose his health and happiness.

20. If lagnesh is placed in 3rd, 5th, 7th constellation from birth constellation, this position will be adverse and unfavourable to the person. He may be sick.

21. If lagnesh is in a debilitated sign occupying houses as stated below lagna-wise, it confirms the disease of related house (bhava)-

    (i) In Aries lagna Mars in 4th house debilitated in sign Cancer creates chest and lungs problems.

    (ii) In Taurus lagna Venus in 5th house debilitated in Virgo provides stomach pain.

    (iii) In Gemini lagna Mercury in 10th house debilitated in Pisces gives backache and knee pain.

    (iv) In Cancer lagna Moon in 5th house debilitated in Scorpio brings watery and earthy digestive problems.

(v)   In Leo lagna Sun in 3rd house debilitated in Libra gives arms and nail pains.

(vi)   In Virgo lagna Mercury in 7th house debilitated in Pisces gives urinary organs diseases.

(vii)   In Libra lagna Venus in 12th house debilitated in Virgo gives eye disease and feet problems.

(viii)   In Scorpio lagna Mars in 9th house debilitated in Cancer gives hip pains or problems.

(ix)   In Sagittarius lagna Jupiter in 2nd house debilitated in Capricorn creates mouth disease.

(x)   In Capricorn lagna Saturn in 4th house debilitated in Aries creates chest and lungs problems.

(xi)   In Aquarius lagna Saturn in 3rd house debilitated in Aries provides nail pains.

(xii)   In Pisces lagna Jupiter in 11th house debilitated in Capricorn gives arms and legs pain.

4.6   Events affecting during dasha Sign in 1st house

In Aries

(i)   **Favourable** - If sign is Aries in 1st house, Mars will be lagnesh. It may be beneficial during its dasha. Strong Jupiter or Sun's dasha period may also keep him healthy and improve his educational status. He may be fortunate leading a prosperous and a comfortable life. He may be well behaved and religious. Weak Mercury dasha may also make him healthy, wealthy and famous.

(ii)   **Unfavourable** - Moon or Venus or Saturn dasha may mould him to immorality lessening his wealth, status, health and peace of mind.

In Taurus

(i)   **Favourable** - Venus will be lagnesh hence its dasha may be good for wealth. If friendly powerful Saturn or Mercury or Rahu dasha is also running, it may shape him corpulent but religious and wealthy. He may improve his status and popularity in his family. He may be well mannered and happy. He may get scholarships.

(ii)   **Unfavourable** - If planet inimical to Venus is there in lagna, it may keep him unhealthy. He may be sickly and poor during their dasha period. His children may also cause troubles affecting his health and mental peace.

In Gemini

(i) **Favourable** - Here Mercury is lagnesh. If Mercury and friendly Venus dasha is running, he may succeed in his business and improve his financial position. He may adopt writing and communicative work and travel frequently. His siblings may help him. He may marry second time.

(ii) **Unfavourable** - If planet inimical to Mercury dasha is running and 7th house is weak and afflicted, he may indulge in immature sex, which may spoil his position and popularity.

In Cancer

(i) **Favourable** - Moon will be lagnesh. If its dasha and strong Jupiter or Mars dasha is in operation, his appearance may be handsome and attractive. His life may be peaceful. He may regard and respect his parents. He may be successful in his efforts. He may lead a comfortable life having his house and conveyance facilities. His parents may also lead a comfortable and respected life. He may be purely religious and perform all the traditional rites and rituals from time to time. He may be long lived.

(ii) **Unfavourable** - If Moon is weak and afflicted, during its dasha, government may impose tax penalty on him. He may incur financial losses.

In Leo

(i) **Favourable** - If Sun and Mars are strong; he may be well known, healthy and wealthy in their dasha period. He may improve his status and beget a son. He may be fond of music and dance.

(ii) **Unfavourable** - If Sun is debilitated or weak, during its dasha; his children may create problems in his business. He may be worried and mentally disturbed.

In Virgo

(i) **Favourable** - Mercury will be lagnesh. If its dasha and friendly but powerful Venus dasha are in operation, he may improve his health and wealth. He may win over his enemies or opponents.

(ii) **Unfavourable** - If Mercury and other than Venus dasha are going on, his enemies or opponents may create troubles. He may suffer from diseases and debts.

In Libra

(i) **Favourable** - Venus will be lagnesh. If its dasha and Mercury or Saturn dasha are running, he may improve his status. His wife may be well behaved and beautiful. His domestic life may be happy and peaceful.

(ii) **Unfavourable** - Other than above planet's dasha may keep him busy in traveling aimlessly and wasting money uselessly for no good cause.

In Scorpio

(i) **Favourable** - Mars will be lagnesh. Mars dasha may be a little bit beneficial. If with Mars Jupiter or Moon or Sun dasha is running, it may be more favourable for further studies. He may be respected and reputed. If Mars is in 4th, 8th and 12th Moksha houses, he may be religious and spiritual. He may also get patrimony and become wealthy.

(ii) **Unfavourable** - If with Mars Saturn or Rahu dasha is in operation, he may indulge in extra marital sex outside and become sick. He may also be a gambler or thief.

In Sagittarius

(i) **Favourable** - Jupiter will be lagnesh. If it occupies 9th house with Mars or Sun during its dasha period, he may be religious, friendly, wealthy and well known. He may lead a happy and comfortable life with his caring wife and good children. He may love and respect his father. He may gain money from him. He may be successful in his ventures. His siblings may also prosper and respect him. If Jupiter is in a friendly sign, his conduct may also be blameless. .

(ii) **Unfavourable** - He may work hard during its dasha period. This excessive hard work may affect his health and happiness.

In Capricorn

(i) **Favourable** - Lagnesh Saturn dasha with friendly Venus or Mercury dasha will make him intelligent and learned. He may join a high level post in government. He may be progressive and successful. He may be wealthy, well known and a man of good conduct and character. He may love and regard his father and elders. He may be religious and travel to many holy places.

(ii) **Unfavourable** - During an inimical planet dasha, he may work in excess time and quantity. This may lose his health, domestic happiness and personal concerns.

In Aquarius

(i) **Favourable** - Saturn will be lagnesh. During its dasha, he may be healthy, wealthy and popular. If with Saturn friendly Venus dasha is going on, it may help him to be courageous, energetic, hard working and successful wealthy person. He may regard and respect his elder siblings. He may be in a high position having good friendly circle especially of opposite sex.

(ii) **Unfavourable** - During an inimical planet dasha, friendly circle of opposite sex may be a problem for him in his own family.

In Pisces

(i) **Favourable** - Jupiter will be lagnesh. If it is powerful, during its dasha, he may be healthy, wealthy and popular having all comforts of life. If with Jupiter friendly Moon or Mars dasha is running, it may make him disciplined and virtuous. He may be active and lead a happy life.

(ii) **Unfavourable** - If an inimical panet dasha is in operation, he may live far away from his birthplace. He may be harsh. He may not be cordial to his family members and relatives. He may be extravagant and develop tendency for gambling. He may lose his health and become sickly.

4.7 Examples – kundlis (From 1st Aries lagna to 12th Pisces lagna)

Kundlis of all 12 lagnas from Aries to Pisces are given below for reference and example purposes with astrological observations, their facts and effects. More examples house-wise of Purush trine (Dharma houses) 1st, 5th, 9th houses are also quoted at the end of this chapter. Three main points have been taken regarding Astrological Observations for examples of every lagna kundli. Three main points are:

1. Lagna considerations

2. Placements, aspects and combinations

3. Conclusion

At first we are taking following twelve kundlis as Example Kundlis No. 4 to 15 with astrological observations, their facts and effects.

Kundli No. 4 Mesh lagna - Retirted Police officer Mr. K.P.S.Gill
  1. Date of birth 29 -12 - 1934,
  2. Time of birth 14 -15 P.M. (IST)
  3. Place of birth Cochin (Kerala) Lat.- 09⁰ / 58' N, Long. - 76⁰ / 14' E.
  4. Birth Nakshatra Hasta - 3
  5. Balance Dasha at birth Moon 04 years - 07months - 18days

BIRTH CHART

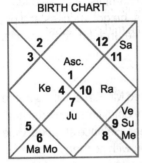

NAVANSH CHART

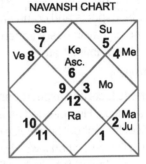

Kundli No. 4.7 (K-4)

Astrological Observations

Aries is the rhythmic, violent, mysterious, acute and impulsive sign. Arieans are active, aggressive, rough and rugged. They resist diseases. They are dynamic, creative, independent, frank, ambitious, energetic, forceful and heroic. They are always in limelight. Their will power is strong. The above Birth Chart being Aries (Mesh) lagna belongs to bold, brave, courageous, forceful and popular police officer Mr. K.P.S.Gill

1. Lagna considerations

Here lagnesh Mars.and Surya lagnesh Jupiter aspect lagna. Chandra lagnesh Mercury is located in 9th house of luck and fortune with Sun, the significator (karak) of the house. Mars and Jupiter made him action oriented, enterprising, powerful and ambitious. Thus lagna is activated. Being born in Hasta nakshatra, he himself is an intelligent, learned, bold, brave and courageous man.

2. Placements, aspects and combinations

Lagnesh Mars, Jupiter and labhesh (11th house owner) Saturn are aspecting Lagna (1st house). Chandra lagnesh Mercury is sitting with the Sun and Venus in 9th house and all are aspecting 3rd house, which indicates power and energy (parakram). From Chandra lagna 3rd house of Mars, sign Scorpio i.e. 8th house, is aspected by Saturn. Bhagyesh

(9th house owner) Jupiter is situated in 7th house in Libra sign, which is owned by Venus, and Venus is in 9th house in Sagittarius sign of Jupiter, hence there is an exchange of signs (Rashi Parivartan Yoga). Venus is in the highest longitude among all other planets, therefore it becomes Atamkarak. In Navansh lagna Ketu is in 1st house and exalted Saturn is in the 2nd house and Sun in its own sign Leo in 12th house made him a fearless and forceful officer and a good administrator. Because of these placements, aspects and combinations, he got success and popularity, honour and dignity in every sphere of life. Indeed he bears all the good qualities of an administrator.

3.Conclusion

All these facts and aspects bestowed Mr. K.P.S.Gill supreme powers in police services. He emerged as a very bold, firm, powerful and fearless police officer throughout his service career. He once stopped violence and terrorism in Punjab, when it was burning with so many problems. He had been the president of the Hockey Players Association of India for a long time. Indian Hockey team won medals and got name and fame all over the world in his time. Now Ketu dasha is operating, that may be normal to keep him energetic, happy and peaceful.

Kundli No. 5 Vrishabh lagna - Famous Singer Lata Mangeskar

1.Date of birth 28 - 09 - 1929

2.Time of birth 21 - 51P.M. (IST)

3.Place of birth Indore (M.P.) Lat. 22⁰ / 43' N. Long 72⁰ / 50' E.

4.Birth Nakshatra Pushya - 4

5.Balance Dasha at birth Saturn 00 years - 01 month - 06days

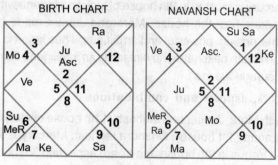

Kundli No. 4.7 (K-5)

Astrological Observations

Taurus sign is next to Aries. It is mild, soft, smooth and submissive sign. Taureans are practical, reliable, patient, determined and focused people. They are tolerant, but when they lose their temper, they become angry and aggressive like a bull. After a short period they become normal. They are fond of pleasure, fun, love, beauty and music. They are amazing in controlling themselves. They are obstinate having certain principles in life. The above given birth chart belongs to the world-famous singer Lata Mangeskar.

1. Lagna considerations

Lagnesh Venus is posited in 4th house of comforts, Chandra Lagnesh Moon is in its own sign Cancer in 3rd house of growth and Surya lagnesh Mercury in its exalted sign with karak Sun is sitting in the 5th house of intelligence. Though none aspects lagna, yet all planets are placed in from 3rd to 5th houses. It is good to be a famous singer. Born in Pushya nakshatra, she is virtuous, righteous, dutiful, good-natured, learned, theist and devotee of Almighty God. She has sweet voice having all these qualities. In Navansh chart. Mercury is rising in the Virgo sign, hence Vargottam, imparting her a sweet voice and power of speech. She got name and fame because of her sweet voice and different type of sweet songs sung by her. Jupiter is situated in lagna and aspects 5th and 9th houses. This made her knowledgeable and fortunate. The owner of speech (voice) Mercury retrogrades and is posited in the 5th house of wisdom. Jupiter, the planet of wisdom is occupying Lagna and aspects the 5th house and also Atamkarak Mercury. Chandra lagnesh Moon is placed in its own sign Cancer (Chandra lagna).

2. Placements, aspects and combinations

In Taurus lagna, the owner Venus is in 4th, the house of comforts as a result of which luxury and success came to her doorstep and she became a world fame singer. She is happy, healthy and wealthy. Jupiter, being the owner of 8th and 11th, the houses of occult knowledge and gains (profits) and fulfillment of desires blessed her supernatural powers in voice. From Chandra lagna Sun and Mercury both are in 3rd, the house of energy and speech. Sun is forming Ubhayachari yoga, Moon Sunpha yoga and Mercury with Sun Budhaditya yoga. All combinations are strengthening her ability to cope with the field of singing.

3. Conclusion

The position of Jupiter and Venus in kendras and Mercury in trine house and that too in an exalted sign, established her as a great singer. Now She is popular all over the world for her sweet songs. She walks in and out of the country to entertain her fans and admirers. Present dasha is also favourable to keep her healthy and happy.

Kundli No. 6 Mithun lagna- Computer Wizard Bill Gates

1. Date of birth 28 - 10 - 1955
2. Time of birth 21 - 30 P.M. (PST)
3. Place of birth Seattle (U.S.A) Lat.47^0 / 36' N.Long.122^0 / 19' W.
4. Birth Nakshatra Uttara Bhadrapad - 4
5. Balance Dasha at birth Saturn 02 years 09 Months 02 Days.

BIRTH CHART

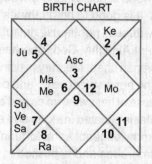

NAVANSH CHART

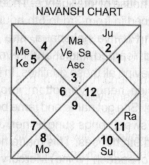

KUNDLI - 6

Kundli No. 4.7 (K-6)

Astrological Observations

Gemini is the sign of intelligence and knowledge. Geminians are planners, versatile, adaptable, emotional, charming, logical, lively, chatty, amazing, amusing, fond of reading and writing, good conversationalist, inventive, progressive and mathematician. Their memory and grasping power is tremendous. The above horoscope belongs to the world famous computer wizard, Mr. Bill Gates, who revolutionized in computers informational technology.

1. Lagna considerations

Lagnesh Mercury is placed in its exalted Virgo sign in the 4th house of comforts with Mars and aspects the 10th house of actions. Chandra Lagnesh Jupiter in 3rd house and Surya lagnesh Venus in its own sign with Sun and Saturn in 5th house, are placed in its adjoining houses on both sides. Therefore lagna is fortified. Being born in Uttra Bhadrapada nakshatra, he is tactful, fond of arguing, prolific in procreation and has aptitude for learning. This is the reason, that he became Computer wizard. In Navansh lagna Saturn, Venus and Mars are posited and adding more power and strength to him. The significator Sun, though it is in debilitated position, yet being in 5th house with Venus in its own sign and exalted Saturn producing Neechbhang Rajyoga made him famous in this field of computers information technology.

2. Placements, aspects and combinations

Lagnesh Mercury is in 4th house with Mars and both aspect 10th house of actions. Mercury is strong being in its exalted sign and is forming Bhadra Yoga. Mars aspects its own sign in the 11th house of gains and profits. Moon aspects 4th house and Jupiter aspects 9th house of fortune and 11th house of gains and profits. Exalted Saturn and Venus both are in sign Libra and both aspects the 11th house of gains and profits. Exalted Saturn with friendly Venus made the person computer wizard and provided him name and fame, dignity and honour in the field of Computers all over the world. Sun is forming Ubhaychari yoga. Exalted Saturn is Atamkarak and it aspects 11th and 2nd houses of gains and financial matters. It is a good position. It bestowed him prosperity and extreme wealth.

3.Conclusion

Though he is a computer wizard and in 2009 first richest person of the world as shown in Forbes Magazine, yet he is suffering from the challenge of piracy in this field of computers because of Rahu aspects Moon in 10th house and its sign in 2nd house. He will have to take more steps to handle this problem. He may progress more but he should try to solve the problem of piracy so that it may come to an end. If it is solved then a new era of prosperity will come to his doorsteps.

Kundli No. 7 Kark lagna- Great Saint Aurobindo Ghosh

1.Date of birth 15 - 08 - 1872
2.Time of birth 04 - 45 A.M. (IST)
3.Place of birth kolkata (W.Bengal) Lat. 22^0 / 32' N. Long. 88^0 / 22' E.
4.Birth Nakshatra Moola - 2
5.Balance Dasha at birth Ketu 04 Years - 00 Month - 14 Days.

BIRTH CHART   NAVANSH CHART

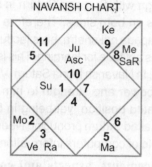

Kundli No. 4.7 (K-7)

Astrological Oberservations

Cancer is the fourth sign of the zodiac. It is emotional, sensitive and changeable. Cancer people are self-reliant, intelligent, imaginative, talkative, honest, easily moveable and attached to the family. Its owner Moon represents mind, feelings and emotions. The above kundli (Birth Chart) belongs to Saint Aurobindo Ghosh, who showed a way of life and served the people.

1. Lagna considerations

Lagnesh Moon is situated in Jupiter's sign Sagittarius and Jupiter is posited in 1st house in Cancer singn of Moon. It is in its exalted sign with friendly Mars, hence lagna is fortified. Surya lagnesh Sun is located in its own sign Leo. Persons born in Moola nakshatra are ease loving, peaceful, are of balanced mind and disciplined, so he was. In Navansh chart Sun and Moon both are in exalted signs in 4th and 5th houses. Sun inclined him for good cause of religion. Significator (Karak) Sun is in 2nd house of financial matters in its own sign with Mercury and Venus. It is a good position.

2. Placements, aspects and combinations

Exalted Jupiter with Mars is posited in lagna and from lagna it aspects 5th house of wisdom and Siddhis (specific knowledge) and 9th house of fortune and religion. Moon and Jupiter are forming Rashi Parivartan yoga, the exchange of signs / houses being Moon in 6th house in Sagittarius and Jupiter in lagna in Cancer in 1st house. Mars being Owner of 5th and 10th houses sitting in lagna with exalted Jupiter creating Neechbhang Rajyoga also supported energy and strength. Moon for mind and Jupiter for heart provided him understanding and power. Sun, Mercury, Venus in royal sign Leo in 2nd house and Moon, Saturn in Sagittarius in 6th house all developed in him mystic and spiritualistic nature. Other than this, Mercury with Sun is forming Budhaditaya yoga. Mercury is Atamkarak also. Sun forming Vasi yoga, Moon Anpha yoga, Jupiter Hansa yoga gave him saintly qualities. Moon in conjunction with Saturn were also responsible for his ascetism and saintly behaviour. He was a famous philosopher of his time.

3. Conclusion

Because of all the above placements, aspects and combinations intelligent and learned Aurobindo Ghosh did penance whole-heartedly with his mind, intelligence and devotion to God. He later on became Yogiraj. He established a religious institution in Pondicherry (India) now called Aurobindo Ashram. This institution reminds us his good works done for the welfare of humanity and the culture of India.

Kundli No. 8 Simha lagna Ex. President Shankar Dayal Sharma

1.Date of birth 19 - 08 - 1918

2.Time of birth 07 - 00 A.M. (IST)

3.Place of birth Bhopal (M.P.) Lat. 23^0 / 16' N. Long.77^0 / 23' E.

4.Birth Nakshatra Poorva Ashadha - 3

5.Balance Dasha at birth Venus 08 Years- 09 Months- 26 Days.

BIRTH CHART

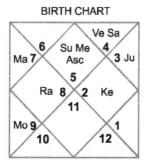

NAVANSH CHART

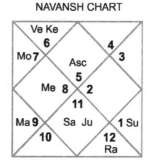

Kundli No. 4.7 (k-8)

Astrological Observations:

Leo is the 5th sign of zodiac. It is the sign of royal planet Sun, king of all the planets hence Leons are dynamic, dominating, active, creative, ambitious, courageous, generous, enthusiastic, broad minded, warm-hearted, frank, truthful, energetic, adaptable and unemotional. They are independent thinkers and good organizers. They have lot of tolerance and mingle with high status and low cast people. The above kundli (Birth Chart) relates to our honourable president S.D.Sharma, who was unanimously elected in his time.

1.Lagna considerations

Lagnesh and Surya lagnesh Sun is in its own sign Leo in lagna, therefore, lagna is extremely activated and powerful. Chandra Lagnesh Jupiter is posited in 11th house. Moon aspects Jupiter and Jupiter aspects Moon. He was born in Poorva-Shadha nakshatra, hence he was peace loving, far-sighted, truthful and friendly. Once he was the only choice as a President of India for all the members of Lok Sabha and Rajya Sabha. In Navansh chart owner of the sign Leo is in its exalted sign Aries in 9th house of fortune and religion. Significator Sun and lagnesh is occupying its own house of lagna in Mool-trikon sign, providing energy, power and strength to the person. He was healthy, wealthy and fortunate enough.

2.Placements, aspects and combinations

Mercury with the Sun is in lagna and forming Budhaditaya yoga. He was a man of literature and a good orator. He was intelligent and learned and reached up to highest level in government as a first citizen of India. Moon and Jupiter aspects each other face to face forming a very good Gajkesri Yoga. Mars, being yogkarak for Leo ascendant, from 3rd house aspects its exalted sign in 6th house and also 9th and 10th houses of Fortune and Karma (actions) forming a kind of Rajyog. This is the notable and remarkable fact, which led him so high to be a first citizen of India.

3.Conclusion

Due to all above facts, he enjoyed the lifelong love of his friends and reached to the highest post of the country, the President of India in the last days of his long political career getting respect and honour all over the world. Mars is the Rajyog Karak. This made him popular. Now he is no more, but he will be remembered years long in the history of democratic India for his deeds.

Kundli No. 9 Kanya lagna Cricketer Sachin Tendulkar
1. Date of birth 21 - 04 - 1973
2. Time of birth 18 - 00 P.M. (IST)
3. Place of birth Mumbai (Maharast) Lat. 18^0 / 58' N. Long.72^0 / 50' E.
4. Birth Nakshatra Jyeshtha - 2
5. Balance Dasha at birth Mercury 10 Years- 08 Months-16 Days.

BIRTH CHART

NAVANSH CHART

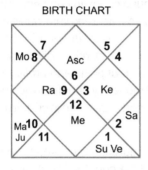
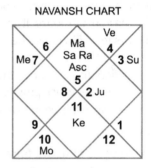

Kundli No. 4.7 (K-9)

Astrological Observations

Virgo is the 6th sign of zodiac. The sign Virgo concerned with Mercury is the sign of intelligence and knowledge. Virgo people are intelligent, knowledgeable, analytical and dutiful. They are methodical truthful, peace-loving, introvert, talkative and economical. They are never satisfied with their achievements. They are kindly and agreeable. The above kundli (birth chart) pertains to our best cricketer Sachin Tendulkar, who is never satisfied with his achievements of the field and tries again and again to be the best in his field.

1.Lagna considerations

Lagnesh Mercury is placed in 7th house and aspects lagna. Chandra lagnesh and Surya lagnesh is one and the same i.e. Mars in its exalted sign Capricorn is situated in 5th house of intelligence. Debilitated Jupiter is sitting in 5th house with exalted Mars, which is creating Neechbhang Rajyoga, also aspects lagna hence lagna is activated. Born in Jayeshtha nakshatra, he is joyful, laborious, energetic, bold, courageous, religious, charitable, have few friends. Navansh lagnesh Sun is posited in 11th house of Mercury of gains and profits, increasing his income. Significator (Karak) Sun is located in 8th house in its exalted sign with Venus, the owner of the houses of fortune and wealth.

2.Placements, aspects and combinations

Virgo is the sign of intellectual. Born in Virgo lagna, the person is intelligent, analytical, dutiful, methodical, truthful, introvert, talkative and economical. He is disciplined and loves peace. He is never satisfied with his cricket achievements. Lagnesh Mercury is placed in 7th house and aspects lagna, which has its own exalted sign Virgo. Jupiter, the owner of 4th and 7th houses is located in 5th house of destiny and education and aspects lagna from 5th house. It gave him movable and immovable property. Exalted Mars from 5th house being the owners of 8th and 3rd houses of courage and hidden talents made him Brad man of India cultivating immense capability of fighting. Owner of 11th house of gains and profits, Moon is placed in 3rd house, which provided all monetary benefits including travel opportunities with in the country and abroad to take part in cricket matches.

3.Conclusion

On the basis of above facts and figures, the cricketer Sachin has got the goals and glory for himself and the country. He always showed his vigour and vitality in every ensuing game of cricket. He is called Master-Blaster Sachin. His future will also be bright and remarkable. This time Venus Mahadasha is running. It will be lucky for him. His future career will be more shining and progressive for him and the country.

Kundli No. 10 Tula lagna Actor/Politician Ex. C.M. N. T. Ramarao

1.Date of birth 28 - 05 - 1923,

2.Time of birth 17-00 P.M. (IST)

3.Place of birth Hyderabad (A.P.) Lat. 17⁰ / 23' N. Long. 78⁰ / 28' E.

4.Birth Nakshatra Swati - 4

5.Balance Dasha at birth Rahu 01 Year - 04 Months - 00 Day.

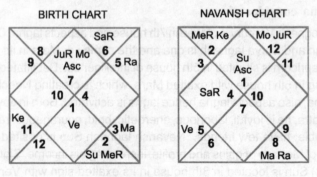

Kundli No. 4.7 (K-10)

Astrological Observations

Libra is the 7th sign of zodiac regarding justice and balance. Librans are smiling, affectionate, easy going, idealist and far-sighted. They are handsome, beautiful, traditional, peace loving and have good qualities of leadership. Their thinking is always positive and favourable. They properly weigh pros and cons before taking any decision. Following considerations belongs to the kundli of actor turned politician N. T. Ramarao, who chaired the post of chief minister of Andhra Pradesh and administered it very well.

1. Lagna considerations

In his kundli lagnesh, Chandra lagnesh and Surya lagnesh Venus is situated in 7th house and aspects lagna, hence lagna is extremely activated. Being born in Swati nakshatra, he was well behaved, intelligent, knowledgeable, dutiful, sweet spoken, religious and charitable. In Navansh lagna Sun is posited in lagna in its exalted sign ànd Jupiter from its own sign Pisces aspects 4th house in its exalted sign, where retrograde Saturn is located and aspects its own sign in 10th house of actions. Significator (Karak) Sun is in 8th house in Venus sign Taurus with Mercury, which accorded him the highest post of administration in the state of Andhra Pradesh.

2. Placements, aspects and combinations

Moon and Jupiter both are posited in lagna and aspects lagnesh in 7th house and lagnesh vice versa. Here Venus is the only planet owner of all the three Lagnas and occupying Kendra bhava the 7th house. Saturn and Mars both aspects each other from their occupied houses. Sun is forming Ubhaychari yoga, Moon Gajkesri yoga, Venus Bheri yoga and Anshavtar yoga. These yogas are best reasons that made him popular as an actor and further turned to be a good politician and took oath as Chief Minister of Andhra Pradesh state and completed his duties well for the welfare of the people of state. He was intelligent, learned, virtuous, religious and theist. Navansh lagnesh Sun is posited in Navansh lagna in its exalted sign and Jupiter from own sign Pisces aspects 4th house in its exalted sign, where retrograde Saturn is located and aspects its own sign in 10th house of Karma (action) providing him luxuries of life and good office.

3. Conclusion

Because of all above good combinations and yogas, for a long period, N.T.Ramarao passed his life smoothly as an actor and politician. He worked for the welfare of the people and got popularity, dignity and honour.

He was in riches. In the later days of his life, his own relatives deceived him. He could not bear it and soon died. He was religious and benevolent. People still remember him for his good and remarkable deeds.

Kundli No. 11 Vrishchik lagna- Ex. P. M. Late Lal Bahadur Shashtri
1. Date of birth 02 - 10 - 1904.
2. Time of birth 10 - 15 A. M. (IST)
3. Place of birth Varanasi (U.P.) Lat..25⁰ / 20' N. Long. 83⁰ / 00' E.
4. Birth Nakshtra Ardra - 2
5. Balance Dasha at birth Rahu 11 Years - 08 Months - 06 Days.

BIRTH CHART

NAVANSH CHART

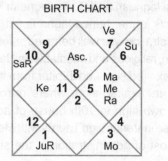

Kundli No. 4.7 (K-11)

Astrological observations

The sign Scorpio is 8th sign of zodiac. It is a mysterious and materialistic sign. Scorpions are committed, loyal, determined, intelligent and generous. They are hungry of affection and love. They are calm and quiet, but when they lose temper, they become roaring in nature. Lal Bahadur Shastri was such a man. At the time of Indo-Pak war, he gave a roaring slogan "Jai jawan Jai kisan". It strengthened our army and countrymen. Such persons do not like flattery. They are diplomatic and revengeful. They wait for the time to take revenge. They are intense lovers. The above horoscope belongs to a capable, peace loving and an honest patriot of India Ex. P.M. Late Lal Bahadur Shastri.

1.Lagna considerations

Lagnesh Mars aspects lagna from 10th house of action (karma) and Chandra Lagnesh Mercury is also placed there in the Leo sign of Royal Sun in 10th house with Mars and Rahu. Royal Sun is situated in the exalted sign of Mercury in 11th houses respectively. It is a good position. So Lagna is fortified. Born in Aridra nakshatra he was genius, gentle, religious and a man of character. Sun is in kendra with Jupiter in Navansh kundli also. Saturn and Moon both aspects each other from their own signs. Significator (Karak) Sun is located in 11th house of gains and profits aspects the 5th house of education and children. God gifted him educated and capable children. They are still maintaining father's dignity and status.

2. Placements, aspects and combinations

From 10th house, 1st house owner (lagnesh) Mars aspects lagna. Chandra lagnesh Mercury is in Kendra. Sun and Mercury are forming Rashi Parivartan yoga (exchange of signs). Therefore it is a good Rajyoga. Venus and Saturn are in its own signs and Mercury in11th house in Chalit kundli are also forming a Rajyoga. Saturn in 3rd house brought him name, fame, respect, honour and popularity among the people of the country and abroad. Saturn as a planet is Atamkarak occupying its own sign in 3rd house provided him more energy and strength.

3. Conclusion

On the basis of above facts, we can conclude that he was an honest, virtuous and most popular Prime-Minister of India. In a very short period he brought name and fame in the development of India. Moon's position in 8th house brought him untimely death out of the country in Tashkant, the then the famous city of Russia. He will always be remembered in the history of India.

Kundli No. 12 Dhanu lagna- Ex. British P.M. Margrette Thacher

1. Date of birth 13 - 10 - 1925,
2. Time of birth 13 - 06 P.M. (Greenwich Time)
3. Place of birth LondonCity (England) Lat.51⁰ / 31' N. Long.00⁰ / 10' E.
4. Birth Nakshtra Magha - 3.
5. Balance Dasha at birth Ketu 02 Years - 10 Months - 06 Days.

BIRTH CHART

NAVANSH CHART

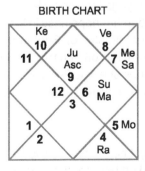
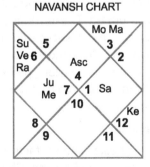

Kundli No. 4.7 (K-12)

Astrological obsevations

Sagittarius is the 9th sign of zodiac. It is philosophical in nature. Sagittarians are humane, hasty, dynamic, sincere, versatile, open minded, frank, missionary, impulsive, creative, enterprising, religious, humble, honest, sacrificing and expansive. They are limited to their areas. It is a fiery sign; hence they are most practical, ambitious and optimistic in life. The above horoscope belongs to Ex. British P. M. Margrette Thacher, who was most practical in administering tackling the problems of the country during her tenure.

1. Lagna considerations

Lagnesh Jupiter is in lagna (1st house). Chandra Lagnesh Sun is strengthening Mars, both sitting in 10th house of Karma (actions) and Mars aspects lagna. Surya Lagnesh Mercury is situated in 11th house with exalted Saturn, which aspects lagna. Therefore lagna is very much activated. Born in Magha nakshatra she is studious, courageous, healthy and wealthy. In Navansh kundli Sun is located in 3rd house of courage in Virgo sign hence Vargottam. From 10th house significator Sun influences lagna and aspects 4th house of lagnesh Jupiter, adding power and strength to friendly Mars, which aspects lagna and lagnesh Jupiter providing her good health, happiness and luxuries in life.

2. Placements, aspects and combinations

Jupiter, the 1st house owner and the karak Sun with Mars all are in Kendra. Owner of 5th house of wisdom sitting in 10th house Mars aspects 1st house (lagna) and Jupiter. Exalted Saturn from 11th house also aspects lagna. Thus lagna is fortified and favourable. From Chandra lagna the planet Venus is in Kendra and lagnesh Jupiter is in 5th house, the trine house in its own sign Sagittarious. Several yogas such as Vesi, Bhaskar and Ravi yogas by Sun, Anpha yoga by Moon, Hansa yoga by Jupiter are formed. These yogas provided her happiness in life. Indeed she proved a most successful Prime-Minister of England. Sun is Atamkarak also. Being friendly to Jupiter, It has offered her the high level post in government for a long period. When she was Prime-Minister U.K. she received honour and dignity in and out of country. She is still popular, healthy and wealthy.

3. Conclusion

On the basis of above facts, she got her desires fulfilled and once became powerful in England. She worked hard for the progress of her country. Lagnesh Jupiter and significator Sun both bestowed her good luck and fortune. She is a bold and powerful lady. Happiness will always continue to be at her doorstep and she will lead a very smooth, happy, healthy and wealthy life.

Kundli No. 13 Makar lagna   Actress Aishwaryarai Bachchan

1. Date of birth   01 - 11 - 1973
2. Time of birth   12 - 00 A.M. (Noon) IST
3. Place of birth Manglur (Karnatak) Lat. 15⁰ / 32' N. Long. 76⁰ / 09' E.
4. Birth Nakshatra Poorva Ashadha - 4.
5. Balance Dasha at birth   Venus 04 Years - 09 Months - 13 Days.

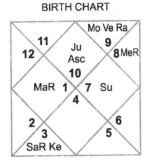
BIRTH CHART

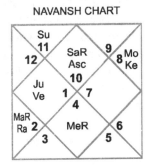
NAVANSH CHART

Kundli No. 4.7 (K-13)

Astrological Observations

Capricorn is the sign of Saturn. So the Capricorneans are sensible, prudent and determined. They are most practical, strong-willed and ambitious. They are quite stubborn in their purposes. They are disciplined, hard working and expert in immediate decision-making. They never compromise with the wrong arguments of others but they focus their aims for the better achievements and adjust to the surroundings and circumstances. The above kundli (birth chart) belongs to the famous actress Aishwarya Rai Bachchan, who takes own decisions to achieve her aims.

1.Lagna considerations

Lagnesh Saturn.is situated in 6th house. Chandra Lagnesh Jupiter is in lagna and Surya lagnesh Venus is located in 12th house with Moon in Sagittarius. Hence Chandra lagna is fortified due to Shubh Kartari yoga (Presence of benefics on both sides of Moon). Born in Poorva Shadha nakshatra, she is friendly, peace loving, far-sighted, kind to elders, loves her husband, truthful, dutiful, goes abroad and wealthy. Debilitated Sun, the significator (Karak) is located in 10th house in Kendra and retrograde Mars also in 4th house in Kendra in its own sign Aries creating Neechbhang Rajyoga. In Navansh chart Sun is placed in Aquarius sign and aspects own sign Leo adding energy to its lagnesh.

2.Placements, aspects and combinations

Significator (Karak) Sun is placed in exalted sign of Saturn in 10th house of actions in Kendra. From 6th house Saturn aspects Venus and Moon is in 12th house. From 4th house friendly Mars, the owner of 4th house in retrograde position, aspects Sun in 10th house and makes Neechbhang Rajyoga. Jupiter is located in lagna and aspects 9th house of fortune in Virgo and the owner of Virgo sign Mercury is placed in 11th house of gains and profits in Scorpio. From 4th house Mars aspects Mercury adding income benefits and resources to the person. From Chandra lagna, Saturn is in Kendra and aspects Sagittarius sign of Jupiter and planets Moon, Venus and Rahu occupy it. From 12th house Moon and other planets also aspect Saturn. Mars is forming Ruchak yoga. This yoga confirms her kingly status.

3.Conclusion

We can conclude that the owner of 8th house Sun is placed in debilitated sign Libra, so in future some sudden ups and downs may come to pass, however she is popular all over the world rolling in riches and getting name and fame, honour and dignity as an actress. Moon being Atamkarak is very good for her prosperity. Nowadays She is healthy and happy. As per future prospects, time is coming, that she may work on her grand father in law's some written episodes or compositions as Saturn aspects 3rd house.

Kundli No. 14 Kumbh lagan- Athlete (Runner) P.T.Usha

    1.Date of birth 20 - 05 - 1964,

    2.Time of birth 01 - 00 A.M. (IST)

    3.Place of birth Calicut(Kerala) Lat.11⁰/ 55' N. Long.75⁰/ 45' E.

    4.Birth Nakshtra Poorva Phalguni-3

    5.Balance Dasha at birth Venus 08 Years- 04 Months- 19 Days.

BIRTH CHART

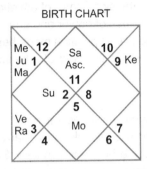

NAVANSH CHART

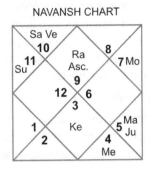

Kundli No. 4.7 (K-14)

Astrological Observations

Aquarius is the 11th sign of zodiac. Being a fixed sign, it is a sign of completion and perfection. Saturn is its owner. It provides more calculative thinking, philosophical views and intuitive abilities. Aquarians are static, independent, unconventional and detached mentaly. They are humanitarian, generous, rational and idealist. They are unpredictable, eccentric and obstinate. The above is the horoscope of the world fame athlete P. T. Usha, who never lose her enthusiasm and energy and ever was rational in performing her duties towards people of the country.

1. Lagna consideration

Lagnesh Saturn is posited in lagna in its own sign Aquarius and Sun is placed in 4th house of comforts and aspects 10th house of Karma (actions) .Sun is covered on both sides by benefics i.e. Shubh Kartari yoga. From 3rd house, Jupiter aspects Moon. Surya lagnesh Venus is situated in 5th house of education. Therefore all lagnas are strong. Born in Poorva Phalguni nakshatra, she is sweet spoken, far-sighted, energetic, successful and charitable. Lagnesh Saturn in Navansh Chart is in its own sign Capricorn in 2nd house. Significator (Karak) Sun located in 4th house as already mentioned, is strengthening the energy of the native to be a good athlete.

2. Placements, aspects and combinations

In Aquarius lagna Saturn's placement in its own and mool-trikon sign is very good and fortunate. Saturn brings happiness, good health and comfortable life along with honour and dignity. It is forming Sasa yoga being in Kendra in its own sign. Saturn and Moon both aspect each other. From 3rd house Mercury, Jupiter and Mars three planets aspect

9th house of fortune and religion. Mars, the significator of athletics and sports, is posited in its own sign in 3rd house of power and energy and aspects its own 10th house of profession. This position made her a top level runner athlete and brought success in the field of athletics and sports all over the world.

3. Conclusion

Therefore above facts of combinations and yogas made her healthy, wealthy, popular and a shining star of India. She took part in many races in India and abroad and secured several medals for the country. She will be known as a good athlete for years. Moon is Atamkarak to fix her mind towards this opportunity. Her future may be good and bright and life may be smooth and peaceful.

Kundli No. 15 Meen lagna-Gurudev Ravindra Nath Tagore

1. Date of birth   07 - 05 - 1861,
2. Time of birth   03 - 40 A.M. (IST)
3. Place of birth Kolkata (West Bengal) Lat. 22⁰ / 35' N. Long. 88⁰ - 23' E.
4. Birth Nakshtra   Revti - 2
5. Balance Dasha at birth Mercury 11 Years - 03 Months - 19 Days.

BIRTH CHART

NAVANSH CHART

Kundli No. 4.7 (K-15)

Astological Observations

Pisces is the 12th and last sign of zodiac. It is the sign of salvation (Moksha). Pisceans are generous, tolerant, intelligent, learned knowledgeable, sensitive and highly equipped with philosophical and spiritual abilities. They are very orthodox, sympathetic and God fearing people. They are fond of drinking water in large quantities every day. They are easily impressed with the feelings and thoughts of the people of their surroundings. The above horoscope relates to such a world fame man, R. N. Tagore, who passed his whole life for the welfare of the people of his region and the country.

1. Lagna considerations

Lagnesh and Chandra lagnesh both Jupiter.is posited in 5th house in the exalted sign Cancer and aspects lagna and Moon in lagna. Surya lagnesh Mars is placed in 4th house of comforts and luxuries and aspects 10th house of karma (actions) of Jupiter. Lagnesh and Chandra lagnesh Jupiter is one and the same, therefore, lagna is extremely activated. Born in Revti nakshatra, he was healthy, heroic, bold, courageous and a man of noble thoughts. He passed his whole life in fulfilling practically for the people of his country, India. Lagnesh and Navansh lagnesh both signs are Pisces, hence lagna and lagnesh both are powerful. In Navansh chart. Mercury the planet of intelligence is in its own sign in 4th house, the house of desires. Significator (Karak) of first house Sun is placed in 2nd house in its exalted sign with Mercury and Venus. It is the house of speech and wealth.

2. Placements, aspects and combinations

Moon is occupying lagna and aspects 7th house, the exalted sign of Mercury, the planet of intelligence. Pisces lagna is beneficial. Jupiter, the owner of lagna is situated in the 5th house in exalted sign Cancer and Moon is in lagna in Pisces. It is Rashi Parivartan yoga i.e. exchange of signs / houses. Mercury in Aries sign of Mars and Mars in Gemini sign of Mercury is also forming Rashi Parivartan yoga. It is very good position, Moon and Mars are in Kendra and lagnesh Jupiter in trine. This made him philanthropic and humanitarian. Mercury with Sun forms Budhaditaya yoga in 2nd house of financial matters.

3. Conclusion

On the basis of above cited yogas and Mercury being planet of intelligence and in kendra from exalted Jupiter, all these confirmed him as a poet, writer and painter of world fame. Though Mars and Ketu caused breaks in his educational career, yet his name and fame, honour and dignity as the founder of Shantiniketan will remain for centuries. Indeed he was a gem of the Golden India.

4.8 Fifth house (Putra Bhava)

This house is known as Putra bhava / Vidhya bhava (House of children and education) It is an auspicious (Shubha) bhava. This bhava (house) deals with children, intelligence and academic qualifications. It shows creativity, artistic talent, imagination and writing of books. It indicates devotion to a cause and provides success to an enterprise with lesser efforts. It represents romance, pleasures, love affairs, short attachments, recreations, emotions, morals, risk, lottery, betting, riches and diplomacy leading to name and fame. It creates religious consciousness, spiritual practices and knowledge of religious books (Shastras) the old Vedic scriptures. Hence this house is also called 2nd house of Dharma (religion).

If the owner or occupying planet is strong and well placed, in conjunction with or aspected by benefics ethical effects on person's life may be noted in mahadasha / anterdasha. If owner of the 5th house in its exalted or own or friendly sign occupies 1st, 9th, 10th, 11th houses will bestow highly beneficial results such as good children, family pleasures and higher education. Planet Jupiter for knowledge and wisdom, Venus for romance and Rahu for diplomacy are closely related to it.

4.9 Owner of Fifth house in various houses

In first house

(i) **Powerful** - By God's grace the person will be intelligent, knowledgeable and a man of high thinking. He may achieve high positions in life such as a minister / secretary / magistrate / judge. He may not like evil-minded persons. Many servants may be under him. He may have a few but very good educated children.

(ii) **Weak** - He may be clever, cunning and evil minded. He may indulge in fraudulent acts and unlawful activities.

In second house

(i) **Powerful** - He will receive money / income from the government working on a good post and by speculations being learned in Shashtras (Hindu religion books). He may have a beautiful wife, well behaved and educated children.

(ii) **Weak** - He may lose his money from government. He may also lose his status and receive disgrace and displeasure. His family may be in trouble. He may be a saint or a priest in a temple. He may lead a lonely life being far away from the family.

In third house

(i) **Powerful** - The person may have capable younger brothers, from whom he will always be getting respect. They may be obedient and trust worthy:

(ii) **Weak** - He may have misunderstandings with his younger brothers. His occupation may be in trouble due to them. He may be a miser and a selfish person.

In fourth house

(i) **Powerful** - The person may be a leader / adviser / administrative officer having big farmlands. He may be long lived leading a happy and prosperous life. He may have one or two good children. He may be respectable and honourable in society.

(ii) **Weak** - He may lose his high position, health and wealth. This situation will bring him disgrace and displeasure. His children may also suffer.

In fifth house

(i) **Powerful** - If fifth house owner is in its own 5th house, it is a very good position. The person will be intelligent, learned and famous. He may be a good mathematician. He may be a head of an institution. He may be religious and father of good children.

(ii) **Weak** – He may be cruel and cunning, forgetful and not keeping his words. He may be a man of wavering mind and unbelievable. His children may die in young age.

In sixth house

(i) **Powerful** - His maternal uncle may be wealthy and popular. Due to him, he may also retain a good position in society. But his children may not be cordial.

(ii) **Weak** - He may be childless and adopt a son from maternal uncle's family, who may not be faithful and obedient to him, else relations with children may be inimical.

In seventh house

(i) **Powerful** - He will be educated, learned, prosperous, respected and charitable having an attractive and charming personality. His family life may be happy. He may have two sons. One of them may go abroad and earn name, fame and a lot of wealth.

(ii) **Weak** - His son may die in a foreign country after getting popularity and fame. So death of the son may affect his health and family life.

In eighth house

(i) **Powerful** - He may be happy, peaceful and satisfied having a few handsome children.

(ii) **Weak** - He may incur loss of property and wealth and may feel unhappy. He may have some disease. This may often lose his temper and peace of mind.

In ninth house

(i) **Powerful** - He may be healthy, wealthy and famous. He may be a teacher or a preacher or an author. He may help in renovating public places such as parks, temples, community centers etc. His children may also prosper and attain high positions.

(ii) **Weak** - He may lose his name and fame in the society and be unlucky and unhappy.

In tenth house

(i) **Powerful** - This is an excellent position for the owner of 5th house. It executes Rajyoga. The person may hold a high office in government and earn goodwill. He may acquire some land. He may be wealthy and religious. One of his sons may bring name and fame to him.

(ii) **Weak** - He may lose his property and prospects. Family may be in trouble.

In eleventh house

(i) **Powerful** - This is a good position and owner of 5th house may aspect its own house from 11th house. The person will be intelligent, learned, powerful, popular, religious and helping hand for others. He may be an author. He may have a few educated children, who may bring success and prosperity to the family.

(ii) **Weak** - His sons may go astray. It may affect his position and popularity bringing him disgrace and displeasure.

In twelfth house

(i) **Powerful** - The person may proceed in search of reality of life i.e. towards moksha (Salvation). He may be religious and spiritual.

(ii) **Weak** - He may be detached from his family. He may be childless and adopt a child, who may not be obedient and faithful to him.

4.10 Planets occupying fifth house

1. Sun

(i) **Positive** - If positive Sun is in 5th house; he may be an intelligent and learned person having good morals and characteristics. He may take higher studies in medicines and administration.

(ii) **Negative** - If Sun's position is negative, he may suffer from heart disease. He may be unhappy and unhealthy being short tempered. He may not be long lived. He may face hurdles in the birth of children.

2. Moon

(i) **Positive** - The person may be God fearing and religious but straight forward. He may be intelligent and learned, truthful and sympathetic. He may be wealthy and have a female child.

(ii) **Negative** - He may be timid and weak. He may fall ill frequently.

3. Mars

(i) **Positive** -He will be intelligent, learned, courageous and a man of firm determination. He may be a physician or surgeon, electrical engineer, criminal lawyer etc.

(ii) **Negative** - He may be short-tempered, deceitful having bad habits, which may lead him to loss of health and wealth. He may suffer from colic disease. He may have loss of children.

4. Mercury

(i) **Positive** - He may be highly intelligent and learned, respected by friends and followers. He may be a good poet or a speaker. He may be a leader. He may be a fan of music. He may have one or two capable children.

(ii) **Negative** - He may lose his position in later years of life because of nervous disorders.

5. Jupiter

(i) **Positive** - He may be intelligent, knowledgeable and God fearing. He may be a good teacher or an advisor or an astrologer. He may be popular among friends and in the society. He may earn profits in his speculations. He may have high position in family and have lovely children.

(ii) **Negative** - If malefics occupy 5th house in an inimical sign; he may be discontented and unhappy on account of progeny.

6. Venus

(i) **Positive** -The person will be wise, happy, romantic and fond of pleasures. He may be a good orator having poetic nature. He may be influential, wealthy and charitable and blessed with affectionate female children. He may have many friends and well wishers.

(ii) **Negative** - Excess of fun and pleasures may affect his health and peace of mind.

7. Saturn

(i) **Positive** -The person may study geology, archeology or other technical subjects. He may be serious in nature hard working and focussed.

(ii) **Negative** -He may be sick and lazy, poor and weak, a rover and evil minded. So he may be unlucky. He may quarrel with his relatives and friends. They may hate him. His domestic life may be miserable. His sons may also bring him sorrows.

8. Rahu

(i) **Positive** - He may be lean and thin but a good diplomat, fortunate and fond of Shastras.

(ii) **Negative** - He may suffer from stomach ailments causing heart problems. His friends and relatives may deceive or misconceive him. He may lose his children.

9. Ketu

(i) **Positive** -The person may be intelligent and study foreign languages and technical subjects.

(ii) **Negative** - He may be short tempered. His own fellowmen may dislike him. He may have stomach problems. His children may not cooperate him.

4.11 Planets placements, aspects and combinations 5th house

Fifth house is the house of children and college / university education, therefore, some questions regarding both the facts or aspects will arise in the mind of a person. Will I be a father? How many children will I have- one or two or more than two, a son or a daughter? Will they live long or die earlier? Will I be childless or adopt a son or a daughter? What educational achievements will I gain in life? The answers regarding children and education may be as under:

1. Person will have children earlier or later

    (i) If the 5th bhava is associated with or aspected by benefics.

    (ii) If owner of 5th house and lagnesh are in 5th house or exchange houses.

    (iii) If Jupiter in 5th bhava and aspected by lagnesh.

    (iv) If owner of 2nd house is in 5th bhava aspected by Jupiter.

    (v) If Navansh lagnesh is in 5th house with the owner of 5th bhava associated with or aspected by benefics.

    (vi) If Navansh lagnesh and owner of 5th bhava both are posited in lagna.

    (vii) If lagna is Aries or Scorpio and Sun in 5th and Saturn in 8th both associate with or aspect by benefics.

2. First born child may be a son

    (i) If owner of 5th bhava is in 1st or 2nd or 3rd house.

    (ii) If Mars, Venus and Moon in 3rd, 6th and 12th signs.

    (iii) If owner of 5th bhava is in the house of Moon or Venus is in conjunction with or aspected by them.

    (iv) If owner of 5th bhava occupies / aspects lagna or lagnesh occupies / aspects 5th bhava.

3. First born child may be a daughter

    (i) If Moon and Venus are in 5th and a malefic in 11th house.

    (ii) If owner of 5th house is placed in 2nd or 8th house

4. Number of children a person may have

    (i) If Sun is in 5th house and aspected by benefics, the person may have three children.

    ii) If lagna is Virgo and Saturn is in 5th house, the person may have five children.

5. Longevity of children may be short

    (i) If owner of 5th bhava is placed in any one of 3rd, 6th, 12th houses and not aspected by benefics.

(ii) If both the sides of owner of 5th house are malefics.

(iii) If 5th bhava is occupied by a malefic and owner of 5th bhava also in conjunction with a malefic.

(iv) If owner of 5th bhava occupies the debilitated sign in Navansh.

(v) If Rahu is in 5th house aspected by Mars.

(vi) If Rahu and lagnesh both occupy 5th bhava or Rahu associates with the owner of 5th bhava.

(vii) If owner of 5th bhava with Rahu and Saturn is situated in 5th house, and aspected by Moon.

6. Person may be intelligent, learned, his memory remarkable-

(i) If Mercury or Venus in its own sign occupies 5th bhava.

(ii) If Jupiter is in 5th bhava.

(iii) If Mercury and Jupiter both occupy or aspect 5th bhava.

7.Person may be dull and have weak grasping power-

(i) If Rahu and Saturn are in 5th house.

4.12 Events affecting during dasha Sign in 5th house

In Aries

(i) **Favourable** - If Mars is powerful, he may be intelligent, religious and popular in the society during its dasha. He may be healthy and wealthy. He may improve his status.

(ii) **Unfavourable** - During dasha period of weak Mars, he may try to grab other's wealth. His children may create problems. Government may go against him. His father may be sickly.

In Taurus

(i) **Favourable** - During dasha period of Venus being Rajyoga karak, he may be lucky. He may lead a smooth and fashionable life. He may be highly placed earning name, fame in the society. He may look after his joint family. He may be a fan of music, singing and dancing.

(ii) **Unfavourable** - If Venus is weak and malefics conjoin it, he may suffer from lung's disease of asthma.

In Gemini

(i) **Favourable** - During Mercury dasha, he may be sympathetic and soft spoken. He may be successful in his efforts. His children may also do well. He may help his siblings. He may have good position in his community.

(ii) **Unfavourable** – During weak Mercury dasha, he may be selfish and miserly and unhelpful to his brothers. He may suffer from a serious illness.

In Cancer

(i) **Favourable** - Powerful Moon dasha may be positive. He may be a teacher or an advisor holding high position in government. He may love and regard his mother. He may be wealthy having a good house and conveyance. He may be virtuous and religious.

(ii) **Unfavourable** - Weak Moon's dasha may be harmful for his mother and his son. His mother may be ailing. This may influence his peace of mind and earnings.

In Leo

(i) **Favourable** - Powerful Sun's dasha may be good for him. He may be wealthy and famous in the society. He may be successful in competitions. His children may respect him. He may go for further studies out side and earn a lot of wealth and popularity.

(ii) **Unfavorable** - Weak Sun's dasha may affect his wealth, health and popularity. He may be childless.

In Virgo

(i) **Favourable** - Powerful Mercury dasha is good and favourable. He may be intelligent and learned. His maternal uncle may prosper. He may get all benefits and comforts of life through him. He may be successful in achieving his aims and objectives.

(ii) **Unfavourable** - Weak Mercury dasha may create tension because of children or having no children. He may be ailing and face stomach problems.

In Libra

(i) **Favourable** - During Venus dasha, he may be lucky, well mannered, truthful, happy and fair in his dealings. He may have faithful and devoted wife. His children may also be good. They may go abroad and earn lot of wealth. Thus he may lead a happy domestic life. He may be long lived.

(ii) **Unfavourable** - If Venus is weak and afflicted; misfortunes may affect his studies and also his children's studies.

In Scorpio

(i) **Favourable** -If powerful Mars dasha is in operation, he may take bold and courageous steps in his studies. His children may also be capable.

(ii) **Unfavourable** - During weak Mars dasha, he may have children problem. He may be childless. He may suffer from respiratory trouble. He may be short tempered. His relations with his wife may not be cordial.

In Sagittarius

(i) **Favourable** - During powerful Jupiter's dasha, he may get favour from government joining a good administrative post. He may write books and earn money. His father may also be in the good books of government. His siblings and son may also help him in his work. He may travel to many holy places. He may be lucky and prosperous and improve his status.

(ii) **Unfavourable** - If Jupiter is weak and its dasha is running, he may have to work more. He may feel unhealthy and become sick. Long journeys may be tiring and also weakening his health.

In Capricorn

(i) **Favourable** - Here Saturn will be the owner of 5th bhava and also of 6th house. Therefore during its dasha, mixed results may favour him. If Venus combines or aspects it and sub period is running, it may bring him good friends, status, popularity, wealth, house, conveyance and all other luxuries in life.

(ii) **Unfavourable** - He may be busy with his tiring duties, it may affect his health and fall sick.

In Aquarius

(i) **Favourable** - Saturn will be Rajyoga karak. During Saturn dasha, he may become intelligent and knowledgeable. He may get a government job through his elder brother. He may write books during this period. People may like him. He may have a large circle of friends. Luck may favour him to become wealthy and famous.

(ii) **Unfavourable** - Large circle of acquaintance may sometimes harm him. He may lose his high position.

In Pisces

(i) **Favourable** - If Jupiter, the owner of 5th house is powerful and well placed, during its dasha, the person may go abroad, take further higher studies and earn his livelihood also. He may reside there leading a peaceful and honourable family life.

(ii) **Unfavourable** - During its dasha period, he may be worried due to his children or having no children. If childless, he may adopt a son. He may spend money on speculations and he may go astray.

4.13 Ninth house (Bhagya Bhava)

This house is known as Bhagya bhava / Dharma bhava (House of fortune and religion). It is an Auspicious house (Shubha bhava) and more powerful than 5th bhava. This bhava indicates father, guru, fortune and religion. It indicates purity, piety, faith, sincerity, higher studies, educational achievements, inventions and researches. It signifies long journeys in country, foreign travels, sea voyages, and philosophy, preaching, dreams, visions, worship, meditation, intuition, charity, sacrifice and faith in Dharma. Hence it is called the 3rd house of Dharma (religion). It cares & proves as a father of the person. If the owner, occupying, associating, aspecting well placed and fortified by the benefic planets, they provide sudden unexpected success and righteousness in many matters in its mahadasha / anterdasha. Jupiter for piety and faith, Rahu for journey abroad and Sun for fatherly help stay very close to it.

This is the key house. It is the result of our past deeds. If a benefic planet occupies this bhava, the person will be most fortunate and religious. He may turn towards higher academic achievements. If there is an exchange between owner of 9th and 10th bhavas and both the owners either in 9th house or in 10th house, it will be a good equation. The person may be serving on a high level post. His father may also be healthy, wealthy and a religious man. If the owner of the 9th house is in conjunction with the owners of angles 1,4,7,10 and 5,11 houses and occupies own house or one of 1,4,7,10,5,11, 2, 3 houses it may provide excellent results by way of financial benefits, job opportunities, happy family life, higher academic achievements, foreign travels overall lucky and prosperous.

4.14 Owner of ninth house in various houses

In first house

(i) **Powerful** - Person may be learned, fortunate and popular. He may be hard working and earn a lot of wealth with his own efforts. He may be handsome and a man of character respected by government and the friends. He may be religious and lead a peaceful, contented and happy life.

(ii) **Weak** - He may be unlucky, unhappy and atheist. He may lose his peace of mind.

In second house

(i) **Powerful** - His father and joint family may be rich and influential. His children may also be good. He may get wealth from his father and become rich.

(ii) **Weak** - He may destroy the paternal property and become poor losing his popularity and mental peace.

In third house

(i) **Powerful** - He may have good relations with his siblings. He may be well mannered, a good orator and a writer earning a lot of money, name and fame through related professions.

(ii) **Weak** - He may be in trouble because of irrational comments in his writings and lose his prosperity and popularity.

In fourth house

(i) **Powerful** - He may get motherly love and happiness. His mother may be a rich lady. He may also be an owner of agricultural land, buildings and vehicles. He may gain from real estate or automobile business.

(ii) **Weak** - If Rahu occupies or aspects 9th house, he may be devoid of motherly love. His early life may also be full of miseries or misfortunes.

In fifth house

(i) **Powerful** - He may attain good achievements in higher education, and be an intelligent and learned. He may be a rich and reputed person in society. He may have moral and religious values and be father of capable sons.

(ii) **Weak** - His sons may be unsuccessful in achievements. His father may also be poor and unhappy. This may affect his mental peace.

In sixth house

(i) **Powerful** - He may earn money through his father and have his own business.

(ii) **Weak** - He may be involved in litigation and be in debts. He may lose relations from maternal uncle's side. He may be in trouble created by his enemies.

In seventh house

(i) **Powerful** - After his marriage, he may have an opportunity to go abroad and earn money, name and fame. He may be wealthy and prosperous there. Father may also go abroad and deal in import and export business. He may be religious and devoted to the God.

(ii) **Weak** - His father may die abroad. Luck may desert him after marriage.

In eighth house

(i) **Powerful** - He may get his paternal property and lead an ideal and religious life.

(ii) **Weak** - His father may die early. He may have to shoulder heavy responsibilities of the family, hence always incur debts. He may have to sell his paternal house.

In ninth house

(i) **Powerful** - This makes a powerful Rajyog. The person may be fortunate enough to earn a lot of wealth, name and fame. He may be a religious and charitable man. His father may also be wealthy and prosperous. Both he and his father may live long.

(ii) **Weak** - If owner of 9th house occupies 6th or 8th or 12th house in Navansh Chart, his father may die in his early age leaving a heavy burden of the family on his shoulders.

In tenth house

(i) **Powerful** - This position also makes Rajyog. He may be a powerful man in the society. He may be generous, sympathetic and religious. He may have all comforts in life. People may respect and regard him.

(ii) **Weak** - He may lose his status, prosperity and all comforts in life.

In eleventh house

(i) **Powerful** - He may obey his elders and become a rich and charitable man. He may be powerful and influential in society. He may perform religious rites and rituals. His father may also be well known and religious.

(ii) **Weak** - His friends or partners may destroy his wealth by fraudulent acts.

In twelfth house

(i) **Powerful** - He may be a religious and a noble man. He may spend money lavishly on charities in religious matters. He may earn name and fame for his father.

(ii) **Weak** - He may suffer from poverty. He may work hard for his livelihood, but still be unsuccessful. His father may also die early leaving him in debts.

4.15 Planets occupying ninth house

1.Sun

(i) **Positive** -The person may be bold, courageous, ambitious and enterprising. He may be a man of good morals and spiritual pursuits. He may be a saint, priest, religious leader or a good astrologer. His sons may also be religious and charitable.

(ii) **Negative** - He may not respect his father. If Sun conjoins either with Moon or Venus, he may suffer from eyesight problem.

2.Moon

(i) **Positive** - He may be intelligent, learned, fortunate and prosperous. He may be generous and charitable. He may go to foreign countries and acquire good immovable property. If Saturn and Mars or Mercury aspect the Moon, he may be a good administrator or leader. He may have many friends.

(ii) **Negative** - If Moon associates with Mars, his mother may have fatal injury, if Venus conjoins, he may indulge in immoral activities and if Saturn joins he may suffer body pains.

3.Mars

(i) **Positive** - He may be generous, charitable and famous. He may deal in arms or weapons business. If Jupiter associates with Mars, he may be learned in Shastras. If Venus combines, he may have many relationships.

(ii) **Negative** - He may neither obey his father nor love his brothers. He may be jealous, proud and short tempered. If Saturn associates with Mars, he may have illicit relations with other women.

4.Mercury

(i) **Positive** - He may be intelligent, learned and a research scholar in Cosmo-mathematics / theology / meta-physics. He may be an astrologer, writer, editor, poet and preacher .If Venus conjoins, he may be a good singer and if Jupiter conjoins, he may be a good orator and a man of wisdom. He may go abroad and deliver lectures on religious topics. He may be wealthy. He may be friendly to his father.

(ii) **Negative** - Mercury is always nearer to Sun, so it may be combust any time. In case of combust Mercury or malefics join it, then relatives may cause troubles.

5.Jupiter

(i) **Positive** -The person may be highly religious, a man of principles and rules. He may be learned in shastras. He may study law. He may go abroad to preach. He may be wealthy and reputed. If Mars aspects, he may be an officer in army. If Saturn combines, he may be a man of character and strive for divinity. He will love his father and brothers to the core of his heart.

(ii) **Negative** - If Jupiter associates with Venus, he may turn to be immoral. This position may defame him.

6.Venus

(i) **Positive** - He may be lucky and travel to many holy places. He may be religious and gain respect everywhere. He may be intelligent, learned and famous. If it combines with Saturn, he may be a good diplomat. He may have good sons.

(ii) **Negative** - If Venus associates with Sun and Moon, he may suffer in quarrelling with opposite sex. If it combines with malefics, he may be penalized.

7.Saturn

(i) **Positive** - The person may lead a lonely life. He may be a saint (Sanyasi) and establish some religious institution. He may be wandering. He may have no siblings.

(ii) **Negative** - If Sun combines, he may not have cordial relations to his father and his sons and if Mercury associates, he may be a man of deceiving nature and an atheist.

8.Rahu

(i) **Positive** - He may be wealthy, religious and famous. He may travel to holy places. He may be fortunate after the age of 42 years.

(ii) **Negative** - He may be miser and impolite. His wife may not respect him. He may be a man of loose morals. He may hate his father and turn to be irreligious.

9.Ketu

(i) **Positive** - The person may be brave and bold. He may save money. He may have a good wife and happy children. He may rise after 48 years of age.

(ii) **Negative** - He may be short sighted, arrogant and also infamous in his community. He may be losing his temper and treating his parents badly.

4.16 Planets placements, aspects and combinations 9th house

This house mainly represents father, fortune, journeys, religion and higher education. He may be healthy, wealthy, successful, charitable and respected in his field and in the community.

1. Father will die early, if Sun is placed with Mars and Saturn in 4th and 10th houses, or if there is a malefic sign in 5th or 9th house from lagna and Sun occupies it or Sun is with malefic in 10th house from Chandra lagna or If Saturn and Mars are in 1, 5, 11 signs in 5, 7, 9 houses from Surya Lagna.

2. If Sun aspects lagna, the person will inherit parental wealth and property.

3. If 9th house has a movable sign and 9th house owner also occupies a movable sign in conjunction with or aspected by Saturn and 12th house owner is strong, the person will be an adopted son.

4. If 4th house owner associates with 9th house owner in 6th house, his father will be extravagant.

5. If 5th house owner is benefic and Sun is well placed, the person will fetch happiness to his parents.

6. If 5th house owner or Sun is afflicted by Saturn or Rahu, the person will bring miseries to his parents.

7. If 1st house of the person and 10th house of his father are in the same sign, the person will be obedient to his parents.

8. If owner of lagna or 1st house of the person and his father are in 6th and 8th houses, they will be indifferent in their thoughts and views.

9. If the Sun and Moon with Mars and Saturn occupy trio houses, he will be an abandoned son.

10. If Mars and Rahu are placed in 11th or 9th houses from lagna, they will cause father's death and if Sun or Moon occupies 4, 7, 10 houses in 1, 4, 7, 10 sign, the person will not perform the funeral rites of his father.

11. If a benefic occupies 9th house, the person will be lucky.

12. If 9th house is occupied by a malefic planet and 6th house by a debilitated planet, the person will suffer in every sphere of life and if Sun being malefic occupies 9th house, the person will be poor and unlucky.

13. If the 11th house owner is in 9th house with 10th house owner, he will be fortunate in every sphere of life and If 9th house owner is in 2nd aspected by 10th house owner or if 9th in 2nd or 2nd in 11th and 11th in 9th house, the person becomes fortunate and wealthy

14. If 3rd and 9th house owners join together in a benefic sign or aspected by benefic, the person's fortune shines with the help of his brothers.

15. If 5th and 9th house owners conjoin or aspect, the person gets prosperity through his sons and If Venus or Jupiter is in 9th house or aspect owner of 9th house, the person will be most lucky.

16. If 1st house and 9th house owners exchange the houses, the person will be fortunate & healthy.

17. If owner of 9th house is in 4, 8, 12 signs and in 3, 6, 9, 12 houses, he goes to pilgrimage for a long time and If Jupiter combines 9th and 10th house owners, the person travels to many holy places.

18. If there is a benefic planet in 9th house from Chandra lagna, the native goes to a long pilgrimage.

19. If Jupiter is posited in 9th house from Moon and Lagna and aspected by Saturn, the person will be a founder of some religious institution.

20. If Jupiter, Sun, and Mercury occupy 9th house, the person will be learned and wealthy.

21. If 12th house owner, from 1st house owner, is placed in a watery sign i.e. 4, 8, 12 sign, the person becomes wealthy and prosperous in a foreign country.

4.17 Events affecting during dasha Sign in 9th house

In Aries

(i) **Favourable** - Mars will be Rajyog karak and if it is powerful, it may bestow good luck with high positions, prosperity and wealth during its dasha. It may develop religious interest. He may be successful in his efforts and improve his status. He may go abroad for higher studies.

(ii) **Unfavourable** - If the owner is weak and ill placed above cited results will suffer during its dasha.

In Taurus

(i) **Favourable** - If Venus is powerful, during its dasha, person may be happy, healthy, wealthy and fortunate. He may be obliged with a good post in government. He may have faithful and caring wife and capable children.

(ii) **Unfavourable** - If it is weak and afflicted, he may lose all the benefits such as conveyance facility, house and motherly love. He may be unlucky. He may be accident-prone.

In Gemini

(i) **Favourable** - If Mercury is powerful; he may be fortunate and successful in his ventures. His siblings may also help him. He may be healthy, wealthy, prosperous, benevolent and religious.

(ii) **Unfavourable** - If Mercury is weak, during its dasha, he may not be able to earn enough money. His siblings may also create problems for him.

In Cancer

(i) **Favourable**-He may achieve his higher academic qualifications. He will love and regard his parents. He may gain property during this period. He may be happy and contended during its dasha period.

(ii) **Unfavourable** -If Moon is weak and afflicted; he may be unlucky and lose his wealth. His father may also suffer from serious illness and die early.

In Leo

(i) **Favourable** - If sign Leo occupies 9th bhava and Sun is strong, during its dasha, he may be a high level officer. He may be financially strong. He may beget a son, lucky for the family. He may be knowledgeable and religious. People may like him.

(ii) Unfavourable - If Sun is in debilitated sign, He may lose his high position and cash balance in its dasha. His higher ups may go against him and it may lessen his father's span of life.

In Virgo

(i) **Favourable** - If sign Virgo is in 9th bhava and Mercury is there and powerful, he may gain benefits through his cousins and enemies.

(ii) **Unfavourable** - If it is weak, he may be unlucky during its dasha. He may not succeed in his ventures. His enemies may harm him. There may be litigation. His father may get injury. He may lose his position.

In Libra

(i) **Favourable** - If sign Libra is in 9th bhava and Venus is strong; he may marry with a well-mannered and dignified lady during its dasha. He may gain benefits through his wife. He himself may earn money through his personal contacts. He may be successful and popular getting all comfort in life. He may have cordial relations with his father and family.

(ii) **Unfavourable** - Weak Venus, during its dasha period, may make him homeless, penniless and unlucky. His father may be sick and possibly die.

In Scorpio

(i) **Favourable** - Powerful Mars may bring him high position and status through government during dasha period. He may be wealthy, popular. He may be religious and get love from father and in return pay due regards to his father. He may gain benefits and status through patrimony.

(ii) **Unfavorable** - If Mars is weak, during its dasha period; he may be mean, selfish and violent. He may be unfortunate and not able to continue cordial relations with his elderly persons of the family. He may be unsuccessful in his efforts. His father may fall ill.

In Sagittarius

(i) **Favourable** -This is a good situation, if 9th house owner occupies its own house. During its dasha, he and his brothers may be prosperous and wealthy. He may be successful in his efforts. His father may also help him in his affairs. He may be religious and a man of simple living and high thinking.

(ii) **Unfavourable** - Weak Jupiter may make him impolite, irreligious, unlucky and cruel to his people. Government officers may also go against him.

In Capricorn

(i) **Favourable** - Saturn being Rajyog karak, If it is powerful, during its dasha, he would be a high level official. He would love and regard his parents. He will be respected in society. He may be religious and travel to many holy and religious places. His character and conduct would be praiseworthy. He would gain property and lot of wealth.

(ii) **Unfavourable** - Weak Saturn may lessen his wealth. He may become poor, tired and unable to spare time to the family and children.

In Aquarius

(i) **Favourable** -This is a good position to attain status and wealth, if Saturn is powerful and aspected by friendly benefics, he may gain everything due to his father's influence in its dasha period. He may earn money through speculations. His elder siblings may also be prosperous and wealthy.

(ii) **Unfavourable** - Sometimes his speculations may go wrong influencing his position and peace of mind.

In Pisces

(i) **Favourable** - If Jupiter is powerful, during its dasha period; he may go abroad and earn money. He may be successful in his ventures. He may be religious and popular.

(ii) **Unfavourable** - If a planet is weak or in adverse nakshatras, the individual may lose his business and earnings during its dasha.

4.18 Example kundlis with astrological observation

Six example kundlis regarding 1st, 5th, 9th houses two each house of Purush Trine i.e. Dharma Houses with astrological observations are given as below:

Kundli No. 16 Ex. Prime- Minister. Late Mr.Rajiv Gandhi

1. Date of birth 20 - 08 - 1944.

2. Time of birth 08 - 11 A. M. (IST)

3. Place of birth Mumbai (Maharastra) Lat. 18^0/ 58' N. Long. 72^0/ 50' E.

4. Birth Nakshatra Poorva Phalguni - 2

5. Balance Dasha at birth Venus 14Years-03Months-09Days.

BIRTH CHART   NAVANSH CHART

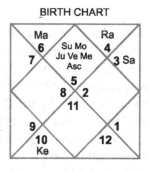 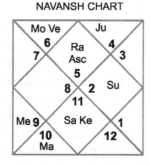

Kundli No. 4.18 (K-16)

Astrological Observations

In this birth chart (Janam kundli) Leo is the ascendant. It is the 5th sign of Zodiac, whom the owner is Sun, the king of all the planets. Sun brings name and fame. Such people are dynamic, dominating, active, creative, ambitious, courageous, generous, broad minded and warm hearted. They mingle with high or low category people. They have lot of tolerance and high thoughts. Rajiv Gandhi, the eldest son of late Smt. Indira Ganhi, was such a man. He was simply a pilot, when he took an oath as Prime Minister of India. Very soon, he obtained prosperity and popularity all over the country and abroad.

1. Lagna considerations

Lagnesh, Chandra lagnesh and Surya lagnesh is one and that is Sun, which is posited in its own sign Leo in lagna (1st house). Thus all three lagnas i.e. Sudarshan Lagnas are common with sign Leo. Therefore lagna is extremely activated. Lagna and Navansh lagna both are also one i.e. Leo, hence Vargottam. In Navansh chart Sun is placed in 10th house. Digbali and exalted Mars and Jupiter both aspect each other. Saturn, the owner of Mool trikona sign Aquarius aspects 9th house. Therefore there is a strong connection amongst all Dharma houses 1st, 5th and 9th houses. Lagnesh and significator (Karak) Sun, occupying lagna in conjunction with four benefics Moon, Mercury, Jupiter, Venus and third aspect of Saturn is in a very good position. Born in Poorva Phalguni nakshatra, he was sweet spoken, far-sighted, capable, dutiful, successful, religious and charitable. He proved all these qualities during his tenure as Prime-Minister of India and tried his best to fulfill his duties and responsibilities for his country and the people.

2. Placements, aspects and combinations

Jupiter being friendly aspects its own signs in 5th house of children and education and also 9th house of fortune and religion. Mars from 2nd house also aspects 5th house of children and education and 8th house of Jupiter and further 9th house of its own sign Aries, the house of fortune and religion adding energy and strength to its friend Jupiter. Saturn is placed in 11th house of Mercury aspects lagna. It also aspects 5th and 8th houses both of Jupiter. Therefore, they are supporting each other being friendly and powerful encouraging and strengthening 1st, 5th and 9th dharma houses and dharma principles. All dharma houses are interrelated. Lagnesh Sun forms Vesi and Bhaskar yoga, Moon Gajkesri and Durdhara yoga, Mercury Budhaditaya yoga. Lagna, lagnesh Sun and Moon all are in odd signs with daytime birth and forming Mahabhagya yoga. These yogas made him fortunate in all the spheres of life. Prior to this administrative post of prime minister, he was a successful pilot.

3. Conclusion

Life, therefore conclude that lagnesh is posited in lagna with the owner of the 5th Jupiter, which aspects 5th and 9th houses and 9th owner Mars aspects 9th house as well. Hence all 1st, 5th and 9th dharma houses are well connected and interrelated. Mr. Rajeev Gandhi was basically a righteous gentleman, devoted to upholding Dharma values during his tenure as Prime-Minister of India; though his life was sacrificed in this process. Really he proved himself very popular and a successful Prime Minister doing developmental work (good deeds) for country's progress. He tried to fulfill all the desires of his mother regarding his country and people. But the presence of the Moon, the owner of 12th house and Jupiter, the owner of 8th house in lagna with Sun and aspect of Malefic Saturn caused leveling of allegations of corruption against him resulting in loss of reputation and life. The birth tithi (lunar date) being *amavashya* (Dark Moon) too caused the sudden ups and downs in his career and untimely death. But he will be remembered for many years to come.

Kundli No.17   Ex. C. E. C. India Mr. T.N. Seshan.

1. Date of birth 15 - 12 - 1932.

2. Time of birth 08 - 30 A.M. (IST)

3. Place of birth Tirunelveli (TN) Lat.08⁰ / 44' N. Long.77⁰ / 42' E.

4. Birth Nakshatra Punarvasu-1

5. Balance Dasha at Birth Jupiter 12years-10months-21days.

BIRTH CHART   NAVANSH CHART

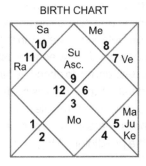
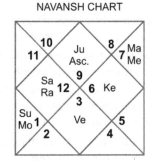

Kundli No. 4.18 (K-17)

Astrological Observations

Sagittarius is philosophical but a fiery sign. Those, who are born in this lagna, are humane, hasty, dynamic, bold, courageous, sincere, optimistic, disciplined, dutiful and religious. They work honestly but are seen aggressive and stubborn. T. N. Seshan proved it during his service period especially, when he was the chief election commissioner of India. His election rules and reforms were remarkable.

1. Lagna considerations

Lagnesh and Surya lagnesh Jupiter is placed in 9th house of fortune and religion in the friendly Sun sign Leo with Mars and Ketu and aspects lagna (1st house) its own house that relates to health and happiness, 3rd house of boldness and courage and 5th house of intelligence and knowledge. Chandra lagnesh Mercury alone is situated in 12th house adjoining to lagna; hence lagna is more powerful and fortified. This is a very good combination of 1st, 5th, 9th houses called Dharma Houses.

2. Placements, aspects and combinations

Lagnesh Jupiter is in 9th house in Leo sign and Sun is in lagna (1st house) in Sagittarius sign, hence there is Rashi Parivartan yoga (exchange of signs). It aspects 5th house also. Mars is placed in 9th house with Jupiter and aspects its own sign Scorpio in 12th house and 3rd house of courage. Dhanesh (2nd house owner) Saturn from its own sign Capricorn and labhesh (11th house owner) Venus from its own sign Libra aspect 5th house. All these connections and interrelations of 1st, 5th and 9th Dharma houses helped him to prove a good administrator. Bhagyesh (9th house owner) Sun in lagna and Dhanesh (2nd house owner) Saturn imparted him sharpness and boldness of voice, discipline and controlling ability. At first he was posted Dy. Commissioner, later on Defence secretary in the tenure of Prime-Minister Mr. Rajiv Gandhi. He has a good knowledge of astrology. Once he advised Prime-Minister Mr. Rajiv Gandhi not to attend Perambudur Chennai programme guessing his fatal death. After it, he was posted Chief Election Commissioner of India. His innovative electoral rules and reforms introduced in his tenure made him so famous, fearsome and popular among political parties and public that he won the prestigious Magsaysay award for goverment service in 1996.

3.Conclusion

In view of the above facts, we can conclude that 1st, 5th and 9th dharma houses are interrelated and reinforced because of lagna owner is posited in 9th house with 5th owner and 9th owner is in lagna producing Rashi Parivartan yoga (exchange of signs between Sun and Jupiter) and Jupiter aspects both 1st and 5th houses. This combination made him popular during his tenure. He is purely an honest, religious and God fearing man. His father-in-law was also religious and a good astrologer. He also has a good knowledge of astrology and believed in its analysis and predictions. He is a man of principles and understanding. His remarkable electoral reforms withstood political pressure made him popular. This is the reason, that the people then called him a dictator, when he was chief election commissioner.

Kundli No. 18 Ex Vice President Bhairo Singh Shekhavat

1.Date of birth 23 - 10 -1923

2.Time of Birth 09 - 30 A.M. (IST)

3.Place of Birth Sikar (Raj.) Lat. 27^0 / 33' N. Long. 75^0 / 09' E.

4.Birth Nakshatra Revti-1

5. Balance Dasha at Birth Mercury 14years-08months-28days.

BIRTH CHART

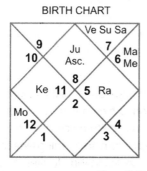

NAVANSH CHART

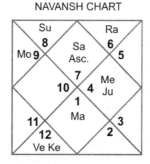

Kundli No. 4.18 (K-18)

Astrological Observations

It is a Scorpio lagna sign birth chart. It is a fixed sign. Such people are committed, loyal, intelligent, determined, love hungry and self-made man. They crush all the obstacles that come in their way and move forward. Mr. Bhairo Singh Shekhavat is one, who has these qualities and he reached up to high-level post. At first he was in state and he chaired as C.M. of Rajasthan three times and then to the post of Vice President Of India.

1.Lagna considerations

Lagnesh (the 1st house owner) Mars is situated in 11th house with exalted Mercury in Virgo sign. Chandra Lagnesh Jupiter is located in lagna aspects Moon in 5th house of intelligence and knowledge and Moon sign Cancer in 9th house of fortune and religion. Moon and lagnesh Mars both aspect each other. Therefore Chandra lagna is extremely activated. Surya lagnesh Venus is posited in its own sign Libra with exalted Saturn and debilitated Sun. It is an example of Neechbhang Rajyoga, which made him a popular political leader.

2.Placements, aspects and combinations

Jupiter aspects its own 5th house of knowledge and Moon, also 7th house of Libra and 9th house of Cancer signs, thus strengthening luck and religious sentiments. Lagnesh (1st house owner) Mars and exalted Mercury being in Kendra from Moon is forming *2nd grade* Rajyog. This is a very good combination and interrelation of 5th, 9th and 1st houses of Purush Trine (Dharma houses). Jupiter being significator of 5th house and placed in 1st house made him an intelligent, learned and a good speaker. He chaired as C.M. of Rajasthan three times continuously and later on he was elected as the Vice President of India. In his horoscope Sun is forming Ubhaichari yoga, Mercury Bhadra yoga being in Kendra from Moon which make him sympathetic and friendly.

3.Conclusion

We can conclude that lagna owner Mars aspects 5th house where 9th owner is placed and aspects lagnesh, 5th owner Jupiter is placed in lagna apects both 5th and 9th houses, making strong corelation amongst 5th, 9th and 1st houses. Venus, Sun, and Saturn are forming Neechbhang Rajyoga in 12th house. This is the best combination. Jupiter in lagna in Scorpio sign and Mars with exalted Mercury in 11th house of gains and profits made him lucky and powerful in political field. Thus he gained honour and dignity not only in the country but also abroad. His future life may not be as bright and influential, as it has been in the past years, because of present unfavourable dasha.

Kundli No. 19 Ex. Dy. Prime Minister Jagjeevan Ram

  1.Date of birth 05 - 04 - 1908

  2.Time of Birth 06 - 00 A.M. (IST)

  3.Place of Birth Arrah (Bihar) Lat.25^0 / 34' N. Long.84^0 / 40' E.

  4.Birth Nakshatra Rohini -1

  5. Balance Dasha at Birth Moon 09years- 05months- 22days

BIRTH CHART   NAVANSH CHART

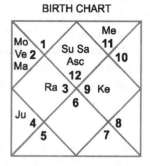 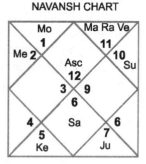

Kundli No. 4.18 (K-19)

Astological Observations

It is a Pisces lagna kundli. Pisces is a dual sign. Such people are honest, generous, sensitive, knowledgeable, disciplined and laborious. They are God fearing and never tired. They reach to their goals with their strong will and abilities / understandings. Mr. Jagjeevan Ram was such a man, who reached Varansi and Delhi from a small village namely Chandwa near Arrah in Bihar state.

1.Lagna considerations

      Lagnesh and Surya lagnesh exalted Jupiter is located in 5th house of intelligence and wisdom and aspects 9th house of fortune and 1st house of health and happiness. Chandra lagnesh is situated in 3rd house of courage and enthusiasm with the Moon, owner of 5th house and Mars, the owner of 9th house. Thus the lagna is highly activated and lagnesh, the 1st house owner Jupiter is powerful. Bhagyesh (9th house owner) Mars aspects its own sign Scorpio in the 9th house. Navansh lagnesh is also Mars, which occupies 4th house of comforts and luxuries.

2. Placements, aspects and combinations

From 3rd house its owner Venus, exalted Moon and 9th house owner Mars and exalted lagnesh Jupiter all aspect 9th house of luck and fortune. From 1st house Saturn also aspects 9th house owner (Bhagyesh) Mars in 3rd house. From 5th house Jupiter aspects its own house -1st house (lagna) also. All these above facts and aspects helped him to reach the post of higher administration in government as Dy, Prime-Minister of India at the time of Mr.Chandra Sekher's Tenure as Prime-Minister of India. Sun is forming Vasi yoga due to planet Mercury in rear house other than Moon and Jupiter Hans yoga being exalted in 5th house from lagna. These yogas extended his status and led him to the higher post of prosperity and dignity, comforts and luxuries, wealth and honour. It indicates a good combination and correlation of all three 5th, 9th, 1st houses known as Dharma Houses.

3. Conclusion

On the basis of above facts, aspects and combinations, we can conclude that ascendant owner Jupiter is placed in 5th house from where it aspects 9th and 1st houses. Owner of 9th house Mars is placed with 5th owner Moon in 3rd house from where they aspect 9th house. Thus there is a strong connection and interrelation amongst 5th, 9th and 1st dharma houses of Purush Trine. While in government, he not only held so many portfolios but also employed a number of downtrodden people in government service. For this act of intelligence and good deeds, people still remember him. Powerful and well placed benefics aspecting 9th house of fortune and religion offered him as much as he desired in fulfilling all his cherished desires and ambitions. Due to him, his only daughter Meera Kumar has been continuing as a parliamentarian since long and at present she is holding the post of speaker in Lok Sabha. Now he is no more but he may be remembered for long.

Kundli No. 20 Aadi Guru Shankaracharya

1. Date of birth 06 - 04 - 0686
2. Time of birth 15 - 30 PM (IST)
3. Place of birth Kaladi (Kerala) Lat. 10^0 / 10' N. Long. 76^0 / 26' E.
4. Birth nakshatra Pushya - 2
5. Balance Dasha at birth Saturn 14 Years 04 Months 04 days

BIRTH CHART

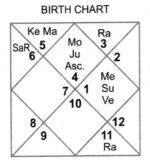

NAVANSH CHART

Kundli No. 4.18 (K- 20)

Astrological Observations

This is a Cancer lagna kundli. Cancer is the emotional, sensitive and unstable sign. Cancerians are self reliant, intelligent, imaginative, virtuous and honest with a good understanding and sense. Aadi Guru Shankaracharya was such a man. By his sparkling intellect, he defeated everyone in the field of arguments.

1. Lagna considerations

Lagnesh and Chandra lagnesh Moon is one and placed in 1st house with exalted Jupiter, the owner of 9th house of fortune and spirituality. Surya lagnesh Mars is placed in 2nd house of speech and voice in Leo sign and exalted Sun with Mercury and Venus is placed in the 10th house in sign Aries. They are forming Rashi Parivartan yoga (exchange of signs). Navansh lagnesh Sun is placed in Moon sign Cancer while Jupiter in Navansh lagna. Therefore lagna is extremely activated and fortified. Born in Pushya naksatra he was capable, knowledgeable, religious and a man of character.

2. Placements, aspects and combinations

In the above birth chart the exalted Jupiter is situated in lagna and aspects the 9th house of fortune and spirituality. It made him wise and religious. It also aspects 5th house of intelligence, whose owner Mars is placed in 2nd house of speech and voice in Leo sign of Sun and aspects 5th house of its own and 9th house of Jupiter. Sun is situated with Mercury and Venus in its exalted sign Aries of Mars in 10th house of actions from where they are influencing and strengthening lagna, Moon and Jupiter. Thus, there is a good connection and correlation of 9th, 1st and 5th dharma houses. They endowed him with a sparkling intellect. Saturn is also aspecting and influencing 5th and 9th houses. All these made him possible to become famous as the head of a religious institution. Moon is in its own sign Cancer in lagna filled Aadi Guru Shankaracharya's mind with spirituality and he wrote the most famous commentaries for the Vedas (Hindu religion books). He was a true devotee of God. Moon is forming Sunpha yoga being planets in 2nd house other than Sun and Gajkesri yoga being Jupiter in kendra from Moon. Exalted Jupiter is forming Hans yoga being in Kendra from lagna.

3. Conclusion

Now we can conclude that 9th house is powerful as its owner exalted Jupiter is sitting with lagnesh Moon in 1st house (lagna) and aspects 5th house. Mars 5th house owner also aspect its own 5th house and 9th house and from 10th Sun is influencing lagna. Thus, all dharma houses 9th, 5th and 1st of Purush trine are interconnected and interrelated. Sign Cancer and Moon in lagna are the significator of feelings and emotions. They made him a man of wisdom and philosophy. Sun, Mercury and Venus gave deep thoughts of karmas (actions) and he became Aadi Guru Shankaracharya.

Kundli No. 21 Deshbandhu Chitranjan Dass

1. Date of birth 05 - 11 - 1870

2. Time of birth 06 - 25 AM

3. Place of birth Calcutta (W.B.) Lat. 22⁰ / 32' N. Long. 88⁰ / 22' E.

4. Birth nakshatra Uttra Bhadrapad 4

5. Balance Dasha at Birth Saturn Years 03 Months 00 Days 07

BIRTH CHART   NAVANSH CHART

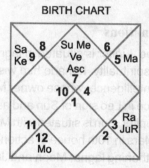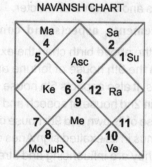

Kundli No. 4. 18 (K-21)

Astrological Observations

This is a Libra lagna birth chart (kundli). Librans are always smiling, easygoing and peace loving. They are handsome, intelligent, learned, man of principles, generous, true patriot, traditional, religious and charitable. Deshbandhu Chitranjan Dass was such a man. Born in Uttra Bhadrapad nakshatra he was tactful, virtuous, fond of arguing and prolific in procreation. He was a top level Barrister of his time in Calcutta high court.

1.Lagna consideratios

Lagnesh and Surya lagnesh Venus is one and occupying its own sign Libra, the lagna (1st house). Chandra lagnesh Jupiter is situated in 9th house of fortune and religion and aspects lagna, 5th house of education of Saturn and also Saturn in 3rd house. Saturn also aspects 5th house and 9th house occupied by Jupiter. Hence lagna is extremely fortified.

2.Placements, aspects and combinations

Lagnesh is placed in lagna in its own sign Libra with Sun and friendly Mercury. Owner of 5th house Saturn aspects its own 5th house from 3rd house and also 9th house and Jupiter situated there. From 11th house Mars also aspects 5th house and 6th house of Jupiter and Moon placed in the 6th house. Hence there is an interrelationship and good connection of 9th, 1st and 5th all Dharma houses of Purush Trine. Jupiter being in Kendra from Moon is forming Gajkesri yoga. It made him wealthy and famous in society. He was one of the capable barristers of Calcutta high court. He was kindhearted, humane, charitable and accommodating to unknown beings. Once he donated all his property and riches to the congress party, which was fighting for India's independence. It was the reason that the people named him Deshbandhu.

Conclusion

We can conclude that above facts of placements, aspects and combinations of planets, especially the position of benefic lagnesh Venus with Mercury is placed in lagna in its own sign forming Malvaya yoga and benefic Jupiter is sitting in 9th house of fortune and religion aspecting lagna, the house of health and happiness and 5th house of intelligence and wisdom. Due to these connections and correlations amongst 9th, 1st and 5th dharma houses, he became so popular among the public that he was named Deshbandhu Chitranjan Dass. He was sympathetic, virtuous and charitable. His sacrificing nature will continue to remind us of his qualities and abilities.

Figure : 4.1 (F-3) First Trine Dharma Houses

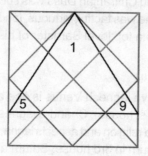

Figure : 4.1 (F-3)

ॐ

Chapter
5

Second Trine Aishwarya Trine (Artha Houses)

5.1 What is Aishwarya Trine? Related houses

In the previous chapter, we have mentioned Purush trine (Dharma houses). They are the most important houses (bhavas). They represent person's childhood, education, success, children, and nature of life and also good luck. Now we will take Aishwarya trine (Artha houses). Aishwarya means the life full of fun and pleasures, luxuries and riches. These are 10th, 2nd, and 6th bhavas. They indicate person's profession, occupation, achievement, livelihood, family life, wealth, status, diseases, troublesome elements, competition and hurdles. Person's good efforts may fetch him affluence and happiness but bad deeds shape him unhappy and painful. It all depends on the placements, conjunctions and aspects of the planets either of benefics / malefics or combination of planets constituting yogas. Sixth house is a malefic house. It provides debts, diseases and creates enemies. House wise effects follow in continuity. First we will take second, then sixth and tenth house. Please see Figure 5.1 (F-4) at the end of Chapter

5.2 Second House (Dhanu Bhava)

This house is known as Dhanu bhava / Kutumb bhava (House of financial matters and joint family) Second bhava deals in financial matters, gains or loss, energy, ability, resources, jewellery, precious stones, bonds, securities, shares, power of speech, memory, imagination, relations with the members in a joint family and early education. It shows accretion, accumulation and also affinity to the studies of Mathematics or Economics. As it rules over family wealth so it is known as the first house of Artha (wealth). It gives a lot of wealth in its owner's or occupying planet's mahadasha / anterdasha. Jupiter is the significator but Mercury is very close to this house. It is Marak bhava (house of death) also. Therefore before analyzing the birth chart person's longevity may be checked. Regarding his / her longevity details, if it is short or medium or long a separate topic of longevity with examples is given in the last chapter.

5.3 Owner of Second house in various houses

In First house

(i) **Powerful** : The person will be a self-made man. He may earn money by his own intelligence and efforts. He may be famous and respectable. If it is in an exalted sign and the owners of 4th, 5th, 7th and 9th houses or Sun associates, he may be healthy and obtain inherited wealth.

(ii) **Weak** : He may be impolite and hate his own family. This behaviour may lose his share of inheritance.

In Second House

(i) **Powerful** : He will be learned and justified. He may earn money through business. He may be charitable and sympathetic and be seen helping others. If the owner is in a favourable constellation and is aspected by benefics, he may be famous in the community. He may marry second time.

(ii) **Weak** : He may be selfish and greedy. He may lose his wealth and become poor. He may also be prone to some constant disease. It may create problems in domestic life. He may be childless.

In Third house

(i) **Powerful** : The person will be intelligent, well mannered and courageous. He is likely to have his own business. His siblings may also help him in business. He may be fond of learning art, music, and dance.

(ii) **Weak** : He may be dishonest, discourteous, quarrelsome and an atheist. His standard of leading a luxurious life may turn him to be a thief.

In Fourth House

(i) **Powerful** : He will have his earning from business, such as automobiles, real estate, etc. He may buy farmlands and buildings. He may be long lived.

(ii) **Weak** : He will be selfish. He will not care for his family and parents.

In Fifth House

(i) **Powerful** : He will be intelligent and learned. He may execute good deeds, and earn name and fame. He may gain wealth through children and speculations.

(ii) **Weak** : He will be miser and ill mannered. His children may suffer for food and education.

In Sixth House

(i) **Powerful** : He will accumulate wealth through hard work overcoming obstacles and competitors.

(ii) **Weak** : He may suffer from diseases in the lower parts of body. His suspicious dealings may cause him penalty or arrest. He may also suffer from eyesight problems.

In Seventh House

(i) **Powerful** : The person and the life partner both will be fond of funs and pleasures. They may accumulate wealth from foreign sources. They may live abroad.

(ii) Weak : He will be extravagant in spending money on funs and pleasures and incur health problems. He may commit suicide.

In Eighth House

(i) **Powerful** : He will inherit parental property. He may also buy some property through his earnings.

(ii) **Weak** : Being fatalist, he may be lazy and deceitful losing his own earnings and inherited wealth. Relations with his brothers may also be sour.

In Ninth House

(i) **Powerful** : The person will be a learned, respected, and religious possessing good health and wealth. He will be skillful, hard working, happy and charitable.

(ii) **Weak** : He may face health problems in his young age and become poor.

In Tenth House

(i) **Powerful** : He may either join government service or he may take business contracts from the government and become wealthy. He will be fortunate and a man of character.

(ii) **Weak** : Business dealings with the government may cause obstacles. He may lose his earned wealth, health and peace of mind.

In Eleventh House

(i) **Powerful** : This is an excellent position for the owner of 2nd house. The person will be wealthy, fortunate, famous, and prosperous.

(ii) **Weak** : Enemies may create problems in the way of his progress and prosperity.

In Twelfth House

(i) **Powerful** : The person may go abroad to earn money or earn through foreign sources.

(ii) **Weak** : He may be poor, indebted, and incur losses due to wasteful expenditure.

5.4 Planets occupying second house

1.Sun

(i) **Positive** -He will be fortunate and wealthy. He may lead a good life in his early age.

(ii) **Negative** - Government authorities may pose him problems. He may be stubborn and quarrelsome. He may have mouth trouble, teeth or eyesight problems. Hence his family life may also be disturbed.

2.Moon

(i) **Positive** - The person will be happy and healthy. He may have a large family and high connections. People may admire him.

(ii) **Negative** - He may have health problems or psychic disorder.

3.Mars

(i) **Positive** - He will be bold, courageous and energetic and earn money with hard work.

(ii) **Negative** - He may be harsh and aggressive and cause disputes in his own family life. He will be dull, evil minded, talkative and poor.

4.Mercury

(i) **Positive** - He will be intelligent and learned. He may be a lawyer. He may take up trading business and become rich. He will be religious and charitable.

(ii) **Negative** - He may suffer from ill health, mental tensions and skin problems.

5.Jupiter

(i) **Positive** - He will be handsome, healthy, sympathetic and a man of good character. He will have a good wife and bold children. He may be wealthy and popular. He may be a poet, writer and or an astrologer. He may be long lived.

(ii) **Negative** - He may be selfish and proud. He may not be good for his father or elders. This may affect his domestic happiness.

6.Venus

(i) **Positive** - He will be fortunate, healthy, wealthy and famous. He will be intelligent and learned. He may possess all the comforts in life. He may have a big family, caring life partner and capable sons. He may deal in gems and jewellery.

(ii) **Negative** - His friends and relatives may cause him problems in business. This may increase his anxieties.

7.Saturn

(i) **Positive** - If Saturn is posited in Libra or Aquarius sign, the person will be popular, healthy and wealthy. He may have good relations with his family.

(ii) **Negative** - If Saturn is placed in signs other than Libra and Aquarius; he may be unsocial, sinful, roaming here and there aimlessly. Family relations may not be cordial. He may be a man of harsh tongue and quick tempered.

8. Rahu

(i) **Positive** - He may travel abroad to earn money to be wealthy and prosperous. If Jupiter aspects Rahu, his earnings may be in affluence.

(ii) **Negative** - His eyesight may be weak. He may feel uneasy, while working. His family life may be unhappy.

9. Ketu

(i) **Positive** - He will be religious and charitable. He may be a good orator. He may get success in navigation work and hospital managements.

(ii) **Negative** - He may have health problems and spend money in treatments.

5.5   Planets placements, aspects and combinations 2nd house

A. The person will be wealthy

1. If the owner of 2nd bhava is in lagna or in its own 2nd house.

2. If the owner of 2nd or 1st or 4th or 11th house conjoins the owner of 10th house. Chaudhry Charan Singh Ex. PM India is the example of it.

3. If the owner of 2nd or 1st or 4th or 5th house is in conjunction with the owner of 11th house.

4. If the owners of 2nd and 11th houses exchange their houses.

5. If owners of 2nd and 11th houses are in exalted sign or in 1st ,4th,7th,10th houses.

6. If Scorpio is lagna and Jupiter is in its exalted sign in 9th house.

7. If Pisces is lagna and owner of 2nd Mars occupies 11th house.

8. If Cancer is lagna occupied by Jupiter and 2nd house owner Sun.

B. Person may be poor

1. If owner of 2nd bhava is placed in 12th house.

2. If 2nd bhava, the owners of 2nd and 11th houses are in conjunction with malefics.

3. If lagna is Taurus or Leo and Mercury being the owner of 2nd bhava with Jupiter occupies 8th house.

C. Person may lose wealth in litigation or debts

1. If Cancer is lagna and owner of 2nd bhava Sun with Saturn occupies lagna.

2. If Cancer is lagna and Sun is in lagna and Saturn in 11th house.

3. If 2nd bhava and owner of 2nd bhava is in conjunction with or aspected by owner of 6th house.

D. Person may be blind

1. If Venus and Moon both with malefics are in 2nd bhava.

2. If owners of 2nd, 12th and 1st houses with Sun or Venus occupy 4th or 8th or 12th house.

3. If owner of 2nd house, 1st house and Sun occupy 2nd bhava.

E. Person may be a good orator

1. If the benefics conjoins the 2nd bhava.

F. Person may be bankrupt

1. If Gemini is lagna and owner of 2nd bhava occupies 8th house with its owner Saturn.

G. Person may be a good actor, singer or musician

1. If Taurus or Libra is lagna and owners of 2nd and 5th houses are in 2nd bhava with Venus. See horoscpe O.P.Nayyar.

5.6 Events affecting during dasha Sign in 2nd house

In Aries

(i) **Favourable** - If powerful Mars, the owner of 2nd house is in 1st house (lagna) and its dasha is running, the person may be a government servant and save some money for future.

(ii) **Unfavourable** - If weak Mars combines with malefics, during dasha period, it may bring him loss of money and property. His relations with the family may not be cordial.

In Taurus

(i) **Favourable** - If Venus occupies its own house and no malefic combines or aspects, during its dasha, he may be happy and prosperous. He may be a good orator. His family life may be happy. He may marry second time.

     (ii) **Unfavourable** - Venus, the 2nd house owner is placed in its own house and if Mars occupies or aspects 2nd house during its dasha, his family life and peace of mind both may be disturbed.

In Gemini

     (i) **Favourable** - If Mercury being 2nd house owner occupies 2nd or 3rd house in conjunction with or is aspected by benefics, during dasha period, he may earn money through writing/ editing/ publishing of books.

     (ii) **Unfavourable** - If malefics conjoin or aspect the owner, he may turn to sinful acts or undertakings.

In Cancer

     (i) **Favourable** - Moon will be owner of 2nd bhava. If it is powerful, during its dasha, he may acquire patrimony. He may join a post of rights in government.

     (ii) **Unfavourable** - If Moon is weak and afflicted, during its dasha, he may lose his job and parental property.

In Leo

     (i) **Favourable** - Sun will be the owner of 2nd bhava and if it occupies 2nd house, during its dasha period, he may earn money through government by doing noble and religious deeds.

     (ii) **Unfavourable** - If Sun is weak and afflicted, during its dasha, his life partner may be in problem at the time of delivery. He may face separation from the joint family.

In Virgo

     (i) **Favourable** - Powerful Mercury may help him in earnings during its dasha. His maternal uncle may be wealthy and his relations may be cordial.

     (ii) **Unfavourable** - If Mercury is weak, during its dasha, he may face litigation or dispute over the paternal property. Relations with the family members may not be cordial. Problems of thefts and debts may also arise.

In Libra

     (i) **Favourable** - Venus will be owner of 2nd bhava. During its dasha, the person will be fortunate and successful in getting all comforts in life.

(ii) **Unfavourable** - Weak Venus dasha may drive him to indulge in extra marital affairs. He may lose his money and position.

Scorpio

(i) **Favourable** - Mars will be the owner. During its dasha, he may acquire prosperity and legacy. He may go abroad for better earnings.

(ii) **Unfavourable** - If Mars is weak and afflicted, during its dasha, he would fail in his enterprises. Domestic disputes may also arise. He may commit suicide.

In Sagittarius

(i) **Favourable** - Jupiter will be the house owner. During its dasha, he would be happy, healthy, wealthy and religious. His father may also be fortunate.

(ii) **Unfavourable** - If the owner is weak and a malefic conjoins or aspects, it may cause loss of money and sour relations in the family.

In Capricorn

(i) **Favourable** - Saturn will be the owner and if it is strong, during its dasha, he may join top-level government post or political leadership and earn wealth and honour.

(ii) **Unfavourable** - If Saturn is weak and without benefic influence, during its dasha, he will abuse his position and loose reputation and status.

In Aquarius

(i) **Favourable** -During the house owner's dasha, he will be healthy and hardworking and earn money. If sub period of Mercury or Jupiter is running, he may earn money through activise lectures on religious epics.

(ii) **Unfavourable** - If Saturn is weak and under malefic influence then its dasha may affect his bank balance and relationship adversely.

In Pisces

(i) **Favourable** - He may go abroad in its owner's dasha period and remain busy in religious pursuits there. He may earn and spend money to lead a luxurious life.

(ii) Unfavourable-During owner Jupiter's dasha, huge expenditure and extravagancies may take place. Domestic affairs may also take an unfortunate turn.

5.7 Sixth House (Ripu Bhava)

This bhava is known as Ripu bhava / Roga bhava (House of enemies and diseases) It is an Inauspicious (Ashubha) bhava. This bhava represents alien elements creating enemies along with debts and diseases. It indicates struggles and obstacles, oppositions and worries, injuries and illness, overall miseries and sorrows. It creates problems of litigation and separation. Person becomes miser and greedy. Sometimes it gives result of double negativity that creates Vipreet Rajyog and increases wealth and prosperity. So this house is also called 2nd house of Artha (wealth). If the planet placed in or owe this house, are weak and afflicted they lead the person to face enemies, to bear diseases and loss of wealth in mahadasha / anterdasha. Mars, Saturn and Rahu all the three planets are close to it. Mars creates struggles, Saturn obstacles and Rahu enemies. This is a Trishadaya house and if natural malefics occupy it, they give good results except for health.

5.8 Owner of Sixth house in various houses

In First house

(i) **Powerful** - He will be bold, brave and courageous. He may take up job either in police or army. He may also be a sportsman.

(ii) **Weak** - He may be inimical to his relations. He may face health problems.

In Second house

(i) **Powerful** - He may go abroad and shine in a foreign country and lead a better healthy and wealthy life.

(ii) **Weak** - He may lose his wealth, health and eyesight. His family life may also be disturbed. His wife may also fall ill.

In Third house

(i) **Powerful** - He may be short-tempered, aggressive and inimical to his brothers but he may be rich.

(ii) **Weak** - It is possible that he may have no younger brother or if he is having, relations may not be cordial.

In Fourth house

(i) **Powerful** - He will live far away from his parents. He may not look after his ailing mother. He may have breaks in education and engage himself in a labour type work / job.

(ii) **Weak** - He may adopt broker's occupation with no profit. His relation with mother may not be cordial and he may run into debts. His family life may be unhappy.

In Fifth house

(i) **Powerful** - He may be an adopted son of his maternal uncle. He may be wealthy and famous and free from debts and will have no enemy.

(ii) **Weak** - His children may be weak, inactive and sick. They may be inimical to him.

In Sixth house

(i) **Powerful** - If 6th house owner occupies its own 6th house; he will be healthy and rich. His maternal uncle may also be famous. He is likely to be in service. He will suppress his enemies.

(ii) **Weak** - If 6th house owner associates with lagnesh, he may suffer from an incurable disease. He may have enmity with friends and relatives.

In Seventh house

(i) **Powerful** - He may marry in nearby relations. He may go abroad with his maternal uncle and earn money.

(ii) **Weak** - His wife may be barren (childless) and sick. Therefore relations may be inimical. Either he may divorce her or she may leave him.

In Eighth house

(i) **Powerful** - If owner of 6th bhava is placed in 8th house, it will be a Vipreet Rajyoga being second bad house (dushta bhava), therefore the person will be rich and famous. He may indulge in outside relations.

(ii) **Weak** - He will face incurable disease and spend money on his illness. Hence he may run into debts.

In Ninth house

(i) **Powerful** - His father may be in judiciary and maternal uncle also on a high level post in government. He may also get a good job and earn money. He will be well known.

(ii) **Weak** - He may entangle in sinful deeds. He may be a poor and ordinary man.

In Tenth house

(i) **Powerful** - He will be honest, religious, pious and charitable and spend more time and money in performing rites and rituals.

(ii) **Weak** - It will affect his business. He may engage in sinful activities and harm the interest of his father.

In Eleventh house

(i) **Powerful** - He will gain money through his enemies. His elder brother may be in judiciary.

(ii) **Weak** - His elder brother may lose his status and health. He may incur loss due to theft.

In Twelfth house

(i) **Powerful** - He may suddenly get unexpected wealth and become rich and famous.

(ii) **Weak** - He may be jealous, violent and a man of destructive nature, that may cause him problems in his profession. He may lose his income and popularity.

5.9 Planets occupying sixth house

1.Sun

(i) **Poiitive** - He will be brave, bold and successful administrator or popular politician. He may become rich. He may win over his enemies.

(ii) **Negative** - He may be inimical to his maternal uncle. If Sun is in conjunction with or aspected by Saturn, he may have long time illness such as heart trouble.

2.Moon

(i) **Positive** -The person will be cool and calm in nature. He may work patiently and successfully in a subordinate position.

(ii) **Negative** - If Moon is in conjunction with or aspected by Mars and Saturn, this situation may give him incurable disease for a long time such as stomach pain due to stone in gall bladder. His enemies may also harm him.

3.Mars

(i) **Positive** - He will be courageous, powerful, victorious and successful high level police officer or army commandant or politician. He may be head of the city or state.

(ii) **Negative** - He may be extravagant. He may be prone to accidents, which may cause him loss of wealth in treatment. His subordinates and relatives may also harm him. If Mars is associated with or aspected by Saturn or Rahu or Ketu, he may undergo a major operation.

4.Mercury

(i) **Positive** - He will be lean and thin. He may be aggressive and quarrelsome. He may leave his education half way.

(ii) **Negative** - If Mars aspects it, his nervous system may break down and if Rahu or Saturn aspects, he may lose his peace of mind and become psychic.

5.Jupiter

(i) **Positive** - He will be educated, learned, soft-spoken, healthy and rich. He may be respectable and famous.

(ii) **Negative** - He may be inactive and irritating being poor in health. He may indulge in speculations. He may be afraid of enemies.

6.Venus

(i) **Positive** - He may have many women friends and no enemy. If there are enemies, he may compromise with them.

(ii) **Negative** - He may suffer from urinary troubles and disease of sexual organs.

7.Saturn

(i) **Positive** - The person will be brave, bold, courageous and friendly and win over enemies. If Saturn associates the 6th house owner, he may be a building contractor.

(ii) **Negative** - He will be an asthma patient. If Mars associates, he may be operated upon and if Rahu joins, he may undergo hysteria shock.

8.Rahu

(i) **Positive** - He will be courageous, healthy, wealthy and famous. He may be long lived. He may earn his livelihood from foreigners.

(ii) **Negative** - If Rahu is in conjunction with Moon and Saturn his private life may be a victim of scandals. He may be mentally disturbed. His enemies may also create problems.

9.Ketu

(i) **Positive** - He may be fond of intuitive and occult science. He may be long lived. He would be afraid of enemies.

(ii) **Negative** - He may be immoral and get in to litigation. Accidents may also occur and create health problems.

5.10 Planets placements, aspects and combinations 6th house

1. If owner of 6th bhava is benefic and powerful, he has no enemy or may win over enemies.

2. If Lagnesh is powerful and owner of 6th bhava is in Lagna, he wins over enemies, like Shri Shankar Dayal Sharma, the President.

3. If Lagnesh is powerful and owner of 6th bhava is in 6th, 8th, or 12th house, it would be Vipreet Rajyoga that is good for earnings and status of the person.

4. If Saturn, Mars or Rahu are in 6th bhava and aspected by benefics, he wins over enemies.

5. If malefics occupies or aspects 6th bhava, due to double negativity, person will have no illness.

6. If owner of 6th house, Mercury or Rahu, conjoins or aspects Lagnesh, the person will be impotent.

7. If owner of 6th bhava is in 8th house with malefics, he may have boils on his face.

8. If owner of 6th house occupies 7th house and owner of 8th house occupies its own house, he may have piles.

9. If Moon and Sun exchange their signs and owner of 6th bhava aspects, the person may be a victim of tuberculosis.

10. If Lagnesh and owner of 6th bhava both are in 6th bhava or in 6th sign Virgo, he may die due to dog bites.

11. If Mars is the owner of 6th house and aspected by Saturn or Rahu, his death may occur due to accident.

12. If owner of 6th bhava is in 12th house aspected by malefics, his eyesight will be weak and he may undergo eye operation.

13. If owners of 6th and 1st houses occupy 1st, 4th, 7th, or 10th house, in conjunction with Saturn, Rahu, or Ketu, he may be confined behind bars.

14. If 6th bhava is badly influenced by all the malefics, the person will be happy and healthy due to double negativity.

15. If Jupiter or Ketu or both are in 6th bhava, the person may be fortunate and wealthy and lead a comfortable life.

16. If Gemini is lagna and Mars being the owner of 6th and 11th houses occupy 5th house, his wealth may be stolen by the thieves.

17. If owners of 4th and 1st houses both combine in 6th bhava, he will have enmity with his mother.

5.11 Events affecting during dasha Sign in 6th house

In Aries

(i) **Favourable** - Mars will be the owner. During its period, he may acquire wealth. He may be enterprising and a man of credit.

(ii) **Unfavourable** - During weak Mars dasha, he will suffer from illness. He may have family disputes and strange relations with his near and dear. If Rahu or owner of 8th or 12th joins, he may suffer from poverty and serious illness. In Navansh, if 6th owner occupies 6th or 8th house from Mars, he may meet untimely death.

In Taurus

(i) **Favourable** - If Venus is powerful, during its dasha, he may be a powerful speaker and travel abroad. He may be enterprising and well known in the community leading a comfortable and happy life.

(ii) **Unfavourable** - During weak Venus dasha, he may suffer from kidney and eye problem. He may be poor in finances. Relatives and friends may become enemies.

In Gemini

(i) **Favourable** - During Mercury dasha, he will be brave and courageous and may take risks in enterprises.

(ii) **Unfavourable** - During owner's dasha, he may be angry but submissive in nature. His relatives and friends may also go against him. He may be sickly with nose, throat, skin and nervous problems.

In Cancer

(i) **Favourable** - If powerful and friendly planets combine or aspect Moon, during its dasha, he will be in riches having his own house and vehicles for conveyance. He will have motherly love and care.

(ii) **Unfavourable** - If Rahu conjoins Moon, during Moon's dasha; his mother may pass away after long illness. He himself may also be prone to fits and disease of hysteria.

In Leo

(i) **Favourable** - Sun will be the owner of 6th house. During its dasha, person will be professionally clever and cunning and earn his livelihood by overcoming obstacles and competitors.

(ii) **Unfavourable** - During owner's dasha, he may have tensions. He may fall a prey to debts and diseases. He may feel scared and unsecured.

In Virgo

(i) **Favourable** - Mercury will be owner. If powerful, he will maintain good health. He will suppress his enemies with his intellect. He will be cautious with his money. He will reside at his birthplace.

(ii) **Unfavourable** - During weak Mercury dasha, he may earn money and pull along with his family and relatives especially with auspicious siblings. His aimless traveling to abroad may lose his health.

In Libra

(i) **Favourable** - If the owner Venus is well placed, during its dasha, he may get all benefits, lot of wealth, comforts in life, dignity and reputation. A male child may take birth in his family.

(ii) **Unfavourable** - His marriage may be disturbed because of ill-healthy wife. She will not be able to give birth to a child. There may also be a trouble in his enterprise.

In Scorpio

(i) **Favourable** - During strong Mars dasha he will rise and progress. He will not only earn wealth, but also status, power and popularity.

(ii) **Unfavourable** – During weak Mars dasha, he may be weak and a man of loose character. He may give in to sinful acts. He may be obstinate and quarrelsome. He may suffer from a serious disease, accident or some trouble in his left eye. Family disputes may also arise.

In Sagittarius

(i) **Favourable** -If, Jupiter is the owner of the 6th house, its dasha may be favourable for native's business and service. He may be religious and benevolent.

(ii) **Unfavourable** - Weak Jupiter's dasha may cause him losses in business. His father may also be in trouble. He may not be able to continue higher education. He may be irreligious and yield to his enemies.

In Capricorn

(i) **Favourable** - Powerful Saturn will make him a good leader well known in public. He may go abroad and earn name and fame there.

(ii) **Unfavourable** - During weak Saturn dasha, he may not be able to build good relations with the superiors or the authorities. Patrimony may be a cause of disputes; his brothers may go in litigation against him. He may incur debts and diseases.

In Aquarius

(i) **Favourable** - Saturn is owner of 6th house. During its dasha, the person will be healthy and happy. He may gain in business or occupation but earnings may not be as much as he deserves.

(ii) **Unfavourable** - He may lose his money due to theft or enemies. He may incur debts and suffer from long-term ailments during its dasha period.

In Pisces

(i) **Favourable** - During powerful Jupiter's dasha, he may have wealth and other comforts in life as house, conveyance etc. He may have good relations with his maternal uncle.

(ii) **Unfavourable** - During weak Jupiter's dasha, he may suffer from stomach problems. His foes may torture him.

5.12 Tenth House (Karma Bhava)

This house is known as Karma bhava / Pitru bhava (House of actions and father) It is one of the most Auspicious (Shubha) bhava in angles. It indicates south direction. From here the Sun is on the maximum height, so this bhava looks like a symbol of height or progress of the person.

This house (bhava) indicates occupation, profession, action, achievements, dignity and status. It ensures power, prestige, name, fame and credit for work done. It provides activities, responsibilities, permanency, promotion, authority, ambition, higher post, success, reputation, pilgrimage to holy places. It shows person's present Karmas (actions) of life and means of livelihood so it is known as house of Artha (wealth). If the benefic planets are around it, good results are seen in mahadasha / anterdasha. Rahu for sudden wealth and Jupiter for religious thoughts are close to it.

5.13 Owner of Tenth house in various houses

In First House

(i) **Powerful** - He will be learned, famous and wealthy. He may start his own business and rise independently. He may establish institutions of public welfare. He will be a self-made man.

(ii) **Weak** - He may be sick in childhood. It may affect on his body appearance. Later on he may pick up his health.

In Second House

(i) **Powerful** - He will rise in life and earn a lot of wealth. He will be fortunate, charitable, happy and respectable. He may adopt his father's business. He may prosper in food business.. He may take up business dealings with the government.

(ii) **Weak** - He will suffer heavy losses in his family business. This may affect his health.

In Third House

(i) **Powerful** - He will be bold and courageous. He will work hard for his livelihood. He may join government service. He may take short journeys. He may be a good orator and a writer. His brothers may help him in his career.

(ii) **Weak** - If owner of 10th bhava is in adverse constellations or in 6th, 8th, 12th houses in Navansh Chart, he may lose his health. He may have inimical relations with brothers.

In Fourth House

(i) **Powerful** - This is an excellent position. He will be fortunate, intelligent, learned and wealthy. He may get motherly love and happiness. He may turn to the real-estate business. He may have a good house and conveyance.

(ii) **Weak** - He may lose his property and wealth. He may be compelled to work on a below status job for livelihood. If owner of 8th house combines or aspects it, his health may also be affected.

In Fifth House

(i) **Powerful** - He will be highly educated, learned and intelligent. His children may also be capable. He may earn lot of wealth through speculations and lead a pious and religious life. He may be a priest or an astrologer.

(ii) **Weak** - He may pass through troublesome circumstances that may change his career and make him dependent on his children.

In Sixth House

(i) **Powerful** - He will hold a post of high authority in judiciary / police / prisons,/ civil hospitals / welfare ashrams. He may be popular and respected as a man of principles and ideals to others.

(ii) **Weak** - If Saturn aspects, he may work on a low salary job and if Rahu combines or aspects, he may suffer disgrace and disaster. Criminal proceedings of court may show him the way to prison.

In Seventh House

(i) **Powerful** - He will be liberal and lusty. His life partner will be matured and educated. He will gain money from wife's family. He will be skillful and well known. He will travel abroad.

(ii) **Weak** - He may have bad sex habits that may bring him disgrace and loss of health and wealth. For livelihood he may have to depend upon his spouse.

In Eighth House

(i) **Powerful** - He may occupy a high level post but for a short period and earn reputation and distinction. He may be long-lived.

(ii) **Weak** - He may see many breaks in his career. He may commit offenses and invite criminal proceedings.

In Ninth House

(i) **Powerful** - If 10th house owner is placed in 9th house and is aspected by Jupiter, he may be a spiritual healer or priest or a writer or editor. He will be fortunate. People will respect and regard him. He will be wealthy and highly successful in his business. He will give due regard to his parents. He may be kind and charitable.

(ii) **Weak** - Malefic planets, if occupies 9th house will shorten the influence of gains or profits and lower the status.

In Tenth House

(i) **Powerful** - It will be its own house. It will give rise to a powerful Rajyog. He will be a learned, truthful, enterprising, wealthy and happy person. He may hold high position in government. The government may honour him. He may be a good politician. If two or three planets conjoin, he may be a head of a big and famous institution. He may be a man of Mathematics. He may be famous and renounce the world.

(ii) **Weak** - He may be dependent in life having no respect, if 10th house owner conjoins 6th or 8th or 12th house owners. He may lose everything that he earned in his life.

In Eleventh House

(i) **Powerful** - He will be honest and sympathetic. He will do such meritorious deeds that people will remember him. He may engage hundreds of people in service and gain respect and honour. He may have many friends. His domestic life may be cheerful and peaceful. His children may also bring him name and fame.

(ii) **Weak** - His friends and brothers may go against him. He may lose his peace of mind and happiness.

In Twelfth House

(i) **Powerful** - He will have to work hard for his livelihood and domestic comforts. He will be God fearing and religious.

(ii) **Weak** - He may indulge in the business of smuggling and may be dishonest. Government may also penalize him with fine or taxes.

5.14 Planets occupying tenth house

1. Sun

(i) **Positive** - He will be intelligent and learned working on a high level administrative post. He may be successful politician. He may be liberal, popular and respectable. Government may honour him. He may acquire ancestral wealth. If Mercury is with Sun, he may be a research scholar. If Venus is with Sun, his wife may come from a rich family.

(ii) **Negative** - If Mars associates, he may be addicted to drinking. If Saturn conjoins, he may lose his mental peace and live with sorrows and worries.

2. Moon

(i) **Positive** - The person will be bold, intelligent, wealthy, pious and religious. He will be helpful and charitable. If Jupiter associates, he may study old literature of Vedas and Upnishadas, astronomy, and astrology. He may be a good astrologer and have many friends. He may lead a happy and prosperous life. He may be a head of some religious institution.

(ii) **Negative** - If Saturn aspects, he may be dull and lazy. He may change his professions frequently and may not be stable, happy or satisfied.

3. Mars

   (i) **Positive** - He will be happy, healthy, famous and wealthy having all comforts of life as house, vehicles etc. He may be a good administrator or a political leader. He may be courageous and aggressive. If Mercury conjoins he may be a good technician or engineer, if Saturn conjoins a leader of poor or downtrodden people and If Venus conjoins a trader of luxury goods.

  (ii) **Negative** - He will have no regard for his mother. If Saturn joins, he may be childless.

4.Mercury

   (i) **Positive** - He will be learned, studious, truthful and popular. He will give due regard to his parents. He will have his own house. He will be fortunate and happy. He will have profound knowledge of astronomy, Cosmo-mathematics and meta-physics.

  (ii) **Negative** - If Saturn and Mercury combine, he may be poor with a low salary job.

5.Jupiter

   (i) **Positive** - The person will be learned and respected. He may hold high position in government. He may be rich, wise, and virtuous. If Jupiter is aspected by Venus, he may protect Brahmins or learned people and if it is aspected by Mars, he may establish educational institutions and be its head. He will be obedient to his teachers (Gurus) and parents.

  (ii) **Negative** - If Rahu combines Jupiter, he may create troubles for subordinates and elders. His reputation will be tarnished.

6.Venus

   (i) **Positive** - He will be social, friendly, famous, and highly influential. He may earn money through luxury goods. He may be passionate and fond of pleasures. He will have many children. He will respect the religious people.

  (ii) **Negative** - He will not be a matured person. His education might be disrupted. His immoral acts will spoil his image.

7.Saturn

   (i) **Positive** - He will be rich and famous. He may work for downtrodden people. He may be a political leader. He may be hard working. He may be an agriculturist if sixth lord conjoins or aspects. He may be an ascetic, totally detached and knowledgeable.

(ii) **Negative** - Saturn at times brings a sudden fall from the high position especially if it is with eighth house owner in Navansh Chart. He would be selfish and mean.

8.Rahu

(i) **Positive** - He will be a learned person and travel abroad. He will be bold and brave. He will engage in a family business. He will be religious and love Vedic literature.

(ii) **Negative** - He will be lazy, talkative, and irregular in his work. His actions might be immoral because of low mentality and utterly selfish motives.

9. Ketu

(i) **Positive** - He will be strong and courageous. He will be religious and may go on a long pilgrimage. He may become a yogi (sanyasi) and renounce the world.

(ii) **Negative** - He will be a liar. He may misbehave with his father. He may commit unlawful activities and face many problems. He may be unfortunate.

5.15 Planets placements, aspects and combinations 10th house

1. If owner of 10th bhava associates with lagnesh, the person may be a successful government employee and earn name, fame and respect.

2. If owner of 10th bhava is in angles or trines (1, 4, 7, 10 or 5, 9 houses) he may be a gazetted officer.

3. If owner of 10th bhava is in 9th or 11th house and owner of 9th or 11th house is in 10th bhava that is exchange of houses, the person will be a good administrator.

4. If Moon and Venus are in 10th bhava, the person may be a doctor.

5. If Vrischik rashi is in 10th bhava or in lagna and Moon with Mars conjoins, he may be a doctor.

6. If in 10th house to 10th i.e. in 7th house, there is Capricorn sign and Mars occupies that, but not aspected by malefics, the person will be head of army or political leader. Sardar Ballabhbhai Patel is an example.

7. If Jupiter as the owner of 10th bhava occupies 5th or 9th house, the person may hold a high level position in the government.

8. If Moon is in 10th house and Jupiter in 5th house, the person will be learned and religious.

9. If owners of 9th and 10th houses and Jupiter are powerful and benefics occupy 9th and 10th houses, then he will be a leading, noble, virtuous and famous person.

10. If 10th bhava or lagna and owner of 10th bhava and lagnesh both are powerful, the person will be famous all over the world.

11. If owner of 10th bhava is powerful and well placed, he will be successful in life.

12. If owner of 10th bhava is in exalted sign and from that exalted sign in tenth bhava Rahu joins, he will be successful in life.

13. If Sun occupies 10th house from Moon, the person's mother may die early.

14. If Mars and Saturn are in 7th house from Sun, his father may die early.

15. If 10th bhava, owner of 10th bhava and significator (karak) Sun are aspected by Saturn, Rahu and owner of 12th, the person may be terminated from government service.

16. If Venus is in 10th from Jupiter's position, the person will be wealthy.

17. If owner of 10th bhava is malefic and occupies 6, 8, 12 houses from his position, he may commit sins.

5.16 Events affecting during dasha Sign in 10th house

In Aries

(i) **Favourable** - Powerful Mars will be Rajyoga karak. It will bring popularity, prosperity and wealth to the native during dasha period. He will be a man of high status and authority. He will be fortunate.

(ii) **Unfavourable** - Weak Mars dasha, If falls in childhood, he may be sick for a long time.

In Taurus

(i) **Favourable** - He will be successful in his profession and earn more wealth. His father may also help him. He may be intelligent and reputed and acquire good status.

(ii) **Unfavourable** - He may suffer from severe cold and cough problems along with his family members.

In Gemini

(i) **Favourable** - During Mercury dasha, his business may improve. He may have good relations with his younger brothers / sisters and help and support them. He may have a sweet voice and good behavior.

(ii) **Unfavourable** - If Mercury is weak, he may act foolishly and lose his status

In Cancer

(i) **Favourable** - During Moon dasha, the person will have house, conveyance, and wealth. He will lead a comfortable and happy life. If Mercury combines, he may take higher education for better future. He will be successful and enjoy all powers and benefits of a government post.

(ii) **Unfavourable** - At times, he may be stubborn and may lose his temperament adversely affecting his status.

In Leo

(i) **Favourable** - If powerful Sun is placed in its own 10th house aspected by benefics, during its dasha, he will be knowledgeable in many branches of education. He may be a high-level government officer and lead happy, healthy, and rich life. He may have a son.

(ii) **Unfavourable** - He may lose his memory. Government may go against him. He may lose his respect and status. Paternal property and wealth may also be destroyed.

In Virgo

(i) **Favourable** - During Mercury dasha, he will join high-level post in government and have better income and status.

(ii) **Unfavourable** - During weak Mercury dasha, he may have bad relationship with his father. His enemies may also cause him tension, pain, and sorrow. He may lose his income. Authorities may go against him.

In Libra

(i) **Favourable** - Venus would be Rajyoga karak as 10th house owner. During its dasha period, the individual will be knowledgeable and may further take up higher studies to be proficient in a field. He will be fortunate and lead a happy family life. He may have all comforts in life and a good status in profession.

(ii) **Unfavourable** - A weak and afflicted Venus dasha will be detrimental to his position and status as well as his married life.

In Scorpio

(i) **Favourable** - He will have a good position and income. He will perform his duties well. He will be long lived.

(ii) **Unfavourable** - He may lose his health and suffer from a serious incurable illness.

In Sagittarius

(i) **Favourable** - Powerful 10th house owner Jupiter's dasha will bestow upon him high position in the government. He will be successful in his endeavors. He may have a son in that period.

(ii) **Unfavourable** - He may have mental tension on account of his professional life. He may invite wrath of his seniors.

In Capricorn

(i) **Favourable** - If Saturn, the 10th house owner is powerful, during its dasha, he will feel efficient and successful in doing his job duties and earn a lot of wealth. He may lead a happy and comfortable life. He may be residing in a big residential accommodation provided by government.

(ii) **Unfavourable** - Weak and afflicted Saturn will make the person to indulge in sins and vices such as gambling, horse race etc.

In Aquarius

(i) **Favourable** - Powerful Saturn in its dasha will generate wealth. His elder brothers / sisters may be highly placed and become happy, healthy, and wealthy.

(ii) **Unfavourable** - Weak Saturn may cause him sufferings. He may also suffer from bad health and undermine his status and position.

In Pisces

(i) **Favourable** - During dasha period of powerful Jupiter, person may go abroad, get a high position there and earn wealth and honour.

(ii) **Unfavourable** - Weak Jupiter dasha may create enemies and powerful competitors. Government may impose penalty and fines. Business or Jobs of his elder brothers and sons may also be affected.

5.17 Example kundlis with astrological observations

Six kundlis as an example are given below regarding 2nd, 6th and 10th houses, two for each house of Aishwarya Trine (Artha houses).

Kundli No. 22 Famous Indudtrialist Mr. Rattan Tata

1.Date of birth 28 -12-1937

2.Time of Birth 06 - 30 A.M. (IST)

3.Place of Birth Mumbai (Maharast) Lat.18^0 / 58' N., Long.72^0 /50' E.

4.Birth Nakshatra-Vishakha-1

5. Balance Dasha at Birth-Jupiter-14years-00month-21days

BIRTH CHART

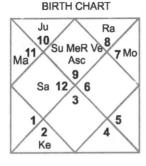

NAVANSH CHART

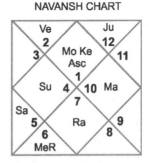

Kundli No. 5.17 (K-22)

Astrological Observations

This is a birth chart of Sagittarius sign, a dual sign. People are bold, courageous, pushing, ambitious and have high aspirations. Rattan Tata is such a pushing man. He has a good understanding how to make others happy and his business flourished? Recently Lakhtakia car sale is an example. Born in Vishakha nakshatra he is a good speaker, pains taker, and deep thinker for the welfare of average man, religious and God-fearing.

1.Lagna considerations

This birth chart belongs to Rattan Tata, who presented a new distinction and direction to the car market by bringing low cost car, price one hundred thousand rupees, so that an average salaried person may fulfill his dream of traveling by car and enjoy life. Lagnesh (1st house owner) and Surya lagnesh Jupiter is posited in 2nd house while Chandra lagnesh Venus with Mercury and significator Sun is placed in lagna, therefore, Chandra lagna is highly activated. Navansh lagnesh Mars is located in its exalted sign Capricorn, while in birth chart it is in sign Aquarius both owned by Saturn. Thus Mars is strengthening his ambition, energy, power, status and business.

2.Planets placements, aspects and combination

Jupiter from 2nd house aspects 6th house of Venus and 10th house of Mercury both occupying lagna (1st house) of its own. Here Sun is forming Ubhaychari yoga and Jupiter and Saturn Rashi Parivartan yoga (exchange of signs). Saturn aspects 6th house owned by Venus. These situations provided him riches and prosperity. He is now world fame industrialist. Significator of 3rd house, Jupiter's friendly Mars also aspects 6th and 10th houses strengthening his eminence and credit. This is a good combination and interrelation of 2nd, 6th and 10th houses known as Artha Houses.

3.Conclusion

On the basis of lagna considerations, planets placements, aspects and different combinations, we can conclude that Rattan Tata was already popular in car market but now after launching low price cars in the market especially in India, made his status and dignity more respectable and honourable amongst common people. Planets in lagna and Jupiter, Mars and Saturn fulfilled all his ambitions of life imparting real shape for his own business providing benefits to the people of the country. It is due to close combination and correlation among 2nd, 6th and 10th houses of Aishwarya Trine called Artha houses. Presently in Venus mahadasha, Saturn anterdasha is in operation. It will raise his business adding lot of wealth and popularity.

Kundli No. 23 Famous Businessman Late Dhiru Bhai Ambani
1.Date of birth   28 -12-1932
2.Time of Birth   06-37 A.M. (IST)
3.Place of Birth   Chorwad (Gujrat) Lat.21^0 / 01' N.Long.70^0 / 14' E.
4.Birth Nakshatra Poorva Ashadha-3
5. Balance Dasha at Birth -Venus   08years. 04months 15days

BIRTH CHART

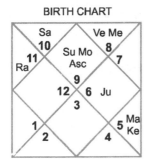

NAVANSH CHART

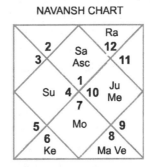

Kundli No. 5.17 (K-23)

Astrological Observations

This is Sagittarius, a fiery sign lagna kundli. Such people are also pushing, ambitious and have high aspirations. Dhiru Bhai Ambani was known as an idol of aspiring entrepreneurs and an efficient businessman of courage and determination. Born in Poorva Sadha nakshtra, he was peace loving, far sighted, fortunate and wealthy. He left a big business kingdom for his sons. Now they are extending it with new dimensions.

1.Lagna considerations

Lagnesh, Chandra lagnesh and Surya lagnesh Jupiter the owner of all lagna's (Sudarshan lagna) is situated in 10th house and influences lagna. In Navansh kundli it is also located in 10th house hence a good position of Jupiter. Therefore Lagna is triple times powerful in his birth chart. It is extremely activated. Venus, the significator of wealth is posited with Mercury. It brings wealth and prosperity by business. Venus is Vargottam being in Scorpio sign in both the charts.

2.Planets placements, aspects and combinations

Both the owners of 1st house of health and happiness and 4th house of comforts and luxuries Jupiter from 10th house aspects 2nd house of wealth and its owner Saturn occupies that house. Jupiter aspects 6th house too. Venus, the 6th house owner and friedly Mercury, the 10th house owner both from 12th house aspect 6th house. Therefore it is a good combination and interrelate 2nd, 6th and 10th houses, called Artha houses. Saturn the 2nd house owner aspects 4th house of comforts and luxuries owned by Jupiter raising its status. Saturn aspects 11th house of income owned by Venus placed in the12th house. Sun is forming Ubhaychari yoga and Moon Gajkesri yoga as Jupiter is in Kendra from Moon, Durudhara yoga as planets are on both sides of Moon (other than Sun) and Amalkirti yoga in 10th house from lagna or Chandra lagna. All these yogas helped him in progressing his business and raising his wealth. He was intelligent, virtuous, benevolent, religious and popular.

3.Conclusion

Thus we can conclude that Dhanesh, the 2nd house owner Saturn and 6th house owner Venus and the Karmesh, 10th house owner Mercury in a short period proclaimed Dhiru Bhai Ambani a famous businessman with riches and prosperity. It is due to Saturn, the 2nd house owner is in its 2nd house, Jupiter in 10th house and aspects 6th house. Venus 6th house owner aspects it and 10th house owner Mercury is with Venus. Hence all Artha houses 2nd, 6th and 10th are well connected and interrelated.

He led a good and comfortable life, when he was in progress and topper in his business but in Mercury anterdasha and Saturn Mahadasha proved him fatal and he left for the final abode on 06-07-2002 leaving his property and business in the hands of his sons and family.

Kundli No. 24 Ex. Prime Minister of India, Smt. Indira Gandhi

1.Date of birth 19 -11-1917

2.Time of Birth 23 -11 P.M. (IST)

3.Place of Birth Allahabad (U.P.) Lat.25⁰ / 27' N.Long.81⁰ / 51' E.

4.Birth Nakshatra Uttra Ashadha-3

5.Balance Dasha at Birth Sun 01year-11months-23days.

BIRTH CHART

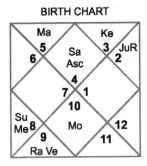

NAVANSH CHART

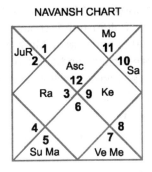

Kundli No. 5.17 (K-24)

Astrological Observations

This is Cancer lagna kundli. Cancereans are imaginative, emotional, sensitive but most successful and take benefits through their opponents. Smt. Indira Gandhi was such a leader, who ruled over India more than fifteen years with perfection and satisfaction with the help of the leaders so called her enemies or opponents. Born in Uttra Sadha nakshatra she was bold, brave, energetic, intelligent and knowledgeable having good understanding of the field.

1.Lagna considerations

Smt. Indira Gandhi, the only child of First Prime-Minister of India Pt. Jawahar Lal Nehrul, was a great and shrewed politician of her time. She was the first Lady Prime Minister of India. Lagnesh Moon is situated in 7th house and aspects lagna and Chandra lagnesh Saturn is already placed in lagna. Surya lagnesh Mars is next to Lagna in 2nd house and aspects Sun the significator of lagna. Therefore lagna is highly fortified. Navansh lagnesh Jupiter is in Vargottam. In birth chart it is located in 11th house and aspects 3rd house. In Navansh kundli it is in 3rd house, hence a good placement.

2.Placements, aspects and combinations

Her birth chart is special one showing three Rashi Parivartan Yogas (exchange of signs) (1) lagnesh Moon in 7th house in Capricorn and Saturn in 1st house in Cancer, (2) Owner of 5th and 10th houses Mars is in Leo sign and Sun is in Scorpio sign and (3) the owner of 11th house Venus is in Sagittarius sign and owner of 6th house Jupiter in Taurus sign. Besides this, Mars aspects Sun and Mercury both sitting in 5th house and 9th house representing fortune and religion. Sun and Mercury aspects Jupiter in 11th house and Jupiter vice versa. Jupiter from 11th house and Saturn from 1st house both aspect 3rd and 7th houses. Saturn aspects 10th house also. Mars is most powerful being the owner of 5th house of education and children and 10th house of karma (actions). This indicates a good connection and correlation of 6th, 10th and 2nd houses, known as Artha houses.

3.Conclusion

On the basis of above aspects, we can conclude that the 6th house is powerful and makes her successful in administration. Jupiter, the owner of 6th and 9th houses of enemies and luck is situated in 11th house of gains, made her popular and wealthy through her political opponents. She took her rivals as friends. Nobody could face her. Once she was defeated in her election as M. P. due to mahadasha of Saturn and anterdasha of Venus. But very soon, she conquered over her enemies and won the next election with a majority of votes. It is because of good relationship of 6th house of Jupiter where Venus is placed and Jupiter in the house of Venus. Mars is sitting in Sun's 2nd house, aspects Sun, which is in Mars house and Saturn aspects 10th house from lagna. This interconnection of 6th, 10th and 2nd houses and exchange of signs (Rashi Parivartan yogas) made her popular. She sacrificed her life at the age of 67 years.

Kundli No. 25   Mr. Barack Obama, Present President, U.S.A.

1. Date of birth 04 - 08 -1961,
2. Time of birth 13 - 06 P.M. (Time Zone -10-00 Hrs.)
3. Place of birth Honolulu (USA) Lat.21° /18' N. Long.157°/ 51' W.
4. Birth nakshatra Krittika-4
5. Balance Dasha at birth Sun Year-01, Months-05, Days-29.

BIRTH CHART   NAVANSH CHART

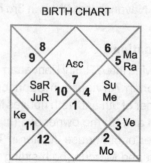
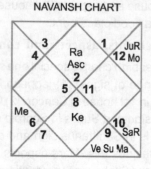

Kundli No. 5.17 (K-25)

Astrological Observations

This is a Libra sign lagna kundli. Its lord is Venus. Librans are reasonable and just. They are popular and have a spirit of sacrifice. They weigh the merits and demerits of a subject like a balance. So Barack Obama balanced his mind to win the Presidential Election and now he is President of U.S.A. Born in Krittika nakshatra, he is handsome, bold, brave, strong, energetic and knowledgeable and keeps good connections in high circles.

1.Lagna considerations

Lagnesh and Chandra lagnesh Venus is in 9th house of fortune. Surya lagnesh Moon is in its exalted sign. Navansh lagnesh is also Venus and there Saturn is in 9th house and Jupiter is in 11th house both retrograde and placed in their own signs, houses of luck and gains. In birth chart significator of 1st house, Sun is in 10th house of karma (actions) and influences lagna. Therefore lagna is extremely activated. It is a good position.

2.Planets placements, aspects and combinations

Mars from 11th house aspects its own sign Scorpio in 2nd house and Pisces sign of Jupiter in 6th house. Moon also aspects friendly Scorpio sign in 2nd house. Saturn and Jupiter from 4th house are in mutual aspect with Sun and Mercury in 10th house. Saturn from 4th house also aspects 6th house that belongs to the retrograde Jupiter is sitting in the 4th house of Saturn itself. Hence there is a good connection and interrelation of 6th 10th and 2nd houses called Artha houses. It indicates good chances of getting lead in his profession. Other yogas are that Sun is forming Ubhaychari yoga being planets on both sides of it other than Moon, Moon is forming Sunpha yoga being a benefic and Saturn, Sasa yoga being in Kendra in its own sign and retrograde Jupiter is forming Rajyoga being in Kendra in the 4th house representing residence, conveyance and luxuries. Mars and Rahu in 11th house indicate huge gains and fulfillment of long cherished desires, being admired by his friends and well-wishers. The owner of 10th is in 8th house, reflects more attention. Nothing comes easily. Present mahadasha of Jupiter and anterdasha of Sun started from August 10th, 2008, it helped him win the election.

3.Conclusion

We can conclude that in mahadasha of Jupiter and anterdasha of Sun, he improved his position in other states and became famous. It is because of interconnections and correlations of 6th, 10th and 2nd Artha houses of Aishwarya Trine as Saturn aspects 6th house belonging to retograde Jupiter and both aspect 10th house of action. Mars aspects its own 2nd house from 11th house of gains and profits. He won the election and took oath as the 44th President of U.S.A. on 20th January 2009. Future may be bright for him. But he would have to take necessary steps to raise and improve the country's economic position which has already gone down. He is to fight with terrorism also. Recently, he is awarded the world's highest Noble Peace Prize of the year 2009.

Kundli No. 26 Ex. President Pak. Mr. Parvej Musharraf

1.Date of birth 11 - 08 - 1943

2.Time of birth 06 - 45 A.M. (IST)

3.Place of birth Delhi (India) Lat.28⁰ / 40' N. Long.77⁰ / 13' E.

4.Nakshatra at birth Jyeshtha-1

5.Balance of Dasha at birth Mercury 15years-o4month-02days

BIRTH CHART

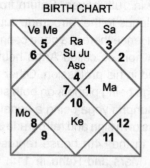

NAVANSH CHART

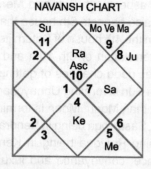

Kundli No. 5.17 (K-26)

Astrological Observations

It is a birth chart of Cancer Lagna. As above stated in Smt. Indira Gandhi's kundlli Cancereans are brave, bold and courageous. They are imaginative and sensitive. They are never afraid of their opponents. They are hard working and steadfast. So Parvej Musharraf is such a man, who administered the country for a long time facing all his opponents. Born in

Jyeshtha nakshatra, he is joyful, disciplined and a good orator but a man of harsh and cruel tongue.

1. Lagna Considerations

Lagnesh and Surya lagnesh debilitated Moon is placed in 5th house of knowledge and Childern. Chandra Lagnesh Mars is placed in its own sign Aries in 10th house and aspects lagna and planets located in lagna, Sun, Jupiter and Rahu. It aspects 4th house of comforts and 5th house of intelligence and Lagnesh Moon posited in 5th house owned by Mars. In Navansh lagna Mercury is in Vargottam occupying 11th house of gains and profits through government.

2. Placements, Aspects, and Combinations

Exalted Jupiter, the owner of 9th house of fortune posited with the karak Sun in 1st house of health and happiness. From lagna Mars is occupying 10th house of profession or occupation in its own sign Aries and from Moon 10th house owner Sun is placed in lagna. Mars and Jupiter both are forming Rashi Parivartan yoga (exchange of signs). Mars, the owner of 10th and 5th houses is Digbali and Atamkarak. It is also forming Rajyoga. Therefore all these yogas proved good and provided him a golden opportunity to be an army officer (a highest post in government). Exalted Saturn in Navansh lagna also indicates army services. In birth chart Saturn aspects 2nd and 6th houses and Mars is situated in its own sign in 10th house. Hence there is a powerful combination of all three 10th, 2nd and 6th houses known as Artha houses of Aishwarya Trine.

3. Conclusion

On the basis of above placements and combinations, we can conclude that Mars is in its own sign Aries in 10th house and aspects lagna and planets Sun and Jupiter. From 12th house, Saturn aspects 2nd house belonging to Sun and 6th and 9th houses belonging to Jupiter. Hence all Artha houses, 2nd, 6th and 10th house are interrelated and reinforced. It is the reason that the native remained for the head of Pakistan Army and ruled over the country for about 8 years as army head and president after crushing and removing all his enemies (opponents) and also all the obstructions . He left the chair, when there was no way. Still he dreams for getting power in government but present mahadasha and anterdasha is not likely to be favourable to him.

Kundli No. 27 Ex P.M. Late Chaudhry Charan Singh

1.Date of birth 23 - 12 - 1902

2.Time of birth 07 - 30 A.M. (IST)

3.Place of birth Nurpur-Merath (U.P.) Lat. 28⁰ / 59' N. Long.77⁰ / 42' E.

4.Nakshatra at birth Hasta-4

5. Balance Dasha at birth Moon 00year- 06months- 18days.

<table>
<tr><th>BIRTH CHART</th><th>NAVANSH CHART</th></tr>
<tr><td>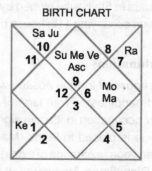</td><td>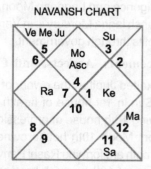</td></tr>
</table>

Kundli No. 5.17 (K-27)

Astrological Observations

It is a kundli of Sagittarius sign. It is a fiery and dual sign. It imparts energy, strength, enthusiasm, vigour and vitality to the person. Chaudhry Charan Singh was from a poor farmer's family. He was ambitious and had high aspirations. His cherished desires fulfilled, when he joined the highest post of Prime-Minister of India. Born in Hasta nakshatra he was bold, courageous, influential and wealthy.

1. Lagna Considerations

Lagnesh and Surya lagnesh Jupiter is situated in its debilitated sign Capricorn in 2nd house of wealth, with the owner Saturn. Chandra lagnesh Mercury is posited in lagna with Venus the owner of 11th house of gains and income and Sun the significator of 10th house of karma (actions). In Navansh lagna Venus, Mercury and Jupiter all benefics are situated in lagna. It is a good position. Chandra lagna is highly fortified.

2. Placements, aspects and combinations

Saturn is placed in its own sign in 2nd house with lagnesh Jupiter and aspects 4th house that belongs to Jupiter. From 2nd house lagnesh Jupiter aspects its 6th house and 10th house where friendly planets

Moon and Mars are placed. They form a Rajyoga. So there is a good connection and correlation of 10th, 2nd and 6th Artha houses. Moon and Mars both aspect 4th house of comforts where Pisces is rising. Mars also aspects 5th house of education and children. Mars is *digbali* in the 10th house of profession and power. Mercury and Venus combination in lagna as owners of 10th and 11th houses and also Mercury and Sun combination in lagna being in Kendra from the Moon created one more Rajyoga, which led him to the highest post in the government as Prime-Minister of India in mahadasha and anterdasha of Mercury and Venus. He not only secured name, fame, honour and authority but also riches and prosperity.

3. Conclusion

We can conclude that Mars is placed in 10th house of actions which belongs to Mercury, sitting in lagna with Venus and Sun and aspects all the three planets in the 1st house, which led him to the politics and made him popular in the community and the region. Saturn is placed in 2nd house in its own sign with Jupiter and Jupiter aspects 6th house of Venus and 10th house of Mercury. Both Venus and Mercury are occupying Sagittarius sign in lagna. Hence there is a strong correlation amongst all 10th, 2nd and 6th Artha houses. Due to these connections, he became the leader of farmers and villagers where life was not good. When he became the Prime Minister of India, he executed the marketing act to reform the condition of farmers and that marketing act is still prevailing. Farmers, to some extent, got its benefits.

Figure : 5.1 (F-4) Second Trine Artha Houses

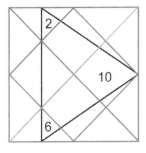

Figure : 5.1 (F-4)

ೞೋೠ

Chapter
6
Third Trine Prakrati Trine (Kama Houses)

6.1 What is Prakrati Trine? Related houses

This is the third trine consisting of seventh, eleventh and third houses (bhavas). They show boldness (parakram), initiative, relations with the life partner, pleasures, procreation, earnings and prosperity in life. They indicate success, status, honour, dignity, mentality and one's over all personality. Are we intelligent and knowledgeable? Are we healthy, wealthy and famous in the society? Are we enjoying fun and pleasures, luxuries and riches in life? Are we modern and fashionable? How is one's nature and temperament? How does one behave with others? Is one a person of character and morality? As already stated Seventh, Eleventh and Third houses come in the category of Kama houses. First we will take over all effects of third house, then proceed to the seventh and eleventh houses. Please see Figure 6.1 (F-5) at the end of Chapter.

6.2 Third house (Bhratra Bhava)

This House is known as Bhratra bhava / Parakram bhava (House of siblings and courage). Though it is one of trishadaya (3, 6, 11) houses yet is also called house of growth. The third bhava shows enterprises and ventures hence it is the house of growth. It indicates mental abilities, studies, intelligence, firmness, boldness, energy, courage, younger brothers / sisters / neighbours, short journeys, communication, expression, writings, contracts, change of residence, passions, desires and happiness in person's life. It is the first house of Kama (fun and pleasures). If the owner or occupying planet is well placed with strong benefics, person may get such benefits and gains in its mahadasha /anterdasha of 3rd house owner. Planet Mars, the significator (Karak) is very close to this house.

6. 3 Owner of third house in various houses

In first house

(i) **Powerful** - He will be lean but tall, brave, and courageous. He may earn money through music, dancing, or acting. He may be a good actor.

(ii) **Weak** - He will be cruel, quarrelsome and man of loose morals. He may have bad relations. He may be poor and stupid.

In second house

(i) **Powerful** - If the owner of 2nd house is benefic, he may be fortunate, wealthy and happy.

(ii) **Weak** - This is not a favourable position. The person will be poor and short lived. He may take undue risks and incur losses.

In third house

(i) **Powerful** - If owner of 3rd bhava is in its own house as a natural benefic, the person will be brave, courageous, friendly and religious. He will gain money through government. He will be happy and healthy. He will have nice brothers and sisters.

(ii) **Weak** - If a malefic is the owner of 3rd bhava or occupies 3rd bhava, he will have sour relations with his younger brothers and sisters.

In fourth house

(i) **Powerful** - If owner of the 3rd bhava is in 4th house, his life will overall be happy. He will be rich. He will gain ancestral property. His brothers may also help him.

(ii) **Weak** - If Mars is weak, he will lose all his property, house and vehicles etc. He himself may rebel against his parents. His domestic life may be unhappy. He may have inimical relations with mother.

In fifth house

(i) **Powerful** - He may be less educated but intelligent. He may have favour from the government. He may be financially strong due to his own children and brothers.

(ii) **Weak** - He may have frictions in the family. His learning and education will suffer.

In sixth house

(i) **Powerful** - He will be respected in society. He will help his brothers. One of his younger brothers may be in army or be a physician. They will be successful in their jobs. If owner of 6th house joins the owner of 3rd bhava in 6th house, he may be a good sportsman and athlete.

(ii) **Weak** - If owner of 3rd bhava with the owner of 6th occupies 6th house, he may suffer with long-term illness. His enemies may also hurt him. He may not have good relations with his brothers.

In seventh house

(i) **Powerful** - He will be fortunate to have a good life partner. He will have cordial relations with his brothers. If owner of 7th house occupies lagna, one of his brothers may go abroad.

(ii) **Weak** - His life partner will be of loose morals. He may be desperate and discontented in his professional life. He may have accidents while traveling.

In eighth house

(i) **Powerful** - He will be long lived. He will get success in career and become wealthy.

(ii) **Weak** - He will suffer from a long-term disease and injure his hands. He may lose his courage. His younger brother may die early. He may be unhappy with his near and dear ones.

In ninth house

(i) **Powerful** - His brothers will prosper and help and respect him. He may take long journeys for improving his status. He may be fortunate after marriage.

(ii) **Weak** - This is not a good position. He may have differences with his brothers and father.

In tenth house

(i) **Powerful** - This is a favourable position. He will be intelligent and fortunate. He will prosper and get help and honour from the government. If owner of 10th house conjoins 3rd house owner or aspects it, he will get good success in his profession.

(ii) **Weak** - His life partner will be aggressive and violent. His domestic life may be unhappy.

In eleventh house

(i) **Powerful** - His hard working habits will bestow him status and prosperity. His brothers may also help him.

(ii) **Weak** - He will be lazy and always dependent on his brothers. He may be frequently ill or sickly.

In twelfth house

(i) **Powerful** - He will be fortunate and happy after marriage. His younger brother may go abroad.

(ii) **Weak** - He will be jealous and aggressive. One of his brothers may also be violent. He may face sorrows, misfortunes, unhappiness, and ups and downs in his service.

6. 4 Planets occupying third house

1.Sun

(i) **Positive** - If Sun is posited in 3rd house, it is a strong position. The person will be brave, bold, courageous, resourceful, and successful. He will be famous in his field. Government may honour him for his good deeds. He may be an author or a poet.

(ii) **Negative** - He will be unhappy with his brothers. They will not give him any credit or respect.

2.Moon

(i) **Positive** - He will be knowledgeable, religious, bold, active, and always fond of traveling. He will not be stable in his profession. He will look after his younger brothers and sisters. His family life will be peaceful and happy.

(ii) **Negative** - He may be miser, cruel, and irreligious and lose his peace of mind.

3.Mars

(i) **Positive** - Mars is the significator (karak) of 3rd house. It makes the person brave, courageous, specialist in many fields and famous in the community.

(ii) **Negative** - Relations with younger brothers and sisters will not be cordial. He may be harsh and violent in nature. He may commit suicide.

4.Mercury

(i) **Positive** - He will be courageous, tactful, and proficient in his work. He may be fond of reading books. He may enjoy short travels. He may be a successful trader and a good neighbour. He may be a poet, an author or a publisher.

(ii) **Negative** - He may be sick and his nervous system may break down.

5. Jupiter

(i) **Positive** - The person will be learned in religious books (Shastras). He will be optimistic and religious. He may travel to distant places. He may have many siblings and good friends. He will earn respect everywhere.

(ii) **Negative** - He will be miser and suffer from ill health. He will be unable to take advantage of opportunities. He would lack in initiative and courage.

6. Venus

(i) **Positive** - He will be knowledgeable and happy, fortunate and wealthy. He will undertake journeys and become successful in his business.

(ii) **Negative** - He will be lazy and miser. He will lack vigour and vitality. He will be poor. He may pass through scandals. He may have more sisters.

7. Saturn

(i) **Positive** - He will be healthy, active and hard working. He will be wealthy. He may join politics and become a leader in the city. He will defeat his enemies. Government might honour him.

(ii) **Negative** - He will lose his high position. His brothers may also suffer from miseries and misfortunes.

8. Rahu

(i) **Positive** - He will be intelligent and learned. He will love his birthplace and reside there till life. He may be long lived.

(ii) **Negative** - He will hate his brothers. People will criticize him on his views and new ideas.

9. Ketu

(i) **Positive** - He will be brave, bold, courageous and earn lot of wealth. He may be quiet modern and fashionable.

(ii) **Negative** - He may suffer injury to arms or neck. He may not have any brother or happiness from the brother.

6. 5 Planets placements, aspects and combinations 3rd house

A. His younger brother may die

1. If owner of 3rd bhava and Mars both occupy 8th house.
2. If Rahu or Ketu occupies 3rd bhava.
3. If Sun occupies 3rd bhava and malefics aspect.
4. If Mars occupies 3rd bhava and malefics aspect.
5. From 3rd bhava, if malefics occupy the angles or triangles.
6. If Saturn alone occupies 3rd bhava.
7. If owner of 3rd bhava is weak or debilitated or combust or in an inimical sign or in 6,8,12 house.

B. His brothers will love and help each other

1. If owner of 3rd bhava and lagnesh combine.
2. If 3rd bhava, owner of 3rd bhava and Mars are in conjunction with or aspected by benefics.

C. He will be brave, bold officer in army or police

1. If owner of 3rd bhava joins powerful Mars, the karak of 3rd.
2. If owner of 3rd bhava, planets occupying 3rd bhava and Mars are powerful. Field Marshal Manekshah is an example.
3. If owner of 10th house and Saturn occupy 3rd bhava and Sun occupies 10th house.

D. His brothers will help in business

1. If owners of 1st and 2nd houses occupy 3rd bhava.

E. He will have one sister
1. If owner of 3rd bhava, Mars and Mercury occupy 3rd bhava.

F. He may be fighter or warrior
1. If Mars, Saturn or Rahu occupies 3rd bhava.
2. If owner of 3rd bhava is in its exalted sign with one malefic and occupies 8th house.
3. If owner of 3rd bhava conjoins with the owners of 6th and 10th houses in its 3rd bhava. Adolph Hitler Chancellor of Germany is an example.

6. 6 Events affecting during dasha Sign in 3rd house

In Aries
(i) **Favourable** - Mars will be the 3rd house owner. During its dasha, he will be successful and fortunate in his efforts. Economically he will be strong. He may travel to short distant places for business purposes. A male child may take birth in the family.

(ii) **Unfavourable** - During its dasha, he may be irritant and aggressive. His siblings may not favour him.

In Taurus
(i) **Favourable** - Venus will be the 3rd and 8th house owner. Its dasha will be favourable for wealth. He will be honest and religious. He may marry more than once.

(ii) **Unfavourable** - During Venus dasha, he will feel lazy and timid. His longevity of life will also be reduced to some extent.

In Gemini
(i) **Favourable** - Mercury will be the owner. During its dasha, he will be bold and brave. His siblings will also be happy. He may take up a government job.

(ii) **Unfavourable** - He may be unhappy with his job. Property disputes in family may also occur. It will affect his wealth. His siblings may be sickly and troublesome.

In Cancer
(i) **Favourable** - Moon will be the owner of 3rd house. During dasha period if it is in conjunction with or aspected by malefics, he may be wealthy and help his brothers. Family relations will be cordial.

(ii) **Unfavourable** - He will not be able to get his mother's love for a long time. He may be totally dependent on his father. Property disputes will occur. .

In Leo

(i) **Favourable** - During Sun's dasha, his life partner may be efficient and influential. She may help in earnings. He may live together his siblings raising his status in the community.

(ii) **Unfavourable** - He will be dependent on his brothers. If Sun with a malefic is placed in 3rd bhava, during dasha, problems will affect his position and profession.

In Virgo

(i) **Favourable** - Mercury will be its owner. If it is placed in 3rd house, he will be successful in his business. During dasha, he may acquire good property, house, car, cash and other amenities of life.

(ii) **Unfavourable** - During Mercury dasha he may not bave cordial relations with his siblings. His enemies may also create obstacles.

In Libra

(i) **Favourable** - During Venus dasha, he may undertake a new job or start a new business of printing and publishing papers and books and earn wealth. If unmarried, he may marry.

(ii) **Unfavourable** - If Venus is in conjunction with a malefic or aspected by malefic, he may indulge in illicit relations within joint family, if Saturn, Mars create Pap Kartari yoga with owner of 3rd bhava.

In Scorpio

(i) **Favourable** - Powerful Mars, during its dasha, will give him long longevity. He will work hard for better status. His siblings may also help.

(ii) **Unfavourable** - He may be sick. His siblings may also be in trouble.

In Sagittarius

(i) **Favourable** - Owner of 3rd bhava Jupiter is the planet of wealth; hence he will earn wealth in its dasha. His younger brothers may also earn. If owners of 3rd and 11th houses are friendly, he will live with his siblings.

(ii) **Unfavourable** - If Jupiter is weak and afflicted, during its dasha, he will not be happy with his brothers and father due to a dispute over property.

In Capricorn

(i) **Favourable** - Malefic Saturn will be the owner. If another malefic conjoins or aspects it, he may adopt a business of printing and publishing during its dasha. He may get favour from government also. He will be happy and successful in his efforts.

(ii) **Unfavourable** - During weak Saturn dasha, he may have relations with hard-hearted persons of opposite sex for his business needs that may hurt and decrease his income.

In Aquarius

(i) **Favourable** - During Saturn dasha, he will be bold, intelligent and hard working. He will earn wealth. His siblings will also help him.

(ii) **Unfavourable** - During dasha, he may not be able to continue education. His health may also be affect.

In Pisces

(i) **Favourable** - During Jupiter dasha, he will go abroad and earn wealth with the help of his life partner and friends.

(ii) **Unfavourable** - If Jupiter the owner is weak, he will be poor and idle. He may not have cordial relations with his siblings. His father may also lose his high position.

6. 7 Seventh house (Jeewansathi Bhava)

This house is known as Jeewansathi bhava / Marak bhava (House of lifepartner and ill health). Seventh bhava is the house of life partner (wife or husband) and also a marak being twelfth to eighth. It indicates marriage, urinary organs, marital happiness, health, sexual diseases, litigation, divorce, separation, partnership, legal ties, bondage, captivity, foreign relations, social status and reputation. It brings the person in public eye with peculiar habits of sensual delights so it is a house of Kama (fun and pleasures). Powerful and well placed benefics fulfill all the desires in their mahadasha / anterdasha. Venus in case of male and Jupiter in case of female being karak are related to it.

6.8 Owner of Seventh house in various houses

In First house

(i) **Powerful** - He will be intelligent, highly educated, learned and clever. He may marry someone, whom he knows from childhood. She may be a classmate or a neighbour or a distant relative. He will travel frequently for his business.

(ii) **Weak** - If owner of the seventh bhava and Venus are weak, he may be adulterous. He may lose his health and domestic happiness.

In Second House

(i) **Powerful** - The person may marry more than once and earn wealth after marriage.

(ii) **Weak** - He may be adulterous and earn money by trafficking in women. He may eat food in death ceremonies. He will be of wavering mind.

In Third House

(i) **Powerful** - He will be kind to his brothers. He will marry late. He may have a female issue.

(ii) **Weak** - He may indulge in adultery or his wife may be indulgent towards his younger brothers.

In Fourth House

(i) **Powerful** - He will be intelligent and learned. His married life will be happy. He will be enjoying all the comforts in life. He will have good children.

(ii) **Weak** - His immature wife may spoil his domestic life. He will have many problems especially regarding conveyance. His wife may go astray.

In Fifth House

(i) **Powerful** - He will be happy, healthy, wealthy, famous and respected. His family will also be well to do. He will be a man of character.

(ii) **Weak** - He will be childless. There may be a trouble in his job or profession. His reputation and regard may fall.

In Sixth House

(i) **Powerful** - He will be bold, energetic, virtuous, and wealthy. He may marry second time.

(ii) **Weak** - His wife will be sick and jealous. He may lead unhappy conjugal life.

In Seventh House

(i) **Powerful** - He will marry in early age. His wife will be healthy and beautiful coming from a reputed family. He will be wealthy and love his wife.

(ii) **Weak** - His wife may die earlier than him. It will give him loneliness and unhappiness. He may indulge in adultery.

In Eighth House

(i) **Powerful** - He may marry second time. He may have all comforts in life, a good house and a vehicle. His wife may also come from a wealthy family.

(ii) **Weak** - Wife may be cruel and sick. Hence there may be problems in married life.

In Ninth House

(i) **Powerful** - He will be intelligent, knowledgeable and clever. He may be famous and wealthy after marriage. His wife may come from a good family. He will be fortunate.

(ii) **Weak** - It is bad for father's health. He may stray out of religious path after marriage. He may lose his reputation and wealth.

In Tenth House

(i) **Powerful** - He will be intelligent and learned. He will gain money from business in a foreign land. His wife will also be adding income to the family. She will be devoted but dominating.

(ii) **Weak** - Wife may be over ambitious and take wrong decisions without thinking of business capacity. It may deteriorate his business career.

In Eleventh House

(i) **Powerful** - He will gain money after marriage. His wife may come from a religious and wealthy family. He will have good children.

(ii) **Weak** - His wife may not keep up her health. This may affect his domestic happiness.

In Twelfth House

(i) **Powerful** - He may travel abroad or reside there in a foreign country for earning. He may go abroad after marriage.

(ii) **Weak** - His married life will not be happy. His wife may be sick. He may incur losses or debts. His enemies may also create problems for him.

6. 9 Planets occupying seventh house

1.Sun

(i) **Positive** - He will be healthy, handsome and fond of traveling. He may like pomp and show. He may use imported goods in his house.

(ii) **Negative** - He may be tactless, abusive, and an egostic. He may incur the displeasure of government. Women may bring him disgrace in life. Relation with spouse will not be cordial.

2. Moon

(i) **Positive** - The person will be intelligent and educated. He will have good nature and balanced mind. He will be a capable and tactful businessman. His wife will be chaste and charming.

(ii) **Negative** - He may have deformed limbs. He may be cruel, jealous and lustful. His mother may not keep good health. He will be moody and lack stability of mind.

3. Mars

(i) **Positive** - He will be generous, intelligent, ambitious, healthy and wealthy.

(ii) **Negative** - Married life may be full of tensions. He himself may be stubborn, tactless and unsuccessful.

4. Mercury

(i) **Positive** - The person will be fair, courteous, faithful, balanced and virtuous. He will be good in accounting, mathematics, astronomy and astrology. He will be religious and devotee to almighty God. He may marry a wealthy woman early.

(ii) **Negative** - He may be cunning, deceitful, and selfish. His spouse may be immature reflecting adversely on his married life.

5.Jupiter

(i) **Positive** - He will be good looking, sympathetic, virtuous, famous, knowledgeable, religious and diplomatic. He may have many followers and friends. His wife may also be beautiful and matured. He may travel to holy places. He may be more famous than his father. He will have capable sons.

(ii) **Negative** - He may expect too much from his spouse and spoil relations.

6. Venus

(i) **Positive** - He will be intelligent, generous, and good-looking. People will regard and respect him. His wife will be chaste, charming, devoted, and faithful. He will take long journeys. He mayl be a good statesman. He may be romantic in nature. He will be successful in his business.

(ii) **Negative** - He will have unhealthy habits or vices. He may be lustful and develop extra relations. He may suffer from venereal diseases.

7. Saturn

(i) **Positive** - He will be virtuous, wealthy and charitable. He may be a politician. His marriage may be delayed. He may be more successful in a foreign land.

(ii) **Negative** - He may suffer from long term diseases of colic pains or illness of genetic organs.

8.Rahu

(i) **Positive** - He may be a good executive. He may get inherited wealth from his parents.

(ii) **Negative** - He will bring ill repute to his family. His wife may also be unconventional and heterodox.

9.Ketu

(i) **Positive** - He may be passionate and lusty and get attracted to opposite sex.

(ii) **Negative** - He may be short-tempered. He may suffer from cancer or leprosy. His wife may be a shrewish lady.

6. 10 Planets placements, aspects and combinations 7th house

1. If benefics are in 7th bhava, the life partner will be devoted and faithful.

2. If malefics are in 7th bhava, there would be problems in married life.

3. If owner of 5th house is in 7th bhava and owner of 7th bhava is in 5th house (exchange of houses) by the owners it indicates love marriage.

4. If Saturn and Mars are aspected by Venus from 7th bhava then husband and wife both will be adulterous and deceptive.

5. If debilitated Jupiter is in the 7th bhava, the person will not be happy with his wife.

6. If Owner of 7th bhava is in 6th house and Venus is weak, the wife will have health problems.

7. If owner of 7th bhava with Mars is situated in 7th house, the wife may keep ill health.

8. If Sun is in lagna (1st house) and Saturn in 7th bhava, his wife will have difficulty in conceiving.

9. If Sun and Saturn are in 6th house, Moon in 7th bhava, and Mercury in 1st house, the wife will not be able to give birth to a child.

10. If Saturn is in 4th house and Mars in 6th house, his wife may be without progeny.

11. If Saturn is in lagna (1st house), Venus in 7th bhava and malefics in 5th house, it will be difficult for birth of a child.

12. If Saturn with Mars aspects Venus with Moon in any house, the person will not marry.

13. If Rahu occupies 7th bhava and is aspected by Saturn and Mars, the person may remain unmarried.

14. If Saturn and Moon are in 7th bhava, person may marry a divorcee.

15. If Saturn and Moon are in 7th bhava and Venus is in Lagna, the person may marry a widow.

16. If Lagnesh is in Lagna and owner of 8th house is either in Lagna or in 7th bhava, the person may marry second time.

17. If Lagnesh and owner of 2nd house are in 6th house and malefics in 7th bhava, the person marry second time.

18. If Mars is placed in one of 1st, 2nd, 4th, 7th, 8th, 12th houses, the marriage of the person may be delayed. It is called Mangleek dosh.

19. If Venus is in 7th bhava in signs excluding Taurus, Libra, and Pieces, his married life may be troublesome.

20. If a malefic is located in 7th bhava and owner of 7th bhava and karak Venus or Jupiter is in 6, 8, 12 houses, his/her family life will be miserable. Actress Rekha is an example.

21. The planets Sun, Saturn, Rahu, owner of 12th house or owner of the sign, where Rahu is situated, have separatists' tendencies. If two of these planets aspect 7th bhava or owner of 7th bhava and the significator (Venus for male and Jupiter for female) husband and wife may take divorce and live separately.

22. If owner of 7th bhava and Mars are in 12th house, the person will be very sexy. His / her married life will suffer.

23. If owner of 7th bhava is in 12th house and owner of 12th house is in 7th bhava i.e. exchange of houses, the person will be extraordinary sensual.

24. If Mars aspects 7th bhava, owner of 7th bhava and karak Venus / Jupiter he/she will be more indulgent in physical relations.

6. 11 Events affecting during dasha Sign in 7th house

In Aries

(i) **Favourable** - If Mars is powerful and favourable, during dasha, his earnings may improve. His married life will be happy. He will travel a lot.

(ii) **Unfavourable** - During weak Mars dasha, he may indulge in adultery. He may suffer from rheumatism or gout. He may not keep his words.

In Taurus

(i) **Favourable** - Venus will be owner of 7th house. During its dasha he may be prosperous and wealthy. Life will be happy.

(ii) **Unfavourable** - He may indulge in adultery, become lazy and idle, postponing his decisions and actions time and again.

In Gemini

(i) **Favourable** - During Mercury dasha, he may get support from his in-laws. Spouse may be beautiful, caring and faithful

(ii) **Unfavourable** - He may take excessive interest in sex life and immoral activities.

In Cancer

(i) **Favourable** - He will be virtuous and religious. His mother will also be happy and healthy.

(ii) **Unfavourable** - During Moon dasha, His domestic life will not be happy with him. He / She may take divorce or live separately.

In Leo

(i) **Favourable** - During Sun's dasha, he will be a knowledgeable, dignified, wealthy and famous in society. He may have good relations with highly placed persons. He will lead a happy life with the spouse.

(ii) **Unfavourable** - He may feel unhappy and dissatisfied with his spouse because of her bad habits.

In Virgo

(i) **Favourable** - During Mercury dasha, he will be bold, energetic, happy and popular having own house, conveyance and other comforts in life.

(ii) **Unfavourable** - He may not have cordial relations with his wife. They both may suffer from ill health. They may be patient of tuberculosis.

In Libra

(i) **Favourable** - During Venus dasha, he will be happy and healthy. He will earn wealth with good partnership in business. His wife may be virtuous and well behaved. Family life will be good.

(ii) **Unfavourable** - The person may seek for extra marital relations outside. He may have rheumatic problems.

In Scorpio

(i) **Favourable** -During Mars dasha, he may join government post and earn prosperity. His wife may be a helping hand. He may start side business.

(ii) **Unfavourable** -During weak Mars dasha, his wife may be unsupportive, irritable, and ill. Domestic life may be disturbed. He may have uncontrollable sex urge.

In Sagittarius

(i) **Favourable** - If powerful and favourable Jupiter dasha is running, he will be fortunate and earn wealth with support of his wife. He will be successful in good relations with others.

(ii) **Unfavourable** - During Weak Jupiter dasha, he will lose his wealth, health, and high position due to his erratic behaviour and undesirable habits.

In Capricorn

(i) **Favourable** - During Saturn dasha, he will earn a lot of wealth. A male child may take birth in the family.

(ii) **Unfavourable** - His career will be disturbed. His wife may also be unhealthy. He may lead an unhappy family life.

In Aquarius

(i) **Favourable** - Saturn will be in mool-trikon sign. During its dasha, he may marry with his lady colleague. He will be happy, healthy and wealthy.

(ii) **Unfavourable** - His peace of mind may be disturbed. His health may also suffer.

In Pisces

(i) **Favourable** - During Jupiter dasha, he may join a government post or be engaged in import and export business. Prosperity and popularity will come at his doorstep. He may be happy, healthy, wealthy and religious.

(ii) **Unfavourable** - His wife may be extravagant. He may incur debts and become prone to secret diseases.

6. 12 Eleventh house (Labha Bhava)

This house is known as Labha bhava / Aaya bhava (House of gains and income) It is known as an inauspicious (Ashubha) bhava, but all the occupying planets give good results. Eleventh bhava represents means of financial gains & profits, success & undertakings, good luck & better health, ambitions, wishes, desires, freedom from miseries, elder brothers / sisters, daughter-in-law, son-in-law, friends, favourites, associations, society and community. It fulfils all the dreams and desires of life, so it is called 3rd house of Kama (Fun and pleasures). Powerful and benefic planets owning or occupying the eleventh house provide all the comforts & happiness in life during mahadasha / anterdasha period. Jupiter, the sinificator is very good to this bhava.

6. 13 Owner of Eleventh houses in various houses

In First house

(i) **Powerful** - If owner of eleventh bhava is in lagna, the person will take birth in a rich family. He will be happy, healthy and wealthy. He may be a good speaker.

(ii) **Weak** - His elder brother may not keep good health. It may affect his business.

In Second house

(i) **Powerful** - He will be successful in all his ventures. He may live with his brothers. If owner of fifth bhava conjuncts or aspects, he will get sudden gains. He may earn money through banking or high level contacts.

(ii) **Weak** - If malefics associate, there will be bickering in family and business will not prosper.

In Third house

(i) **Powerful** - He may earn his living through fine arts. His brothers, neighbours and friends may also help him in his earnings.

(ii) **Weak** - His brothers may create problems and he may lose his money. His efforts may not succeed.

In Fourth house

(i) **Powerful** - He may adopt real estate business. He will be wealthy. His mother may be prosperous and a lady of high status. His maternal uncle may also be helpful. He may enjoy all comforts in life and lead a happy and luxurious life.

(ii) **Weak** - If malefics influence, he may lose his property and become on road.

In Fifth house

(i) **Powerful** - He may have good children, who may progress in life. He will be knowledgeable in Shastras and earn money through education or speculations. He will be pious and religious.

(ii) **Weak** - He may be a gambler and indulge in bad habits. He may suffer from diseases of heart or digestive organs.

In Sixth house

(i) **Powerful** - He will earn money through maternal uncle or by litigation or running ashrams or hospitals. He may go abroad.

(ii) **Weak** - He may be involved in litigation and court cases. He may fall ill and lose his health and wealth. His enemies may also harm him.

In Seventh house

(i) **Powerful** - He may marry a rich and influential lady coming from a reputed family. He may prosper in foreign countries. His wife may be dominating.

(ii) **Weak** - He may indulge in trafficking women or similar immoral activities.

In Eighth house

(i) **Powerful** - He will be born in a rich family and long lived. He may inherit parental property.

(ii) **Weak** - He will lose his money through thieves and cheaters. Adverse constellations may force him for begging.

In Ninth house

(i) **Powerful** - He will be fortunate and wealthy. Government may honour him. He may lead a luxurious life. He may be religious and charitable and establish religious and charitable institutions.

(ii) **Weak** - He will incur wasteful expenditure on tours and travels or father's treatments.

In Tenth house

    (i) **Powerful** - He will earn wealth by hard work. His elder brother will also help him. He will attain top position and be honoured by government.

    (ii) **Weak** - He may earn money through foul means, which may create problems and invite punitive actions from government authorities.

In Eleventh house

    (i) **Powerful** - If the owner is in its own bhava, the native will earn money easily. He will have all comforts in life such as house, conveyance and other luxury items. He will have obedient children. His elder brother will also be wealthy and prosperous and help him life long. He will have many good friends.

    (ii) **Weak** - He will be careless in spending money. He may incur heavy expenditure on medical treatments for self and his elder brothers and sisters.

In Twelfth house

    (i) **Powerful** - He will earn wealth through foreign sources, and import export in bulk.

    (ii) **Weak** - His elder brother may suffer from some chronic disease. He may spend money and time on his treatment. He may also be extravagant in spending for a luxurious style of life or on medical treatment / hopitalisation of family members.

6. 14 Planets occupying eleventh house

1. Sun

    (i) **Positive** - He will be powerful and wealthy. He will have a few children. He will achieve success and honour. He may live long.

    (ii) **Negative** - He may suffer from stomach pain or other ailments or troubles.

2. Moon

    (i) **Positive** - He will be generous, sympathetic and wealthy. He will have good children. He may live long. His friends and servants will love him. He may have all comforts and luxuries in life.

(ii) **Negative** - His generosity may result in loss of earnings and comforts of life.

3. Mars

(i) **Positive** - He will be bold and courageous. He will be wealthy and famous. He may buy land and building. He may take part in politics. He may be influential in community.

(ii) **Negative** - He may have false pride and harsh tongue. He may be short tempered.

4. Mercury

(i) **Positive** - He will be handsome, healthy and man of morals. He will be intelligent and learned. He may be honest and popular. He may have good children. He may be virtuous, wealthy and prosperous.

(ii) **Negative** - His friends or neighbours may create problems in his profession.

5. Jupiter

(i) **Positive** - He will be wise, intelligent, and knowledgeable. He will be handsome, contented, and wealthy. He may rise in his business / profession and spend money for good causes. He may have many friends. Government may honour him.

(ii) **Negative** - He will have false pride and create unhappiness and dissatisfaction.

6. Venus

(i) Positive - He will earn wealth and lead a comfortable life. He may have many friends. He may be virtuous and charitable.

(ii) Negative-He will have weakness for women / sex and may suffer from urinary problems.

7. Saturn

(i) **Positive** - He will be hard working and a successful businessman. He will employ many persons. He may also be a successful politician. He may earn money through government sources. He may be childless.

(ii) **Negative** - He may indulge in party politics and lose his wealth and domestic happiness.

8. Rahu

(i) **Positive** - He will earn money through foreigners. He will be hard working and long lived. He may have few children. He may be famous abroad.

(ii) **Negative** - He may not be an intelligent and learned. He may suffer from ear disease.

9. Ketu

(i) **Positive** - He will be noble, generous, and charitable. He will be healthy and long-lived.

(ii) **Negative** - He will not be an intelligent one. His habits of gambling, horse racing or speculative deeds may result in heavy losses.

6. 15 Planets placements, aspects and combinations 11th house

1. If benefics occupy 11th bhava, the person earns money through noble and fair means and if malefics occupy then by foul and unfair means.

2. If owners of 2nd and 11th bhavas are friendly to lagnesh, person earns money through noble and fair means.

3. If two or more than two powerful planets occupy 11th bhava, the person will be knowledgeable and virtuous. He will have a faithful wife, good children, house, conveyance, ornaments, clothes and other luxuries of life.

4. If weak, debilitated, combust planet occupies 11th bhava, the person will lose all his happiness and comforts in life.

5. If owner of 11th bhava is in angles or triangles (1,4,7,10,5,9) houses, he will be rich.

6. If owner of 11th is in 10th house, owner of 10th in 9th house and owner of 9th in 11th bhava, the person will achieve great heights in his profession.

7. If ascendant is Aries and Sun is placed in its own sign Leo in 5th house and Jupiter in 11th bhava, the person will be wealthy.

8. If Pisces is ascendant and Mars is in its exalted sign Capricorn in 11th bhava and aspects its own sign Aries in 2nd house, he will be wealthy.

9. If Pisces is ascendant and Mars is in its exalted sign in 11th bhava and Moon from its own sign Cancer in 5th house aspects Mars, he will be extremely rich.

10. If owner of 11th bhava is in its exalted sign in birth chart or Navansh chart, he will be wealthy.

11. If owner of 11th and 9th houses with Moon are in 11th bhava and aspected by lagnesh, he will be wealthy.

12. If Saturn is in 11th bhava and Venus with Mercury in its own sign either in Taurus or in Libra occupies 5th house, he will be wealthy.

13. If Leo or Scorpio is ascendant and Jupiter occupies 5th house in its own sign either in Sagittarius or in Pisces, the person becomes extremely rich.

14. If owner of 11th bhava is in 5th house and owner of 5th house is in 11th bhava and Moon is in its own sign Cancer in 4th house, the person becomes wealthy and fortunate.

15. If owner of 11th bhava, Moon and owner of 5th house are in 9th house, the person will be very fortunate and wealthy.

16. If owner of 11th bhava occupies its exalted sign with Venus and Lagnesh is placed in angles (1, 4, 7, 10) houses, he will be fortunate and wealthy at young age.

17. If owner of 11th, 1st, 2nd, and 9th houses occupy 5th house and aspect 11th bhava, the person will be knowledgeable, virtuous, famous, fortunate, and immensely wealthy. Mr. Richard Milhous Nixon Ex. President USA. is the example.

18. If lagnesh is in 11th bhava, the person gets wealth from various sources.

6. 16 Events affecting during dasha Sign in 11th house

In Aries

(i) **Favourable** - During owner Mars dasha, he will have to work hard to fulfill his ambitions. He may be a good speaker.

(ii) **Unfavourable** - Weak Mars will bring him debts and diseases. His health may be affected.

In Taurus

(i) **Favourable** - If Venus is powerful; during its dasha he will be extremely wealthy. He will lead a happy and successful life. He will be a good speaker.

(ii) **Unfavourable** - Weak Venus dasha makes the person selfish, mean and miser. He may be unhealthy and prone to sex diseases.

In Gemini

(i) **Favourable** - Mercury is the owner of 11th house. This is also a good position for the person's progress and success. He will earn a lot of wealth. He will be well known. His children will also be capable. His elder brother will be knowledgeable and intelligent.

(ii) **Unfavourable** - If mercury is weak, during dasha he may try to acquire wealth by foul means but he will fail. He may suffer from colic pains and become sick.

In Cancer

(i) **Favourable** - Powerful Moon, in its dasha, will support for higher education. He may join government service. He will earn a lot of wealth. He will be popular among friends and relatives.

(ii) **Unfavourable** - If Moon is weak and afflicted, its dasha will spoil his health as well as create problems in his occupation or service.

In Leo

(i) **Favourable** - He will be religious and man of character and principles. He will be well known, happy, healthy and wealthy. He will also be virtuous, capable and successful. His domestic life will be peaceful.

(ii) **Unfavourable** - If Sun is weak and afflicted, its dasha will produce adverse results causing bad health. His children may pose problems.

In Virgo

(i) **Favourable** - If the owner Mercury is powerful, during its dasha, he may earn money through his maternal uncle. He may reside in a foreign country.

(ii) **Unfavourable** - If Mercury is weak, during its dasha he may be unhealthy. He may suffer from ear troubles. His enemies may also create problems.

In Libra

(i) **Favourable** - Powerful and favourable Venus, if it is in 11th house, during its dasha, native may accumulate wealth. His wife may guide and encourage him to improve his status.

(ii) **Unfavourable** - He may have strong sex urge and indulge in adultery. He may be badly sick and prone to accidents.

In Scorpio

(i) **Favourable** - If owner Mars is powerful, he may gain wealth and prosperity during its dasha period.

(ii) **Unfavourable** - If Mars is weak and afflicted, he may be unsuccessful and suffer losses in his ventures. His friends may also deceive him.

In Sagittarius

(i) **Favourable** - Powerful Jupiter will give money through government service during its dasha. He may go abroad and accumulate wealth. His siblings may also earn money and become rich.

(ii) **Unfavourable** -If Jupiter is weak and under malefic aspect it will adversely affect his progress. His brothers may also lose their status. He may be sick.

In Capricorn

(i) **Favourable** - If Saturn is powerful he will gain money through government. He will work for the welfare of common people. It will give him name and fame. His father and elder brother will also be successful and wealthy.

(ii) **Unfavourable** - He may suffer from chronic disease. Friends may turn in to foes.

In Aquarius

(i) **Favourable** - If Saturn is powerful and favourable, he may work hard and accumulate wealth during its dasha. His elder brothers / sisters may also be wealthy and prosperous.

(ii) **Unfavourable** - If Malefics conjoin or aspect, it may affect his progress and success during its dasha. He may lose his reputation and suffer from chronic disease.

In Pisces

(i) **Favourable** - If Jupiter the owner of 11th house is powerful, during dasha, he would easily earn money. He may marry second time. He may go to a foreign country. His elder brothers and sisters would help him.

(ii) **Unfavourable** - If Jupiter is weak and afflicted, during dasha, his health would suffer. He will lose his peace of mind and his reputation be at stake.

6. 17 Example Kundlis with astrological observations

Six kundlis regarding 3rd, 7th and 11th houses, two for each house of Prakrati Trine (Kama houses) are given below

Kundli No. 28 Ex. Chanceller Germany, Mr. Adolph Hitler

1. Date of birth 20 - 04 -1889

2. Time of Birth 18 - 38 P.M. (European Time)

3. Place of Birth Braunau (Austria)Lat.48⁰ /16' N. Long.13⁰ / 02' E.

4. Birth Nakshatra Poorva Ashadha-1

5. Balance Dasha at Birth Venus 18years-06months-10days.

BIRTH CHART

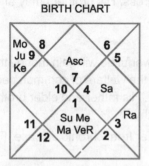

NAVANSH CHART

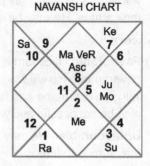

Kundli No. 6.17 (K-28)

Astrological Observation

This is a Libra sign lagan kundli. Librans want a happy and harmonious life. They may not be highly educated, but they are intellectuals. They weigh the merits and demerits of the subject and work accordingly. They are good speakers and have a spirit of sacrifice. Adolph Hitler was such a man of intelligence and possessed speech power. He persuaded the people with good speech and conversation. Born in Poorva Ashadha nakshatra, he was far sighted and fortunate.

1. Lagna considerations

Lagnesh Venus, Surya lagnesh Mars and Karak Sun all placed in 7th house, aspect lagna. Mars from 7th house also aspects 2nd house that deal with speech and conversation. From 3rd house Chandra lagnesh Jupiter also aspects Venus, Mars, Karak Sun and Mercury of speech. Lagnesh Venus is Atamkarak and in Navansh lagna it is placed in lagna with lagnesh Mars. So in both ways lagna is extremely strong.

2.Planets placements, aspects and combinations

Saturn from 10th house influences lagana (1st house) and lagnesh Venus, Mercury, Mars and Sun in 7th house. Chandra lagnesh Jupiter, owner of 3rd house and located in 3rd house with Moon and Ketu aspects Mars the significator of 3rd house placed in 7th house and also Lagnesh Venus, Sun and Mercury. From 3rd house Jupiter aspects 11th house of Sun of gains and profits also. In Navansh chart Saturn is situated in its own sign Capricorn in 3rd house. Thus, it is a good connection and interrelation of 3rd, 7th and 11th houses known as Kama Houses of Prakrati Trine. These aspects made Adolph Hitler a powerful army officer in Germany in local battles. He established his own party and named it Nazi Party. He became the Chancellar of Germany later on. In his chart Moon is performing Gajkesri yoga being in Kendra from Moon and Mars, Ruchak yoga, (Mahapurush yoga) being in Kendra in its own sign Aries. Jupiter is forming Hans yoga being in its own sign in Kendra from Moon and Venus Anshavtar yoga being in Kendra from the movable lagna. Because of these yogas (Combinations), kingly pride and boldness came to him and he ruled over Germany for about a decade.

3.Conclusion

Therefore we can conclude that Adolph Hitler was so powerful in speech that his name still shines not only in the history of Germany but also in Europe. He was the man, who preached the German how to attract public with a good speech and fight for their rights. It happened due to interrelation and correlation of 3rd, 7th and 11th houses known as Kama houses of Prakrati Trine. He was bold and fearless and knew the tacts to rule the country. When Rahu mahadasha and Sun anterdasha started in the year 1945, he and his wife Eva Braun married just 45 hours earlier they committed suicide.

Kundli No. 29 Ex. Cricketer and Now M. P. Mr. Azhruddin
1. Date of birth 09 - 02 - 1963
2. Time of Birth 22 - 25 P.M. (IST)
3. Place of Birth Hyderabad (A.P.) Lat.17⁰ / 23' N. Long.78⁰ / 28' E.
4. Birth Nakshatra Magha-3
5. Balance dasha at Birth Ketu 02years - 00month -25days

<table>
<tr><td>BIRTH CHART</td><td>NAVANSH CHART</td></tr>
</table>

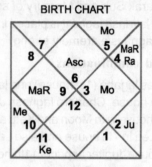
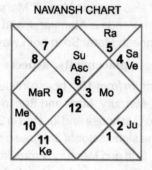

Kundli No. 6.17 (K-29)

Astrological Observations

Above is the horoscope of Padamashri awardee cricketer now parliamentarian Mr. Azhruddin. Its lagna sign is Virgo. Virgo people are fond of changes. They are very conscientious and capable in handling the work even in unfavourable situations. Mr. Azhruddin is such a bold man, who left his captainship soon after he was blamed for match fixing. Being born in Magha nakshatra he is studious, courageous and God fearing.

1. Lagna considerations

The lagnesh Mercury is situated in the 5th house relating education with Chandra laganesh Sun and Surya lagnesh Saturn sitting in Capricorn sign. Navansh lagnesh is also Mercury located in 5th house in the same sign Capricorn of Saturn. Hence Mercury is Vargottam. In Navansh chart Mercury from 5th house and Saturn from 11th house aspects each other. Besides, Saturn aspects Navansh lagna. Therefore lagna and lagnesh both are very strong.

2.Planets placements, aspects, and combinations

Mars the significator and 3rd house owner is placed in 11th house in its debilitated sign Cancer with Rahu. Dispositer of 11th house Moon located in 12th house is aspected by Badhak planet Jupiter owner of 7th house. Placed in 11th house with Moon, Rahu aspects both 3rd and 7th houses. All lagna (Sudarshan lagna) owners in birth chart Mercury of lagna, Sun of Chandra lagna and Saturn of Surya lagna aspect 11th house. Saturn aspects 7th house also, while Jupiter is placed in Aquarius. Thus it is a good connection and correlation of 3rd, 7th and 11th Kama houses of Prakrati Trine. More combinations are that Sun is performing Ubhaichari yoga being planets on both sides other than Moon, Moon Gajkesri yoga being Jupiter in Kendra from Moon and Mercury Budhaditaya yoga being with Sun in 5th house. These yogas have made him intelligent, learned, popular and a wealthy Cricketer.

3. Conclusion

All the above stated facts made his debut in test matches in 1984-1985 in Venus-Saturn dasha with a century against England. Then he was awarded Padamshri and Arjun awards. He became captain of the team in 1990 Venus-Mercury dasha. It is due to good interrelationship of 3rd, 7th and 11th Kama houses of Prakrati Trine. During dasha period of 12th house owner Sun-Jupiter in 1996 his performances deteriorated and he was removed from captaincy. In April 2002 during Moon-Moon dasha, he was banned from playing cricket on the charges of match fixing. But now in Moon-Venus dasha, he won the parliamentary seat in recent 2009 Loksabha elections.

Kundli No. 30 Actress Politician J. Jai Lalitha Ex. C. M. Tamilnadu

1. Date of birth 24 - 02 - 1948

2. Time of Birth 15 - 00 P.M. (IST)

3. Place of Birth Mysore (Karnataka) Lat.12^0 / 18' N. Long.76^0 / 39' E.

4. Birth Nakshatra Magha -3

5. Balance dasha at Birth Ketu 03years-04months-09days

BIRTH CHART   NAVANSH CHART

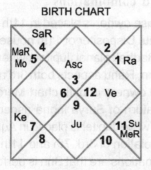 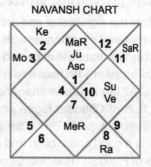

Kundli No. 6.17 (K-30)

Astrological Observations

This is a Gemini sign kundli. Gemini individuals are always carefree, joyous, positive and strong. They are well educated and intelligent. They can adapt themselves in any circumstances. So J. Jai Lalitha is very bold, brave and untiring. After Ramchandran, She became the supremo of AIDMK Political party in Tamilnadu. Indeed she is a famous film actress turned politician. Born in Magha nakshatra she is bold, studious, courageous, fearless and God fearing.

1. Lagna considerations

Lagnesh Mercury is placed in 9th house with Sun and is aspected by Moon and Mars. Chandra lagnesh Sun is placed in 9th house, aspects 1st house (lagna). Surya lagnesh Saturn is situated in Moon sign Cancer in 2nd house next to lagna. Mercury the planet of speech and dramatic abilities situated in 9th house is in a good position. Navansh lagnesh Mars is in its own sign Aries with Jupiter known for skills in taking and achieving objectives (goals). Hence Chandra lagna is activated.

2. Planets placements, aspects and combinations

Exalted Venus occupying 10th house influences lagna and aspects 4th house of Mercury forming Malavya yoga (a Mahapurush yoga) being in kendra. Jupiter 10th house owner occupying its own house from 10th to 10th i.e. in 7th house in its own sign Sagittarius, strengthening the house and performing Hansa yoga (again a Mahapurush yoga) being in kendra. This is a diurnal chart. In karma house (10th house) Malavya yoga influenced her towards Venus related qualities and abilities. She is healthy, mentally alert, capable, learned and wealthy having clear thoughts. Moon and Mars combination added more power to increase such abilities. Thus she proved herself as a very good actress. Anpha yoga and Chandra-Mangal yoga formed by Moon and Amalkirti yoga formed by Venus made her lucky, fortunate, religious and benevolent.

3. Conclusion

So all the above facts and dimensions such as Jupiter being placed in its own 7th house is aspecting 11th and 3rd houses fulfilled all her desires providing all comforts in life. There is a good connection and interrelation of 7th, 11th and 3rd kama houses of Prakrati Trine, which made her a famous actress. Later she joined C. Ramchandran AIDMK party and turned to politics and became the chief minister of Tamilnadu after Ramchandran. Nowadays she is the Supremo of the AIDMK party and has a say in public and state / central politics. She is a bold and powerful lady because of aspect of Sun on 3rd house of its own.

Kundli No. 31 Famous Hollywood Singer, Madonna Louise Ciccone

1. Date of birth 16 - 08 - 1958

2. Time of Birth 07 - 05 A.M. (EST)

3. Place of Birth Bay City (MI U.S.A.) Lat 43^0 / 35' N. Long. 83^0 / 53' W.

4. Birth Nakshatra Poorva Phalguni-2

5. Balance Dasha at Birth Venus 12years-07months-05days

<table>
<tr><td align="center">BIRTH CHART</td><td align="center">NAVANSH CHART</td></tr>
<tr><td>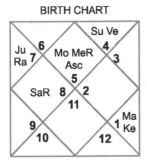</td><td>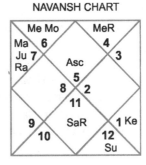</td></tr>
</table>

Kundli No. 6.17 (K-31)

Astological Observations

This is fiery sign Leo lagan kundli. Such people are speedy, energetic, bold, brave, courageous and commanding. Being fiery sign, at lagna it gives authority, brilliance and high ambition. Hollywood Pop icon Madonna Louise Ciccone is such a lady, who is a pop singer sings songs with speed and long (high) sound. Her first self-titled album came in market in the year 1983, when she was 25 years of age. Now she is a writer, dancer, producer, director, designer, author, actress, and an entrepreneur etc. Being born in Poorva Phalguni nakshatra she is sweet spoken, far sighted, successful and popular.

1. Lagna considerations

Lagnesh and Chandra lagnesh Sun is situated in Moon sign Cancer in 12th house with Venus. Surya lagnesh is placed in Lagna in Sun sign Leo with Mercury, the planet of speech and artistic abilities. Navansh lagna is also Leo. Mercury, Moon and Venus are in adjoining houses to lagna and Sun aspects Mercury, Moon and Venus. Therefore, lagna and lagnesh both are most powerful.

2. Planets placements, aspects and combinations

The planet of speech and voice and singing abilities, Mercury, the owner of 2nd house is posited with Moon in lagna and the planet of speed and energy Mars in its own sign Aries is located in 9th house of luck and fortune. Saturn is occupying Mars house i.e. 4th house of luxuries and aspects Mercury and Moon. From 3rd house of strength and power Jupiter aspects Mars sitting in the 9th house of fortune and also 7th house of Saturn and 11th house of Mercury. From lagna (1st house) Moon and Mercury aspects 7th that belongs to saturn. These aspects and interrelations of 7th, 11th and 3rd Kama houses of desires (fun and pleasures) made her an intelligent and successful Pop Star. Now she is not only a pop star but also has many artistic and dramatic qualities and therefore she is writer, dancer, film producer and director, fashion designer, actor, author and so on. In Navansh chart Saturn is located in its own sign Aquarius in 7th house, so 7th house is most powerful to make her a pop singer.

3.Conclusion

Thus we can conclude that Madonna emerged as a very good pop star in a short period of time in U.S.A., Canada and Europe. It is due to the strong connection and reinforcement of Jupiter placed in 3rd house aspecting 7th and 11th houses all Kama houses of Prakrati Trine. She earned a lot of wealth and popularity. Jupiter being Vargottam and Sun Atamkarak both topped her in every sphere of dramatic and artistic productions and programmes continuously after 1983. Her name is written in Guinness Book Of World Records.

Kundli No. 32 A Brave Industrialist Nusli Wadia

1. Date of birth 15 - 02 -1944

2. Time of birth 13 - 30 P.M. (IST)

3. Place of birth Mumbai (Maharastra) Lat.18^0 / 58' N. Long.72^0 / 50' E.

4. Nakshatra at birth Swati-1

5. Blance Dasha at birth Rahu 15years-01month-16days

BIRTH CHART	NAVANSH CHART
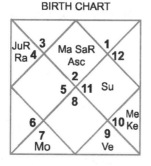	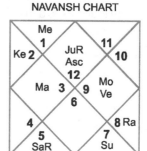

Kundli No. 6.17 (K-32)

Astrological Observations

This is a Taurus lagna kundli. Such people have much endurance and patience. They are ambitious and cheerful. They want to lead a happy and luxurious life. They start their work at the right time. Business Tycoon Nusli Wadia from a Persian family, is such a man, who worked hard to set up his business and to compete others. Born in Swati nakshatra he is well behaved, learned and dutiful.

1. Lagna Considerations

Lagnesh and Chandra lagnesh Venus is located in 8th house in Sagittarius sign of Jupiter and Jupiter with Rahu is placed in 3rd house of Courage in its exalted sign Cancer. Surya lagnesh Saturn is placed in lagna with Mars owner of 7th house and significator of 3rd house. Navansh lagnesh Jupiter is posited in lagna in its own sign Pisces and Venus in 10th house with Moon in Sagittarius sign. Thus, lagna is fortified.

2. Placements, Aspects, and Combinations

Exalted Jupiter is situated in 3rd house with Rahu aspects 7th house of Mars placed in lagna rising sign Taurus and 11th house of gains and profits its own sign Pisces and in same sign Pisces in Navansh lagna. Thus Jupiter is strong and powerful. Lagnesh Venus is Atamkarak and Vargottam in a good position. Saturn is placed in lagna and aspects 3rd house of courage strengthening its power and also of Jupiter, the owner of 11th house of gains and profits. It aspects 7th house also and Mars from lagna aspects 7th house of its own sign Scorpio and Venus, the lagnesh in 8th house. Thus it is a good interrelationshih amongst 11th, 3rd and 7th houses known as Kama houses of Prakrati Trine. Jupiter from Moon is located in 10th house i.e. in Kendra, hence it is forming Hansa yoga that makes a man healthy, wealthy, prosperous, and famous all over the country.

3. Conclusion

On the basis of above facts, we can conclude that 11th house of gains and profits, its owner and Karak Jupiter is most powerful. Being placed in 3rd house it aspects 7th and 11th houses connecting all Kama houses of Prakrati Trine. This is a strong correlation and reinforcement amongst 11th, 3rd and 7th kama houses of Prakrati Trine. Business tycoon Nusli Wadia raised his prosperity, wealth, status and dignity due to the position of Jupiter. Wherever he competed in business, he won the battle and defeated his opponents. From 30-07-2008 Mercury –Saturn dasha is going on and come to an end on 29-11-2010. It may be normal but later on Ketu dasha may be bright and beneficial.

Kundli No. 33 A Famous Bollywood Actor, Mr. Amitabh Bachchan

1. Date of birth   11 - 10 - 1942

2. Time of birth   16 - 00 P.M. (IST)

3. Place of birth   Allahabad (U.P.) Lat.25⁰ / 30' N.Long.81⁰ / 30' E.

4. Nakshatra at birth   Swati-2

5. Balance Dasha at birth   Rahu 13years-00month-18days.

BIRTH CHART

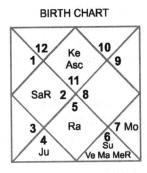

NAVANSH CHART

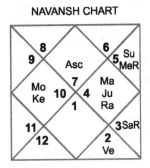

Kundli No. 6.17 (K-33)

Astrological Observations

This is a Janam kundli (birth chart) of sign Aquarius. It is a sign of completion and perfection. It is a fixed sign, so such people stick to their principles. They work persistently in all their undertakings. They prefer secluded places and go in deep meditation. Bollywood actor Amitabh Bachchan known as Big B is an intelligent, knowledgeable and religious man, who has these qualities and deserves records. Being born in Swati nakshatra he is well behaved, knowledgeable, dutiful and theist.

1. Lagna Considerations

Lagnesh Saturn is posited in 4th house of comforts and aspects lagna providing him a balance of mind, maturity, stability and sober outlook to be a millennium man and Ketu transiting in lagna as a planet of salvation, spiritualism, intuition and perfection produces magnetism in his personality. Chandra lagnesh, Surya lagnesh and Navansh lagnesh all are in 8th house. Therefore Lagna is extremely activated.

2. Placements, Aspects, and Combinations

Exalted Jupiter being Vargottam and significator of 11th house is placed in 6th house and aspects 10th house of Profession owned by Mars. Mars with Sun, exalted Mercury and debilitated Venus from 8th house aspects 11th house of Jupiter so 11th house is getting full support and strength. Mars also aspects its own sign Aries in 3rd house of strength extending its power, energy and intelligence with the help of Sun and exalted Mercury. Saturn, the lagnesh, aspects exalted Jupiter and 10th house. Rahu from 7th house aspects 11th house and 3rd house so there is a good relationship amongst 11th, 3rd and 7th houses of fun and pleasures known as Kama houses of Prakrati Trine. Here one truth is notable that Jupiter being in Kendra from Moon is forming Gajkesri yoga and exalted Mercury and debilitated Venus a Neechbhang Rajyoga (Vipreet Rajyoga) for a long life. These yogas made him Big B.

3. Conclusion

We can conclude that he got name, fame, popularity, prosperity and wealth in lagnesh Saturn dasha from 1971 to 1990. His films namely Anand and Zanjeer made him famous. People saw in him an image of angry young man. It is all because of strong connection and correlation of 11th, 3rd houses, which are aspected by Mars and 7th house between benefics. Though in Rahu anterdasha June 1985 to April 1988, gave him a setback of political tensions and ketu anterdasha January 2007 bad health controversies and hardships that seem to have gone now. Let us hope for him a bright future.

Figure : 6.1 (F-5) Third Trine Kama Houses

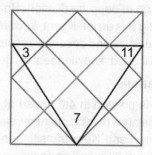

Figure : 6.1 (F-5)

৪০০৪

Fourth Trine Vairagya Trine (Moksha Houses)

7. 1 What is Vairagya Trine? Related Houses

Vairagya Trine is the fourth and last trine of a birth chart. Vairagya means 'Virag' or 'Vairag' that is far away from fun and pleasures and devotion to God. It consists fourth, eighth and twelfth houses (bhavas). Twelfth house is the last house. They represent motherly love, house, conveyance, higher education, longevity of life , peace, harmony, unexpected troubles, disgrace, divine knowledge, union with God, depth, suddenness, liberation and emancipation. They lead us towards Moksha, so they are called Moksha Houses. They remind us of our good or bad actions that we have done so far. Vairagya actually takes us to the divinity and union with God to reform us, if we have been wrong and we are still wrong. This is the right time to be honest and in the service of Almighty God. First we will take fourth house then eighth and twelfth. Please see Figure 7.1 (F-6) at the end of Chapter.

7. 2 Fourth house (Matru bhava)

This House is known as Matru bhava / Sukha bhava (House of motherly love and happiness). This house (bhava) indicates motherly love, home, environment, private affairs, ancestral property, fields, farms, buildings, hidden treasure, vehicles and higher education. It represents happiness and peace of life. Being Nadir, it is the end of enterprise. It brings emancipation from the cycle of rebirth. Hence it is called the first house of Moksha (salvation). If the owner of the house (bhava) and occupying planets are not afflicted, it provides every happiness in the life of a person during its mahadasha / anterdasha. Moon is closely related to this house. Ketu's conjunction or aspect leads to Moksha.

7. 3 Owner of fourth house in various houses

In First house

(i) **Powerful** - The person may be intelligent and knowledgeable coming from a rich family. He may be obedient and loyal to his parents. He will get mother's love in abundance. He may own agricultural lands, buildings, and conveyance and improve the status of the family. He may inherit ancestral property.

(ii) **Weak** - The above mentioned significations would greatly suffer. He and his father may be poor and ancestral property may be auctioned.

In Second house

(i) **Powerful** - He may be wealthy and lucky. He may be highly educated. He may inherit property from maternal grandfather or uncle. His domestic life may be happy.

(ii) **Weak** - If owner of fourth bhava is natural malefic, it may create property disputes in family.

In Third house

(i) **Powerful** - He may be generous, sympathetic and a man of character. He may work hard to earn his livelihood. He may be a self made man.

(ii) **Weak** - He may quarrel with his mother or stepmother and lose paternal property. His domestic life may also be unhappy.

In Fourth house

(i) **Powerful** - The person may be happy, healthy, and man of principles. He may be the owner of agricultural lands, buildings, and vehicles. He may gain ancestral property. His parents may love him. His mother may live long. He may enjoy a happy and peaceful life. If owner of 11th house conjoins or aspects 4th bhava, he may get hidden treasure. He may be religious.

(ii) **Weak** - He may lose his property and peace of mind, if malefics occupy the house.

In Fifth house

(i) **Powerful** - He may be intelligent and highly educated. He may be religious and charitable. He may be loved and respected by the people in his community. He may be prosperous. He may get ancestral property also. He may hold high position in government. He may be fortunate and famous. His mother may be from a rich family.

(ii) **Weak** - If malefics conjoins or aspects, his position and property may fall.

In Sixth house

(i) **Powerful** - He will work hard to improve his business and accumulate wealth.

(ii) **Weak** - He will be selfish, mean and short tempered. He may not get mother's love and ancestral property. His enemies may cause troubles. This may lose domestic happiness.

In Seventh house

(i) **Powerful** - He may generally be happy and get good education. He may have lands and buildings. He may gain more from maternal grandfather. His family life may be happy.

(ii) **Weak** - He may have stepmother who would not like him. He may suffer litigation on property and lose that property.

In Eighth house

(i) **Powerful** - He may get sudden money through lottery or some hidden treasure and become wealthy. His mother may live long and love him.

(ii) **Weak** - His mother may not be happy with him. He may lose ancestral property. He may be either important or weak in sex. His domestic life may not be happy.

In Ninth house

(i) **Powerful** - He will be fortunate, knowledgeable, and religious. He may travel to holy places. If there is a movable sign in 4th bhava, he may also go abroad to acquire wealth. He will love his family. People will respect him.

(ii) **Weak** - His mother's health would. His assets may go his brothers in law.

In Tenth house

(i) **Powerful** - He will be learned, fortunate and wealthy with lands and buildings. He will succeed in his professional career. He may be a chemist or doctor, lawyer or judge. His mother will be long lived. He will vanquish his enemies.

(ii) **Weak** - If owner of 4th bhava is weak and afflicted, he may lose his reputation and position.

In Eleventh house

(i) **Powerful** - He will be kind and generous, happy and contended. He may undertake real estate business and become wealthy. He will be a self-made man. He will also inherit wealth from his mother.

(ii) **Weak** - He is likely to incur heavy expenditure on mother's treatment.

In Twelfth house

(i) **Powerful** - He may go abroad and acquire wealth and properties there.

(ii) **Weak** - He may lose his property and happiness and die abroad in miserable conditions. His mother may have short life.

7. 4 Planets occupying fourth house

1. Sun

(i) **Positive** - He will be handsome and attractive. He will inherit ancestral property. He will take interest in medical science and philosophy.

(ii) **Negative** - He may be cruel and aggressive. He may not have good relations with the members of family. He may be mentally worried. He may think to join politics, but he will be unsuccessful.

2.Moon

(i) **Positive** - He will be happy and contended with his family life. He will get mother's love. He may join politics. He will have his own house, conveyance and all other comforts in life. He will be wealthy.

(ii) **Negative** -His mother may die earlier. He may be proud and quarrelsome. He would be fond of sensual pleasures.

3. Mars

(i) **Positive** - He may earn money from agriculture land crops. He may have property and conveyance. He may join politics and become successful.

(ii) **Negative** - He will be deprived of motherly love. Relations with friends and relatives may not be cordial. If Mars joins with Rahu or Ketu, he may have untimely death or commit suicide.

4. Mercury

(i) **Positive** - He will be intelligent, knowledgeable and fortunate. He will be a good speaker. He will have all comforts in life such as house, vehicle. He may be fond of music and dance. He may be religious and charitable.

(ii) **Negative** - He will be lazy and timid. Government authorities may proceed against him.

5.Jupiter

(i) **Positive** - He will be intelligent, learned virtuous and religious. He may be an astrologer. He will be quite happy, fortunate and respected. Government may honour him. He will love his mother. He may hard work in achieving aims and objectives. He will have a peaceful happy domestic life. He will be honest and practical in his actions and habits.

(ii) **Negative** - He may face allegations and lose his position and reputation.

6. Venus

(i) **Positive** - He will be handsome, helpful, charitable, proficient, fortunate and powerful. He will be long-lived. He will love and regard his mother. He will be fond of funs and pleasures. He will lead a comfortable life with good assets. He will love music and arts.

(ii) **Negative** - Opposite sex may harm him. He may indulge in sensual pleasures and incur loss of his assets and reputation.

7. Saturn

(i) **Positive** - He may be fortunate and happy under influence of benefics. His life may be comfortable but for a short period.

(ii) **Negative** - He will be deprived of mother's love. He would face problems in acquiring house, conveyance facility and other comforts in life. He may suffer from the diseases of lungs and heart. He may lead a lonely life.

8. Rahu

(i) **Positive** - He will be wealthy and have many servants. If Rahu is in Aries or in Taurus or in Cancer sign the person may get happiness from his brothers. He may have a few good friends.

(ii) **Negative** - He will be cruel, aggressive, unhappy, untruthful and unfaithful. He would not be healthy.

9.Ketu

(i) **Positive** - He may go to a foreign country and earn his livelihood there. Thus he may have to leave his native place.

(ii) **Negative** - He may be lazy and unemployed. He will hardly earn his living. He will be deprived of his mother's love. He may go abroad and live there.

7. 5 Planets placements, aspects and combinations 4th house

1. If owner of 4th bhava is in 3rd house it may give a little immovable property, land and building.

2. If owner of 4th bhava occupies 6th or 8th or 12th house and Mars or Saturn occupies 4th bhava, the person loses all comforts, assets and peace of mind.

3. If owner of 4th occupies 6th or 8th or 12th house, it indicates loss of mother's health.

4. If owner of 4th bhava occupies lagna and Venus occupies 4th bhava, the person will have vehicles, jewellery, gems and good bank balance.

5. If 4th bhava and owner of 4th bhava both are in "Papkartari Yoga" means both sides surrounded by malefics, he loses all comforts in life such as property, vehicles etc.

6. If owners of 2nd, 4th and 12th are in angles or triangles, he may acquire property and vehicle easily.

7. If owner of 4th bhava either with Venus and Moon or with Jupiter and Moon occupies angles or triangles, the person gets the best of facilities of conveyance and comforts.

8. If Moon, Mercury, Jupiter and Venus all four benefics occupy 4th bhava or occupy angles or triangles, the person is virtuous and fortunate enough and lead a peaceful comfortable family life.

9. If owner of 4th bhava is in lagna or in 7th house, he will have a good house easily and early.

10. If owners of 4th bhava and tenth house exchange their houses, called "Gopurmas" the person gets lands and buildings easily.

11. If owner of 4th bhava is debilitated and Sun joins the person's property will be under the control of government.

12. If lagnesh and owner of 4th bhava are in friendly signs and occupy good houses, he will get motherly love.

13. If owner of 4th bhava and Moon are in 4th bhava, he will get motherly love in abundance and if aspected by benefics for a long period.

14. If owner of 4th bhava is in 12th house and owner of 12th house is in 4th bhva or exchange of houses, relations with mother would be strained.

15. If owner of 4th bhava and Mars are in favourable signs and houses, the person may join an officer's post in army.

16. If Moon is in 4th bhava with malefics or is aspected by malefics, his mother may have short life.

17. If 4th bhava and owner of 4th bhava both are in conjunction with or aspect by the Sun, Saturn and Rahu, the person is transferred many times from one place to another. He always resides far from his birthplace.

18. If Rahu is in 4th bhava with other malefic or is aspected by malefic, he becomes hypocrite.

19. If 4th bhava, owner of 4th bhava and Moon are in conjunction with or aspect by lagnesh, the person is intelligent, popular and successful politician in his country. Johnson Ex. President USA.

20. If 4th bhava, owner of 4th bhava and Moon all are in conjunction with or is aspected by Rahu, the person is rebellious and revolutionary.

21. If 4th bhava, owner of 4th bhava and Jupiter are aspected by malefics, the person is always seen as sad and unhappy in life.

22. If sign Cancer, Moon, 4th bhava and owner of 4th bhava all four are aspected by malefics, the person will suffer from chest diseases such as tuberculosis, pneumonia, cough, asthma, pleurisy etc.

7. 6 Events affecting during dasha Sign in 4th house

In Aries

(i) **Favourable** - If Mars the owner of 4th house is powerful, during its dasha, he will be happy, healthy, and wealthy. His mother will also be happy and healthy. He may take up higher studies. He would acquire property and vehicles. He may get married, if not married so far.

(ii) **Unfavourable** - During weak Mars dasha, his mother may fall ill. He may suffer from hypertension or heart problems.

In Taurus

(i) **Favourable** - It Venus, 4th house owner is powerful, during its dasha, the native will be fortunate, rich and lead a comfortable family life. The wealth may come from mother's side. He may get good government job and gain dignity and status. He will be intelligent and learned. He will have his own house and conveyance.

(ii) **Unfavourable** - If Venus is weak and afflicted, he may be selfish, mean, and greedy and join bad company. He will not keep cordial relations with his mother. He may be unlucky and sad, facing problems in acquiring house and conveyance.

In Gemini

(i) **Favourable** - Mercury being the owner of 4th, if powerful, the person will be healthy and hard working. He will take bold decisions to succeed in his business. He will earn a lot of wealth. His mother will love him. He will have his house and conveyance. He will be popular.

(ii) **Unfavourable** - If Mercury is weak, during dasha, he may not keep cordial relations with his parents. He may lose his property. He may be sick and poor.

In Cancer

(i) **Favourable** - If Moon is strong far from the Sun and without malefic aspect, during its dasha, he may have good relations in political field. He will flourish his business. He will be wealthy and famous leading a peaceful life. He will have cordial relations with his parents. Mother will be happy and healthy.

(ii) **Unfavourable** - If Moon is weak and near to the Sun, he may strain relations with his wife and children. He may suffer from disease of lungs.

In Leo

(i) **Favourable** - If Sun is strong, during its dasha, he will be well known and popular. He will get all love from his father. He will be religious and charitable. He will get favour from government. He will earn wealth through his own efforts and acquire own house, conveyance facility etc.

(ii) **Unfavourable** - If Sun is weak the under malefic aspects, during dasha period, he may not be in position to pursue higher studies. He may be physically and mentally weak. He may lose his property and other items of luxury.

In Virgo

(i) **Favourable** - During Mercury dasha, he will lead a happy life. He will be hard working and earn a lot of wealth and property.

(ii) **Unfavourable** - If the owner is weak, his parents may feel tension and mother remain sick. His mental peace may also be disturbed. He may be inclined to act unfairly to earn more money. His property may be in dispute. His domestic life will also be disturbed.

In Libra

(i) **Favourable** - During strong Venus dasha, he will be intelligent and learned. He will lead a comfortable life. He may start automobile business. He may gain profits from agriculture.

(ii) **Unfavourable** - If Venus is weak and afflicted, he may lose his patrimony. He may have poor health. Relations in family will be strained.

In Scorpio

(i) **Favourable** - During powerful Mars dasha, he may get hidden treasure or some money from lottery ticket. He may join good post in government. He will get name and fame, dignity and honour.

(ii) **Unfavourable** - During weak and afflicted Mars dasha, he would lose his property, status and popularity. Parents will be unhappy. Domestic life and his peace of mind will be disturbed.

In Sagittarius

(i) **Favourable** - If Jupiter is strong, during its dasha, he may be knowledgeable, popular, happy, and religious.

(ii) **Unfavourable** - During weak Jupiter dasha, his children may be in trouble and problems may crop up with regard to properties and conveyance.

In Capricorn

(i) **Favourable** - Saturn in Libra ascendant is Rajyog karak. Therefore during strong Saturn dasha, he will be happy and wealthy. He may spread his profession. Government may honour him. He will accumulate wealth and property by his own efforts.

(ii) **Unfavourable** - Weak Saturn dasha may bring a separation between him and his parents. He will lose his mother's love. His profession will be adversely affected.

In Aquarius

(i) **Favourable** - He will be rich. He will earn money through agriculture or real estate. He will look after his father. He and his father may go abroad.

(ii) **Unfavourable** - During strong Saturn dasha, he may have poor health. He may be prone to chronic diseases of heart or lungs.

In Pisces

(i) **Favourable** - Being lagnesh and owner of 4th house Jupiter, if strong and well placed, during its dasha, he would make addition to his assets. He will be popular among friends and foes.

(ii) **Unfavourable** - During weak Jupiter dasha, he will feel lazy, foolish and insecure, while abroad. His family life may be unhappy. His parents may also be dissatisfied. He may live in a rented house. He may indulge in sinful activities.

7. 7 Eighth house (Aayu bhava)

This house is known as Aayu bhava / Mirtyu bhava (House of longevity and death) Eighth house (bhava) indicates span of life and the end of life. It represents inheritance, legacies, wills, insurance, pension, gratuity, accidents, accidental death by drowning / fire / suicide, miseries, misfortunes, sorrows, worries, disgrace, disappointments, defeat and loss due to theft and robbery. It disrupts routine life of the person. It reminds us to keep union with Almighty God for moksha (salvation). Hence it is known as the 2nd house of Moksha (salvation). The malefic planet suddenly attacks and ends the life. Mars & Saturn are very close to it.

7. 8 Owner of eighth house in various houses

In First house

(i) **Powerful** - If owner of 8th bhava being powerful occupies lagna, it is very good for longevity of the person. If powerful lagnesh also joins, longevity of life will increase and he may be long lived.

(ii) **Weak** - He may be poor. He may fall in heavy debts. He may suffer body pains. He may face allegations and lose reputation.

In Second house

(i) **Powerful** - If owner of 8th bhava is in 2nd house and aspects own eighth bhava, his longevity will increase.

(ii) **Weak** - He may suffer from eye and tooth troubles. He will be unhealthy. Thus domestic life will not be happy. He would suffer monetary losses.

In Third house

(i) **Powerful** - Third house is 8th house from 8th bhava, hence it is treated a house of longevity. If owner of 6th house also joins, he may earn money through writings and editing.

(ii) **Weak** - His siblings may be unhappy and create problems. He may have ear disease. He may suffer debts. He will be lazy, timid and ugly. If owner of 3rd joins, his sufferings may be unbearable.

In Fourth house

(i) **Powerful** - If owner of 6th house joins, the person may feel happy, but for a short period.

(ii) **Weak** - The person may lose his peace of mind. His mother may also suffer ill health and die early. He may lose his ancestral property, land, building, vehicles etc He may be forced to go abroad, where he will face many troubles and loss of money. His family life will also be unhappy.

In Fifth house

(i) **Powerful** - If owner of 8th bhava is in trio houses from Navansh lagna, he will lead a good moderate life. He will have a few children. He will be long lived. He may undertake research work.

(ii) **Weak** - His children may entangle in a crime. Misunderstandings may also arise between him and his father. He may suffer from stomach problems or nervous debility.

In Sixth house

(i) **Powerful** - If owner of 6th house joins, that will be Vipreet Rajyoga, he may get sudden wealth, house, vehicles etc. He will win over enemies. Litigation will also be advantageous for him.

(ii) **Weak** - He may incur ill health. He may lose his bank balance in litigation or theft. He may suffer the danger of snakes-bites or drowning in deep water.

In Seventh house

(i) **Powerful** - If owner of 8th and 7th houses both are powerful and occupy 7th house, he may undertake journeys to foreign countries on diplomatic missions and may be well known and reputed.

(ii) **Weak** - His wife may suffer ill health and die early. He himself will be ill. Domestic life will not be happy. He may incur heavy losses in business partnership.

In Eighth house

(i) **Powerful** - The person will be long lived and enjoy all happiness in life. He will acquire agricultural land, building, conveyance, position and power through his own merit.

(ii) **Weak** - He may have loose morals. He may get entangled in wrong deeds. He may suffer ill health. He may fail in his undertakings and suffer from heavy loss of money and position.

In Ninth house

(i) **Powerful** - If owner of 8th bhava with benefics occupies 9th house, he may get father's property. His life may be harmonious. He may have good relations with his relatives and friends. He will be long lived.

(ii) **Weak** - He himself may create obstructions in his progress. His relatives and friends may also add problems in his work. If karak Sun is in debilitated sign, it may affect father's longevity or health and he may incur loss of wealth.

In Tenth house

(i) **Powerful** - He will be hard working. He may get a good post beyond his merit and his career become bright for some time. He may earn a lot of wealth and reputation. If owner of 8th from Navansh lagna occupies 6th, 8th, 12th houses, he may get more benefits or gains through insurance in case of death of his elders.

(ii) **Weak** - Because of loose morals and habit of bickering, problems may arise in the progress of his career. He may lose his position and wealth.

In Eleventh house

(i) **Powerful** - If the benefics join the owner of 8th bhava in 11th house, he may get help from his near and dear ones to carry on his business for better gains. His life may be smooth. He may be long lived.

(ii) **Weak** - His elder siblings may go against him and relatives also create problems and troubles in his career and domestic life. His business may suffer. He may run in to debts.

In Twelfth house

(i) **Powerful** - If owner of 8th occupies 12th house and owner of 12th house is in 1,4,7,10,5,9 houses, he may earn substantial wealth. He may establish religious institutions and become its head. He will get respect and reputation.

(ii) **Weak** - He will be extravagant. He may use his earnings in sinful activities. He may be restless and wandering and lose his position and reputation.

7. 9 Planets occupying eighth house
1.Sun

(i) **Positive** - If Sun occupies 8th bhava in its exalted sign or own sign, the person will be long lived. He will be handsome and attractive. He may be a good speaker. If Sun joins owner of 8th bhava or owner of 11th house, he may earn money through speculations and become wealthy and well known. A male child may take birth in the family.

(ii) **Negative** - He may be dull and short tempered. Some spots may be seen on his face. His eyesight may also be weak. He may be anxious and worried.

2.Moon

(i) **Positive** - He will be intelligent, generous and sympathetic. He will acquire wealth and other comforts in life through legacies and inheritance.

(ii) **Negative** - His mother may die early. He may have weak physical and mental health. If Mars and Saturn conjoin, his eyesight may be weak. His longevity may also suffer.

3. Mars

(i) **Positive** - He may be a good administrator. He may marry second time. He may have a few children.

(ii) **Negative** - He will be poor and short lived. His wife may die early. He may marry second time but he will not be happy. He himself may become drunkard and a man of loose morals. His health may suffer. He may be aggressive and harsh in tongue. He will be unbelievable.

4. Mercury

(i) **Positive** - He will be learned in many subjects. He will be generous, courteous, believable and famous. He will be a good orator. Government may honour him. He will inherit money and live long.

(ii) **Negative** - He will be thin and weak but arrogant. He may be mentally disturbed or suffer from nervous problems.

5. **Jupiter**

(i) **Positive** - He will be sweet spoken and well behaved. He may be a good writer or author. He may live long. His death will be peaceful.

(ii) **Negative** - He may suffer from colic pains, diseases of urinary organs, diabetes or obesity. He would be bereft of happiness and contentment.

6. **Venus**

(i) **Positive** - The person will come from a rich family. If Venus is in exalted sign in 8th bhava, he will earn money through speculations or occult sciences. He will be handsome and studious. He may lead a luxurious life.

(ii) **Negative** - His mother may die early. He may suffer from the diseases of genetic organs, impotence and eyesight etc.

7. **Saturn**

(i) **Positive** -He will be intelligent and learned. He will be liberal, sympathetic and long- lived. He will be hard working. He will have a few children.

(ii) **Negative** - He will be timid, talkative, dishonest and cruel. He may suffer from disease of generative organs and colic pains. His domestic life may be unhappy.

8. **Rahu**

(i) **Positive** - He may be hard working and earn his living through insurance or lottery type business.

(ii) **Negative** - He will be passionate, boastful, quarrelsome and short tempered. His behaviour may be questionable for others. He may suffer from disease of private organs.

9. **Ketu**

(i) **Positive** - If benefics aspect ketu in 8th bhava, person may settle abroad and become wealthy. He may enjoy better life.

(ii) **Negative** - He may suffer from some chronic disease. If Rahu is in lagna or Saturn in 8th bhava, he may have Cancer disease.

7.10 Planets placements, aspects and combinations 8th house

1. If owner of 8th bhava is malefic and occupies 11th house, the person becomes Alpaayu (short span of life).

2. If lagnesh is weak, malefic occupies 8th bhava and owner of 8th is debilitated, the person is Alpaayu (short span of life).

3. If owner of 8th bhava with a malefic or with Lagnesh is in 6th or 12th house, the person is Alpaayu (short span of life).

4. If owner of 8th bhava and Mars are in lagna, the person becomes Madhyaayu (middle span of life).

5. If owner of 8th bhava is benefic and occupies 11th house, the person is Dirghaayu (long span of life).

6. If the owner of 8th bhava or Saturn is in 8th bhava, the person is Dirghaayu (long span of life).

7. If Jupiter, Venus and Mercury are in 8th bhava or in 2,5,8,11 signs, the person becomes studious but hardhearted.

8. If owner of 8th bhava is in 2nd house, the person becomes an enemy of own and a thief.

9. If a person is born in daytime and Moon with Mars occupies 8th bhava, he will have one eye.

10. If any retrograde planet occupies 2 / 12 / 6 / 8 house, the person's eyes suffer from squint.

11. If owner of 2nd house or Jupiter karak of 2nd house is in 8th bhava, the person is deaf.

12. If Moon and Rahu both are in 8th bhava, the person will be a patient of Hysteria disease.

13. If Saturn is in 8th bhava and Mars is in 7th or 9th house, there may be chicken pox spots on person's face.

14. If Saturn is in 8th bhava and Rahu or a malefic is in lagna, the person suffers stomach pain.

15. If owners of 5th and 12th houses are in 6/8/12 house, the person suffers from heart disease.

16. If owner of 8th bhava is weak and malefic is in 8th bhava and also malefic aspects lagna, the person suffers from liver disease of low or no hunger (mandagini).

17. If owners of 8th, 11th and 6th houses are in 8th bhava, person suffers accidental death through weapon.

18. If 8th bhava and owner of 8th bhava both are aspected by malefics, the person travels to abroad.

19. If owners of 8th and 3rd houses are benefics and occupy lagna or 5th house, the person becomes a scientist or a researcher.

20. If owners of 2nd, 5th and 1st houses with Mercury occupy 8th bhava, the person is an inventor.

21. If in 8th bhava sign is Taurus and occupied by Rahu, it gives sudden wealth. It may be through lottery.

22. If Jupiter or Moon is in 8th bhava in 4/8/12 sign and aspected by malefics, the person suffers from tuberculosis.

23. If Jupiter is in 8th bhava and malefics are in angles (1,4,7,10 houses) not aspected by benefics, it will create Rajbhang Dosha.

7. 11 Events affecting during dasha Sign in 8th house

In Aries

(i) **Favourable** - If Mars owner of 8th bhava is strong, during dasha, the person will be fortunate and long lived. He will lead a comfortable life. He will take interest in occult sciences.

(ii) **Unfavourable** - During weak Mars dasha, he may be physically weak and sick. He may be charge sheeted for theft. He may meet with an accident.

In Taurus

(i) **Favourable** - If Libra is lagna and lagnesh Venus also the owner of 8th bhava is strong, during its dasha period, the person will earn much wealth and lead a luxurious life with long longevity.

(ii) **Unfavourable** - If Venus is weak and unfavourable, during its dasha, he may meet loss his wealth. He may not keep his words. It will lessen his age.

In Gemini

(i) **Favourable** - If strong Mercury, the owner of 8th occupies its own 8th bhava, during its dasha the person may acquire landed property and wealth to lead a comfortable life.

(ii) **Unfavourable** - During weak Mercury dasha, he will not have good relations with his siblings. He may suffer from nervous and skin problems. His business may also deteriorate. His friends may create problems.

In Cancer

(i) **Favourable** - If Moon is powerful being owner of 8th bhava, during its dasha, he may earn money and lead a smooth and peaceful life.

(ii) **Unfavourable** - During weak Moon dasha, he will not have cordial relations with his parents. Property disputes and litigation may arise in inheritance. He may suffer from psychic problems.

In Leo

(i) **Favourable** - If owner Sun is powerful, during its dasha, he will be intelligent, learned and wealthy. He will have a few children. He will be long-lived and healthy.

(ii) **Unfavourable** - During weak Sun dasha, his income may not be much. His health may be poor. His longevity may suffer.

In Virgo

(i) **Favourable** - He will win over his enemies. He will be successful in litigation and gain property, status and dignity. If lagnesh Saturn aspects it, he will be long-lived.

(ii) **Unfavourable** - During Mercury dasha he may suffer from snakebites or drowning in water.

In Libra

(i) **Favourable** - During Venus dasha; he may marry second time or have company of a good woman. He will acquire property and wealth.

(ii) **Unfavourable** - Hibusiness or partnership may be dissolved. He may have extra marital affairs. He may not live long. He may incur sudden losses.

In Scorpio

(i) **Favourable** - Mars being lagnesh and owner of 8th house, if strong, during dasha, he will be happy, healthy and prosperous. He may get legacies and earn money through foreign resources. His wife will also add to his income. He will be long-lived.

(ii) **Unfavourable** - Weak Mars dasha will turn him to be a man of loose morals. His wife may also be unfaithful. Property disputes in family may arise and litigation may start. He may lose his status and dignity. His domestic life may become unhappy and painful.

In Sagittarius

(i) **Favorable** - During strong Jupiter dasha, his near and dear ones, relatives and friends would be very helpful. His longevity will increase. His acts would be charitable and philanthropic.

(ii) **Unfavourable** - If Jupiter is weak and afflicted, ill luck would desert him. He would not be virtuous and religious. His father may fall sick or there may be differences with his father. Family life may be disturbed.

In Capricorn

(i) **Favourable** - Saturn will be owner. If it is strong, during its dasha, he may join a government post but compensation will be below expectations. He will be long-lived, spiritual and detached.

(ii) **Unfavourable** - If Saturn, owner of 8th bhava is weak, during its dasha, he may be unemployed. He may face insults in family and outside. Some elderly relative may expire. He may face poverty and unhappiness.

In Aquarius

(i) **Favourable** - During Saturn dasha, he may accumulate money for his living and become happy and long-lived. He would take interest in philosophy and spiritualism.

(ii) **Unfavourable** - He may face serious financial problems in business and incur heavy debts. His and his wife longevity may decrease. They may face health problems.

In Pisces

(i) **Favourable** - If Jupiter is strong, during its dasha he may accumulate wealth and raise his status. Male child may take birth in family. He would be virtuous, religious and charitable.

(ii) **Unfavourable** - During weak Jupiter dasha, he may fall prey to snake bites or poisoning. His father may also face problems.

7. 12 Twelfth house (Vyaya Bhava)

This house is known as Vyaya bhava / Moksha bhava (House of loss and salvation) The twelfth bhava is the house of unexpected troubles, restraints, separation, depletion, negation and loss of life. It is the last house of birth chart. It brings miseries and misfortunes, sorrows and sins, imprisonment and disgrace. It rules over monetary losses, extravagancies, wastage, sympathy, charity and divine knowledge (moksha), the ultimate goal of human life, the state after death. Hence it is known as 3rd house of moksha (salvation). Planets placed in and planet owning the house are responsible for bad and evil results in their mahadasha / anterdasha. Saturn is very close to it, the most malefic.

7. 13 Owner of twelfth house in various houses

In first house

(i) **Powerful** - He will be handsome and sweet spoken. If the sign is 3/6/9/12 he will travel in the country and abroad.

(ii) **Weak** - He will be literate but feeble minded and weak in health. If 1st house owner occupies 12th house, the person will be selfish, miser and greedy.

In second house

(i) **Powerful** - If owner of 12th bhava is a benefic, he will be happy, healthy and religious. He will spend money for good causes. He will be a good speaker. He will be dignified and powerful. His earnings would be from foreign sources.

(ii) **Weak** - He may lose his wealth and become poor. His eyesight may be weak and dim. He may indulge in useless talks.

In third house

(i) **Powerful** - He will work hard on an ordinary job and earn his living. He will spend money for the betterment of his siblings.

(ii) **Weak** - He may be timid and ugly. He may suffer from ear disease and no happiness from his younger brothers.

In fourth house

(i) **Powerful** - He may go abroad to earn his living. He will lead a simple life. His mother will be fortunate. If Venus is strong he would acquire gadgets of comforts.

(ii) **Weak** - He will not be able to get his mother's love and blessings. She may die early. He will be deprived of comforts of land, buildings and conveyance. He will be anxious and worried. He will lose his mental peace and family happiness.

In fifth house

(i) **Powerful** - He will be religious and travel to many holy places. He would have good children.

(ii) **Weak** - He will have a weak mind. He will be childless. His domestic life will be unhappy.

In sixth house

(i) **Powerful** - If it creates Vipreet Rajyoga, the person will be happy, healthy, wealthy and prosperous. He will enjoy all comforts in life. He will win over enemies. Litigation will also be advantageous. He will be long-lived.

(ii) **Weak** - If malefic joins, he may be jealous, short tempered and unhappy. He may be involved in adultery and likewise sinful activities. Family happiness will elude him.

In seventh house

(i) **Powerful** - He may marry out of caste or out of country and become happy but for a short period.

(ii) **Weak** - He will be illiterate and poor. He may indulge in adultery. His married life would be miserable.

In eighth house

(i) **Powerful** - The person will be knowledgeable in shastras and occult subjects. He will be religious, righteous, famous and sweet spoken. People will like him. He will be rich and lead a luxurious life. He may earn money through death benefits and legacies.

(ii) **Weak** - He may go astray and become a victim of bad habits and immoral activities. His health and longevity may suffer.

In ninth house

(i) **Powerful** - He will be generous, sympathetic and healthy. He may go abroad and prosper there. He may undertake pilgrimage and earn money through related activities.

(ii) **Weak** - He will lead a lonely life. He will have no relation with family and friends. He will be selfish and unfortunate. His father may die early.

In tenth house

(i) **Powerful** - He will be hard working and earn a lot of wealth. He may invest money in agriculture for more gains. He may take long distant journeys for his profession.

(ii) **Weak** - He may be unhappy in life. Government may punish him. He may incur losses and lack support from family and friends.

In eleventh house

(i) **Powerful** - He may deal in import and export business. He may earn name and fame apart from money.

(ii) **Weak** - His expenditure would be more than income. He would be unfortunate with regard to happiness from progeny.

In twelfth house

(i) **Powerful** - He will be righteous, generous, virtuous and religious. He will enjoy peaceful and comfortable life. He will spend money on religious and charitable activities.

(ii) **Weak** - He will be restless worker and lead an aimless life. He may indulge in adultery.

7. 14 Planets occupying twelfth house

1. Sun

(i) **Positive** - He will be brave, courageous and energetic. His sons will also be good and hard working. He may go to a foreign country and become wealthy and prosperous.

(ii) **Negative** - He will not be successful in life. He may have secret enemies. He may suffer loss of a limb of body. His eyesight may also be weak. He may be engaged in disgusting occupations. His self-confidence would be low. Government may punish him.

2. Moon

(i) **Positive** - If Moon with Jupiter and Venus occupies 12th bhava, the person is wealthy. He may spend money on charity and auspicious events.

    (ii) **Negative** - He will be selfish, jealous, hard-hearted and mischievous. He will like to live in solitude far from the community. He may suffer from some deformity in limbs. His eyesight may be weak. If Saturn joins, he will be dull and idle.

3. Mars

    (i) **Positive** - If Mars in 12th bhava and malefics in 7th and 8th houses, he may marry second time and enjoy life with two wives. He may go abroad or make earnings from foreign sources.

    (ii) **Negative** - He will be short tempered, selfish, greedy but extravagant. He may have skin disease or sleep disorders. He may lose his wealth. He may divorce his wife.

4. Mercury

    (i) **Positive** -The person will be learned in shastras, knowledgeable, religious and charitable. He may be a good writer. He will have a few children.

    (ii) **Negative** - He may indulge in extra marital relations. He will lose health and wealth. He may suffer from nervous or skin problems.

5. Jupiter

    (i) **Positive** - He will be happy and liberal. He will help others. He may be a yogi (sanyasi) by nature.

    (ii) **Negative** - He may be lazy and evil minded. He may lead a lascivious life, which is not good for progeny, wealth and family happiness.

6.Venus

    (i) **Positive** - If Venus occupies Pisces its exalted sign he will be handsome, attractive, healthy and wealthy. He may have all comforts in life and company of good women.

    (ii) **Negative** - He may be idle and lazy and keep busy in sinful activities, hankering for the women outside for comforts of bed. He may have poor eyesight. His life will be miserable. He may suffer from venereal diseases.

7. Saturn

    (i) **Positive** - He may work hard and become wealthy. He may go abroad and make handsome earnings.

(ii) **Negative** - He will be lazy, harsh and jealous. He may be immoral and extravagant. Government may punish him and he may be jailed. He will have many enemies. He may not keep good health.

8. Rahu

(i) **Positive** - He may settle abroad and become wealthy and prosperous. He will help others or donate money for good causes. He will be hard working.

(ii) **Negative** - He will not be a man of character. His eyesight may be weak. He would incur wasteful expenditure on travels and treatments of diseases.

9.Ketu

(i) **Positive** - He may turn to be a Tantrik Sanyasi and give spiritual discourses (a way to salvation) to the people. He may go abroad and live long.

(ii) **Negative** - He may have poor health. He may wander aimlessly spending money for no good cause. He may befriend to the low caste people.

7. 15 Planets placements, aspects and combinations 12th house

1. If benefics occupy or aspect 12th bhava, the person will be generous, sympathetic, and charitable.

2. If planets are in exalted or in own sign in 12th bhava, the person will be philanthropist or helping hand to others.

3. If there is 1 / 4 / 7 / 10 sign in 12th bhava and Saturn occupies or aspects 12th bhava, he will travel frequently.

4. If Venus is in 12th bhava in any sign excluding Virgo sign and owner of 9th aspects Venus, the person will be extremely wealthy.

5. If Venus is in 12th Bhava from the house Jupiter occupying, the person will be extremely wealthy, prosperous, and fortunate.

6. If owner of 12th bhava is in 3rd /6th / 8th house and they are occupied or aspected by malefics or forming Papkartari yoga, the person will be extremely wealthy.

7. If owner of 12th bhava occupies 12th bhava in conjunction with or aspect by Venus, the person will be extremely wealthy and lead a luxurious life.

8. If Venus alone occupies 12th bhava, the person will be extremely wealthy.

9. If Venus is in 12th house from lagna or chandra lagna or surya lagna, the person will be extremely wealthy, prosperous, and fortunate.

10. If exalted Venus occupies 12th bhava, the person will be extremely wealthy, prosperous and lucky.

11. If owner of 12 th house is in its exalted, own or friendly sign, the person gets all comforts in life easily.

12. If owner of 12th bhava is in 9th house, the person is religious and travels to holy places.

13. If owner of 12th is in lagna, the person is handsome and sweet spoken.

14. If owner of 12th is strong and weak planets occupy 12th bhava, the person loses his wealth.

15. If owners of 6th and 8th houses being powerful occupy 12th bhava, the person becomes bankrupt.

16. If Sun is in conjunction with lagnesh and owner of 12th and malefics aspect, the person will be poor.

17. If lagnesh and owners of 6th and 8th houses are in 12th bhava, the person loses all items of comforts in life.

18. If owner of 12th bhava is in conjunction with or aspect by owner of 7th house, the person becomes the slave of bad habits. He will be most sexy and womanizer.

19. If Sun and Moon are in 6th or 12th houses, person's married life will be unhappy.

20. If Rahu is in 12th and owner of 12th is in 8th house, the person definitely loses one of his limbs or part of the body.

21. If Sun and Moon are in 12th bhava and a malefic joins or aspects, he may lose one eye.

22. If Sun, Venus, and lagnesh all occupy 6 /8 /12 house, the person may be blind.

23. If Sun and Moon both are in 12th bhava having almost same longitudes and not aspected by benefics, he may be blind.

7. 16 Events affecting during dasha Sign in 12th house

In Aries

(i) **Favourable** - Mars will be the owner of 12th. During Mars dasha if a benefic anterdasha is running, his health will remain intact, he will be bold, and hard- working. He will gain wealth, conveyance and other comforts of life in the first half of anterdasha.

(ii) **Unfavourable** - During Mars dasha, if a malefic planet's anterdasha comes, he will suffer from respiratory troubles. He will be extravagant and immoral. Government may terminate his services. He may be put in to prison. His domestic life will be ruined.

In Taurus

(i) **Favourable** - If Venus is in 12th and its dasha is running with anterdasha of a benefic, he will be healthy, generous, polite and religious. His wife will also faithful and caring. He will be wealthy and spend his money for good causes. He will enjoy luxuries and lead a comfortable and happy family life in the first half of anterdasha.

(ii) **Unfavourable** - During malefic planet's anterdasha, he may lose his health. He will be irresponsible and people will not believe him. Enemies or thieves may trouble him. He may lead a poor and painful life.

In Gemini

(i) **Favourable** - If Mercury occupies its own 12th house, during Mercury mahadasha and anterdasha of a benefic planet, he may travel in country and abroad and earn a lot of wealth. He will be benevolent and religious. People will like and listen him. He will be healthy and popular in community.

(ii) **Unfavourable** - If a malefic planet's anterdasha is running, he may be unhappy with his siblings. They may create problems in his progress. He may be harsh in tongue and become irreligious. Family life may not be happy.

In Cancer

(i) **Favourable** - If owner Moon's dasha is going on, he will be a man of simple living and high thinking. He may go abroad for his living and earn wealth.

(ii) **Unfavourable** - During dasha period, he will feel depressed. His mother may fall sick. He may lose property and comforts. This will disturb his sleep and mental peace.

In Leo

(i) **Favourable** - If Sun being owner occupies 12th house, then its mahadasha and anterdasha of friendly benefic will make him healthy, wealthy and religious. Government will honour him. He will be popular. He will perform traditional rites and rituals from time to time. He will travel to holy places and shrines for peace of mind and happiness.

(ii) **Unfavourable** - During a malefic planet's anterdasha, he may spend a good amount of money on family and children, but they may create troubles for him. They may attack on him. He may lose his money and peace of mind. He may travel aimlessly.

In Virgo

(i) **Favourable** - It Mercury will be the 12th house owner, during its dasha, the native may get a high position and improve his status. He may be a famous writer. He may travel abroad and become wealthy. He will be intelligent self-made man.

(ii) **Unfavourable** - During Mercury dasha, if it is placed in 12th with a malefic, he will grow enmity with very near and dear ones. He may develop illicit relations with opposite sex. His children may also create trouble to him. He may be poor and unpopular.

In Libra

(i) **Favourable** - If Venus occupies 12th being owner, during its dasha, he may travel abroad and earn a lot of wealth. He may lead a happy, peaceful and dignified life. He will be famous in his community. Government may honour him.

(ii) **Unfavourable** - During Venus dasha his wife may fall ill or become extravagant. He may incur debts. He may be mentally disturbed. He may indulge in adultery and be hospitalized.

In Scorpio

(i) **Favourable** - During Mars dasha, he will gain money through business and improve his status. He will lead comfortable and prosperous life. He will be a good orator. He may live long.

    (ii) **Unfavourable** - During its owner's dasha, he may be prone to accidents. Married family life may also be disturbed. He may lose his property and bank balance. His brothers may go abroad.

In Sagittarius

    (i) **Favourable** - During Jupiter's dasha, he may go abroad for further education and earn money for livelihood there. He will enjoy comfortable life. He will be religious, happy and healthy.

    (ii) **Unfavourable** - If anterdasha of a malefic is running, he will be selfish, mean, and arrogant. He may not be successful in his profession. He may not be able to pursue his higher education. He may be fed up with this world.

In Capricorn

    (i) **Favourable** - During Saturn's dasha, he may get a good job and lead a hard working but happy life. He may go abroad and earn wealth.

    (ii) **Unfavourable** - His near and dear ones may create troubles for him. Property disputes may arise. Government may impose penalty. He may incur losses.

Aquarius

    (i) **Favourable** - During Saturn dasha, he may go abroad and become rich. His elder brothers and sisters may also be rich. He may get all respect and honour in the family. A male child may bear in his family.

    (ii) **Unfavourable** - He may lose his business because of the problems created by his blood relations. The thieves may attack on him. Fire may break out in his house. His health would be affected.

In Pisces

    (i) **Favourable** - The owner of 12th house will be Jupiter, during its dasha, he may go abroad and prosper there. He will be in riches. He will be religious, famous and a helping hand to others.

    (ii) **Unfavourable** - During its mahadasha and anterdasha of a malefic, he may be unhealthy. His enemies or thieves may attack on him. His behaviour may change. He may incur heavy expenses.

7. 17 Example kundlis with astrological observations

Six example kundlis regarding 4th, 8th and 12th houses two for each house of Vairagya Trine i.e. Moksha houses are as below

Kundli No. 34 Ex. President India, Late Sarvapalli Radha Krishanan

1. Date of birth 05 - 09 - 1888

2. Time of Birth 13 - 40 P.M. (IST)

3. Place of Birth Tirutani (TN.) Lat.13⁰ / 11' N. Long.79⁰ / 38' E.

4. Birth Nakshatra Magha-3

5. Balance dasha at Birth Ketu 01year-11months-05days

BIRTH CHART

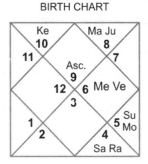

NAVANSH CHART

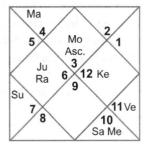

Kundli No. 7.17 (K-34)

Astrological Observations

This horoscope relates to Sagittarius ascendant. People are intelligent, learned, philosopher, orator, statesmen, religious and God fearing. Dr. Sarvpalli Radha Krishanan was such a versatile scholar, who completed his duties and responsibilities honestly in country and abroad. Being born in Magha Nakshtra he was studious, courageous, dutiful, religious and God fearing.

1. Lagna Considerations

Lagnesh is situated in 12th house adjoining to lagna with Mars. Chandra lagnesh and Surya lagnesh is one and that is significator Sun placed in 9th house of fortune and religion in own sign Leo and aspects lagna. Being Significator (Karak) of 9th and 1st house Sun is powerful. In Navansh lagna Moon is located in lagna in sign Gemini of Mercury, hence Chandra kundli is extremely activated.

2.Planets placements, aspects, and combinations

From 12th house Jupiter aspects 4th house, the house of comforts and 8th house of philosophical thoughts. In 12th house sign Scorpio is friendly, in 4th house its own sign Pisces and in 8th house its exalted sign Cancer is rising. So there is a good connection and interrelation of 4th, 8th and 12th (Moksha) houses of Vairagya Trine in this birth chart. The placement of Sun and Moon in 9th house is not only powerful but also beneficial and favourable. Mars with Jupiter is performing Rajyoga. Exalted Mercury with debilitated Venus in 10th house is also forming Neechbhang Rajyoga. Lagna sign being an odd sign, is performing Mahabhagya yoga. Leo sign in 9th house is also an odd sign and its owner Sun is placed with Moon, strengthening native's fortune. Primarily he served as a teacher and after that he became an administrator and lastly 1st citizen of India. Other yogas are formed Ubhaichari yoga by Sun being planets on both the sides other than Moon, Durdhara yoga by Moon being both sides planets other than Sun, Bhadra yoga by Mercury being exalted in 10th house. All these yogas provided him success, prosperity, riches, status, dignity, honour, popularity and all the happiness in life.

3. Conclusion

On above facts and combinations, we can conclude, if fortune favours, a man can touch the heights. In case of Sarvapalli Radha Krishnan it is true. Primarily he was a well-known teacher, this is the reason that the teachers of India celebrate his birthday as Teacher's Day on 5th September every year. Later on he joined so many posts of administration in country and out of country and in U.N.O. etc. as chancellor, chairman, ambassador and so on. He fulfilled all his duties successfully. It is because of aspects and combinations of planets as stated above especially by two friendly planets Jupiter and Mars interconnecting and correlating 4th, 8th and 12th Moksha houses of Vairagya Trine. In the days of Jupiter's mahadasha, he was elected as President of India continuously for two tenures, a period of 10 years. Now he is no more but his name in the history of India will live long.

Kundli No. 35 Gurudeva, Sri Sri Ravi Shankar, (Preach Art of Living)

1. Date of birth 13 - 05 - 1956
2. Time of Birth 05 - 10 A.M. (IST)
3. Place of Birth Papanasam (TN.) Lat.08⁰/ 42' N.Long.77⁰ / 23' E.
4. Birth Nakshatra Mrigshira-3
5. Balance Dasha at Birth Mars 02years-04months-29days

BIRTH CHART   NAVANSH CHART

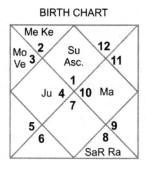
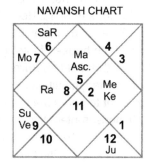

Kundli No. 7.17 (K-35)

Astrological Observations

It is a Mesh lagan kundli owned by Mars. Such people are confident, courageous, enterprising and ambitious. They have high aims and goals. They think, judge and complete them in time smilingly, smoothly and sympathetically. Shri Shri Ravi Shankar ji preaches "Art of Living" with the help of meditation and breathing system called "Sudarshan Kirya" Being born in Mrigshira nakshatra he is good natured, easy going and sweet spoken.

1.Lagna Considerations

Lagnesh and Surya lagnesh Mars is situated in 10th house of Karma (actions) aspects lagna. It is occupied by exalted Sun, the owner of 5th house of intelligence and wisdom. The house of comforts 4th is occupied by exalted Jupiter. Chandra lagnesh Mercury is posited in 2nd house next to lagna. Navansh lagnesh is also Mercury and Vargottam. Sun is powerful in lagna hence lagna is extremely activated.

2. Placements, Aspects, and Combinations

Kundli's three 1st, 4th, 10th houses called kendras are occupied by exalted planets Sun, Jupiter and Mars. Lagnesh Mars from 10th house is performing Ruchak and Kuldeepak yogas being exalted in kendra. It makes native's face magnetic and attractive. In astrology lagna and 4th house are known as centre of Yama and Pranayama. The owner of 9th and 12th houses of fortune, religion and salvation exalted Jupiter is located in 4th house of comforts. It is performing Hansa yoga being in Kendra and aspects lagnesh Mars. Because of this position of Jupiter Swamiji Sri Sri Ravi Shankar has been famous in the field of spiritualism. Exalted Sun owner of 5th house of intelligence sits in lagna, strengthened his leadership in this field. Saturn and Rahu in 8th house of samadhi (meditation) added the situation of vairagya and salvation made him to be a great saint to serve the mankind. Jupiter from 4th house aspects 8th and 12th houses interrelating and reinforcing 4th, 8th and 12th houses (houses of salvation). Venus and Moon in 3rd house provided him courage and popularity. Hence all the three 4th, 8th and 12th houses are correlated and connected favourably and are beneficial to the native.

3. Conclusion

We can conclude that Art of Living is not a new thing and everybody knows but to implement it or to shape it in an easy way is a little bit hard. So Swamiji did it because of Moon in 3rd house with Venus. Breathing system and meditation method both inculcated by Swamiji is full of sweet, attractive and religious songs. They give peace to the people. They come and feel relieved from the sorrows. In 2nd house Mercury and Ketu both are Vargottam. They made his personality so magnetic that people love and follow his preaching and ways. Saturn is in its own Anuradha Nakshatra. It leads him towards this type of meditation and devotion to Almighty God. For this social service, he was bestowed "Yoga Shiromani" award in 1986 by the President of India. It is all due to interconnecting and reinforcing made by exalted Jupiter. Now Saturn mahadaha is running, which may increase his popularity and number of followers.

Kundli No. 36 Missile Man Ex. President Dr. A. P.J. Abdul Kalam
1. Date of birth 15 - 10 - 1931
2. Time of Birth 11 - 55 A.M. (IST)
3. Place of Birth Rameshwaram (TN.) Lat.09⁰ / 17' N.Long.79⁰ / 18' E.
4. Birth Nakshatra Jyestha-1
5. Balance Dasha at Birth Mercury 13years-07months-18days

BIRTH CHART

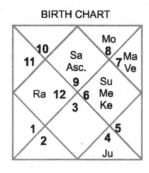

NAVANSH CHART

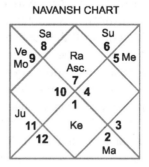

Kundli No. 7.17 (K-36)

Astrological Observations

The above kundli of Sagittarius lagna belongs to our Ex. President of India A.P.J. Abdul Kalam, primarily a scientist, who invented missile for the protection of Army and the Country. Missile is such a weapon, if it is thrown or fired to a definite target or place, it destroys the target. Sagittarians are courageous, pushing, honest, hard working and inventive persons. They are successful in government service. Dr. A. P.J. Abdul Kalam has successfully completed his 5 years tenure as President of India. Being born in Jyeshtha nakshatra, he is joyful and charitable.

1. Lagna Considerations

Lagnesh Jupiter is situated in 8th house of research and scientific inventions in its exalted sign Cancer and aspects Moon in 12th house adjoining lagna. Surya lagnesh Mercury is placed in 10th house in its exalted sign Virgo with Sun and Ketu and influences lagna. Chandra lagnesh Mars is in 11th house with Venus in Libra sign. Navansh lagnesh Mercury is in Leo sign while Sun in Virgo sign (Rashi Parivartan in Navansh). Sun the significator of 1st and 10th houses influences lagna. Therefore lagna is fortified.

2. Placements, Aspects, and Combinations

Lagnesh Jupiter sitting in 8th house of research and scientific inventions in its exalted sign is powerful. It aspects 12th house owned by Mars and 4th house of its own interrelating 8th, 12th and 4th all Moksha houses of Vairagya Trine. Saturn alone is posited in lagna and aspects 7th and 10th houses and three planets, Mercury, Sun and Ketu. It aspects 3rd house having the sign Aquarius the owner Saturn itself. Jupiter is placed in Navansh in Aquarius. Saturn situated in lagna and aspecting exalted Mercury in 10th house, made Dr. Abdul Kalam a scientist, who invented Missile and became famous. Because of Saturn in Sagittarius lagna. Dr kalam got everything easily. From 8th house exalted Jupiter added more strength to provide him research abilities. Sun is performing Vesi yoga being two planets ahead other than Moon and Ravi yoga being Sun in 10th house of actions and Moon Durudhara yoga having planets on both sides other than Sun. These yogas helped him to be healthy, happy, honest, virtuous and a man of high calibre.

3. Conclusion

On the basis of above placement of planets, we can conclude that Jupiter played a very important role from 8th house of science and research being in an exalted sign aspecting 12th and 4th houses to make him famous and to be known as a missile man all over the world. Thus, there is a strong connection and correlation of 8th, 12th and 4th Moksha houses of Vairagya Trine. Saturn from lagna is aspecting Mercury, Sun and Ketu in 10th house also assisted Jupiter to strengthen Dr. Kalam's popularity. Thus 8th house is Very powerful.

Kundli No. 37 Great Scientist, Mr. Albert Einstein

1. Date of birth 14 - 03 - 1879

2. Time of Birth   11 - 30 A.M. (European Time)

3. Place of Birth   Ulrichen (Swz) Lat.46⁰ / 30' N. Long.08⁰ / 18' E.

4. Birth Nakshatra Jyestha-2

5. Balance Dasha at Birth Mercury 09years-08months-04days.

BIRTH CHART

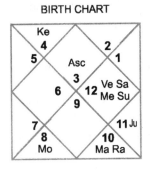

NAVANSH CHART

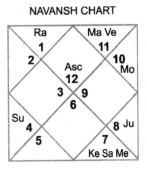

Kundli No. 7.17 (K-37)

Astrological Observations

This is the Gemini sign lagna Kundli. It belongs to Scientist Albert Einstein. Geminians are intelligent and learned. They quickly grasp things. They are versatile and restless. They spend much time to take the decisions. Albert Einstein was a scientist, who wrote the theory of " special relativity and general relativity ". He was awarded Noble Prize in the year 1921 for his discovery regarding " Law of Photoelectric Effect".

1.Lagna Considerations

Lagnesh Mercury with Sun, Venus and Saturn is placed in 10th house. They all influence lagna. Surya lagnesh Jupiter is posited in 9th house of fortune also aspects lagna. Chandra lagnesh Mars with Rahu is situated in its exalted sign Capricorn in 8th house of science and research. Navansh lagnesh is Jupiter sitting in 9th house and Mercury with exalted Saturn and Ketu are in 8th house in Navansh. Thus lagna is fortified.

2. Placements, Aspects, and Combinations

As already stated that lagnesh is placed in 10th house in its debilitated sign with exalted Venus. They are performing Neechbhang Rajyoga. Owner of 10th house Jupiter is in 9th while 10th owner Saturn is situated in 10th house. They are forming Rashi Parivartan yoga. Saturn is stronger than Jupiter that made Einstein great scientist of his time. Einstein was a loyal supporter of his partymen. Exalted Mars is powerful and placed in 8th house and Moon placed in debilitated sign Scorpio, owned by Mars in 6th house aspects, 12th house of Venus. Debilitated Mercury exalted Venus, Sun and Saturn, all located in 10th house, aspect 4th house of comforts. Owner of 5th house Venus and owner of 9th house Saturn, are in association and positive and favourable. But 8th house is strongest; hence there is a good combination and correlation amongst 8th, 12th and 4th Moksha houses of Vairagya Trine.

3. Conclusion

We can conclude from the above facts that Einstein was a man of scientific mind. He studied Physics and wrote about 300 articles. For his discovery of law of photoelectric effect, he was awarded Noble Prize in the year 1921. He was thoughtful and a slow talker, but he was very firm in his studies and views. His firmness and thorough knowledge of physics and related theories made him popular all over the world. It was all due to correlation and reinforcement amongst 8th, 12th and 4th, all Moksha houses of Vairagya trine.

Kundli No. 38 Famous Maharishi Sri Raman

1. Date of birth 30 - 12 - 1879

2. Time of Birth 01 - 10 A.M. (IST)

3. Place of Birth Madurai (TN.) Lat. 09⁰ / 56' N.Long.78⁰ / 60' E.

4. Birth Nakshatra Punarvasu-3

5. Balance Dasha at Birth Jupiter 05years-11month-17days.

BIRTH CHART   NAVANSH CHART

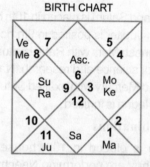 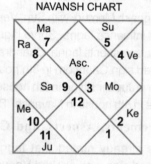

Kundli No. 7.17 (K-38)

Astrological Observations

This is a Virgo lagna kundli. Virgo people are fond of quick changes. They are conscientious and capable of handling the work even in unfavourable situations. Bhagwan Maharishi Raman was such a man, who attained realization after involving in so many unfavorable activities but later on he became a famous saint (Maharishi).

1. Lagna Considerations

Here in his birth chart lagnesh and Chandra lagnesh Mercury is posited in 3rd house of courage with Venus in Mars sign Scorpio and aspects 9th house of fortune. Surya lagnesh Jupiter is placed in 6th house and aspects Moon in 10th house of Mercury. Moon from 10th influences lagna, house of Mercury. Navansh lagna is also Virgo. Significator of 1st and 10th house Sun with Rahu is located in 4th house owned by Jupiter, aspects Moon in 10th house of Mercury, therefore lagna is fortified.

2. Placements, Aspects, and Combinations

Rahu with Sun is placed in 4th house, aspects Mars in 8th house in its own sign Aries and 12th house sign Leo. Rahu and Sun are posited in Sagittarius of Jupiter which aspects 12th house sign Leo of Sun. Thus, there is a connection of 12th, 4th and 8th houses known as Houses of Moksha (Salvation). Saturn in Jupiter's sign Pisces in 7th house and Jupiter in Saturn's sign, in Aquarius in 6th house are performing Rashi Parivartan yoga. This yoga made him recluse. Moon and ketu combination in 10th house added more strength to the native to be alone to attain Moksha (Salvation). Mercury and Venus combination in 3rd house afforded him harmonization of soul, mind and intellect. These combinations granted him the divine powers to reach the Almighty God for getting salvation. Thus connection and correlation of 12th, 4th and 8th Moksha houses of Vairagya Trine helped him to be a great saint (Maharishi).

3. Conclusion

Therefore we can conclude that except Saturn, which is located in 7th house and aspects 9th, 1st and 4th houses, other planets led him towards to commit wrong things but later on Sun and Rahu, Moon and Ketu, Mercury and Venus combinations and aspects of brought change in his behaviour. Jupiter is aspecting 12th house and Moon, Ketu and Saturn 4th house and Mars in its own sign is placed in 8th house. Thus interrelations and correlations of the 12th, 4th and 8th houses of Vairagya Trine opened a right way to attain divinity (Moksha) and to make him a Maharishi (Saint).

Kundli No. 39 Sikh Dharam Founder, Shri Guru Nanak Dev Ji

1. Date of birth 15 - 04 - 1469
2. Time of Birth 13 - 40 P.M. (IST)
3. Place of Birth Nankana Sahib(Pak.) Lat.31^0 / 27' N. Long.73^0 / 42' E.
4. Birth Nakshatra Mrigshira-2
5. Balance Dasha at Birth Mars 05years-00months-01day

BIRTH CHART   NAVANSH CHART

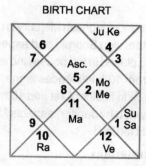
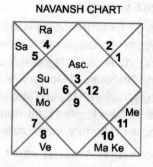

Kundli No. 7.17 (K-39)

Astrological Observations

This is a Leo sign kundli owned by powerful Sun, the king of all planets. Leo born people are sympathetic, generous and helpful to the mankind. They have great faith in friends and relatives. They head the community and establish their own organization. Guru Nanak Dev Ji was such a man, who founded a new sect of religion namely Sikh Dharam. Now Sikh Dharam followers and Sikh Gurudwaras are all over the world. Born in Mrigshira nakshatra he was healthy, happy, good natured, easy going and a soft spoken.

1. Lagna Considerations

Lagnesh and significator Sun in its exalted sign Aries is situated in 9th house with debilitated Saturn. Chandra lagnesh Venus in its exalted sign Pisces is placed in 8th house. Surya lagnesh Mars is posited in 7th house in Saturn's sign Aquarius and aspects Lagna. Navansh lagnesh Mars is placed in its exalted Capricorn and aspects Saturn sitting in Leo sign. Therefore lagna is activated.

2. Placements, Aspects, and Combinations

Four exalted planets are placed in the birth chart. Jupiter in its exalted sign Cancer with Ketu is powerful posited in 12th house of spiritualism and salvation. From 12th house Jupiter and Ketu both aspect 4th house of comforts and also 8th house of long life. Thus, there is a very good combination of 12th, 4th and 8th houses known as Moksha houses. This made him a religious preacher. Exalted Venus from 8th house aspects 2nd house of speech. Sweet voice gave him popularity. Exalted Sun aspects 3rd house, where Libra sign is rising. Exalted Moon and Mercury both aspect 4th house of Mars, that aspects lagna from 7th house. Moon and Mercury combination led him towards attainment of spiritual knowledge. The placement of exalted Sun in 9th house and of exalted Moon in 10th house is a 2nd grade Rajyoga. This indicates a combination of soul, mind and religion. Exalted Sun with Saturn is inclined to spiritualism and devotion to Almighty God. These exalted planets and their aspects made him the founder of a sect of Hindu religion now known as Sikh Dharam. You can see the followers of Sikh Dharam all over the world.

3. Conclusion

While concluding the facts, we see that Jupiter is placed in its exalted sign in 12th house of spirituality and Salvation aspects 4th house of comforts and its own 8th house of long life has creating an interrelation and strong connection amongst 12th, 4th and 8th Moksha houses. Besides, the position of 9th house is also strong. Sun, the lagnesh is placed in its exalted sign Aries aspects lagna and 9th house owner Mars also aspects lagna. Moon in 10th house in its exalted sign Taurus with Mercury also influences lagna and 10th house owner Venus is placed in its exalted sign Pisces adjoining to 9th house of fortune and religion. All these planetary placement and ideas related to them encouraged him to serve the mankind and preach them devotion to God, earned by honesty and shared with others.

Figure : 7.1 (F-6) Fourth Trine Moksha Houses

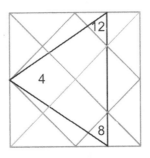

Figure : 7.1 (F-6)

ॐ

Chapter

8

Significance of Yogas
(Combinations)

8. 1 What is yoga?

The word yoga is derived from its root Yuj, which means to join or unite. In Vedic astrology Yoga means a special planetary combination or association either in auspicious houses or inauspicious houses of a birth chart. Yogas reveal native's inherent inclinations, possibilities of political power and influence, wealth, asceticism, miseries, debts, dishonesty, corruption etc. But it is a notable fact that the combination of combust planet is no combination (yoga). Good combination (disposition) improves the status of the person and gives name, fame, dignity, prosperity, honour, wealth and a good health while bad disposition mars the status of the person and makes his life miserable, desperate and sorrowful. He may become sick and poor. Following are some yogas properly defined such as Rajyogas, Panch Mahapurusha yogas, other special yogas and Nabhas yogas:

8. 2 Important Yogas

1. Rajyogas, Vipreet Rajyoga, Neechbhang Rajyoga

The following are some important Rajyogas, Vipreet Rajyoga and Neechbhang Rajyoga. They bring name, fame, wealth, honour and authority to the person, in whose chart these yogas are formed.

(i) When three or more planets exalt or rise in their own signs occupy the angles (kendras) in a birth chart.

(ii) When a debilitated but retrograde planet occupies benefic house in a birth chart.

(iii) When Moon occupies 4th or 7th or 10th house and Jupiter aspects it from his occupied house.

(iv) When one planet out of owners of 2nd, 9th and 11th houses should be in kendra from Chandra lagna and Jupiter as the owner of 2nd or 5th or 11th house.

(v) When three or more planets posses digbal (Directional strength). Digbali planets means Mercury and Jupiter should be in east or in 1st house, Moon and Venus in north or in 4th house, Saturn in west or in 7th house, Sun and Mars in south or in 10th house.

(vi) When owners of 9th and 10th are either in their own houses or exchange houses and owners of 5th, 7th and 6th are in their own houses.

(vii) When any two owners out of the owners of 3rd, 6th, 8th, and 12th houses exchange their houses. It is called Vipreet Rajyoga.

(viii) When the owner of a sign aspects its own sign in the house, where a debilitated planet is situated. It is called Neechbhang Rajyoga.

(ix) When owner of a sign in which one will be debilitated and other exalted should be in kendras from lagna or Chandra lagna. It is called Neechbhang Rajyoga.

2. Dhanik yoga

When the following combinations are formed, it is called Dhanik yoga. The person is wealthy or extremely wealthy.

(i) If any one of the owners of 11th, 10th, 4th, 5th, 1st, and 2nd houses is with the owner of 9th house.

(ii) If any one of the owners of 11th, 4th, 5th, 1st, and 2nd is with the owner of 10th house.

(iii) If any one of the owners of 1st, 2nd, 4th, and 5th is with the owner of 11th house.

(iv) If any one of the owners of 2nd, 4th, and 5th is with the owner of 1st house.

(v) If any one of the owners of 5th and 4th is with the owner of 2nd house.

(vi) If owners of 4th and 5th sit together.

3. Daridra yoga

When the following combinations are formed, it is called Daridra yoga. The person is poor or extremely poor.

(i) If any one of the owners of 2nd, 1st, 4th, 10th, 5th, 7th, 9th, 3rd, and 11th is with the owner of 6th house.

(ii) If any one of the owners of 4th, 2nd, 1st, 10th, 5th, 7th, 9th, 3rd, and 11th is with the owner of 12th house.

4. Saubhagya yoga

If any two out of the owners of 1st, 2nd, 4th, 5th, 7th, 9th 10th, and 11th exchange their signs   (Rashi Parivartan), it is called Saubhagya Yoga.The person is Lucky. He is happy, healthy, wealthy and popular. He earns his name and fame helping others in the community.

5. Durbhagya yoga

If any one out of the owners of auspicious houses that is 1st, 2nd, 4th, 7th, 10th, 5th, 9th and 11th houses and any one out of the owners of inauspicious houses that is 3rd, 6th, 8th and 12th houses exchange signs / houses, it is called Durbhagya Yoga. The person is Unlucky. It causes ups and downs, miseries, sorrows and struggles in the life.

6. Lagnadhi/Chandradhi yoga

When all three benefics, Jupiter, Venus and Mercury are posited in 6th, 7th and 8th houses either from lagna or Chandra lagna, this yoga is formed. The person is honest, polite, sympathetic, virtuous, trustworthy, happy, wealthy and popular. He wins over his enemies.

7. Satyavadi yoga

When a benefic planet occupies 10th house from Lagna or Chandra lagna, this yoga is formed. The person becomes honest, truth loving, wealthy and prosperous. He is well known and reputed till life. He is a man of character always helping the community. It is also called Amala or Amalkeerti yoga.

8. Asatyavadi yoga

The person becomes a perfect liar, if owner of 2nd house occupies the houses of Saturn or Mars and malefics joins 1st, 4th, 7th, 10th, 5th and 9th houses.

9. Chatussar/Vasumati Yoga

When all benefics and malefics both occupy kendras i.e. 1st, 4th, 7th, 10th houses, it is called Chatussar yoga. When only benefics occupy upachayas i.e. 3rd, 6th, 10th and 11th houses, it is called Vasumati yoga. In both the situations the person is independent, authorititative, wealthy, reputed and well known in the country blessed with good children.

10. Panch Mahapurush yogas

When planets are in exalted signs or in own signs and occupy kendras from lagna, they form Panch Mahapurush yoga. Planet wise yogas names are different. The person becomes healthy, handsome, famous, wealthy and long-lived. He is blessed with devoted family and all comforts in life as house, conveyance facility etc. More qualities are as under:

(i) **Mars** in exaltation / in own sign forms Ruchak yoga. The person may be high-level officer in army or police. He may be a ruler or wrestler or a good sportsman.

(ii) **Mercury** in exaltation / in own sign forms Bhadra yoga. The person will be strong and helping hand for others.

(iii) **Jupiter** in exaltation / in own sign forms Hans yoga. The person is a man of character and religious or devotee to God.

(iv) **Venus** in exaltation / in own sign forms Malavya yoga. It gives a happy and comfortable life with loving and caring wife and children.

(v) **Saturn** in exaltation / in own sign forms Sasa yoga. It gives leadership and riches. He may be a head of a community / village / city / state or party.

11. Kahal yoga

When owners of 4th and 9th houses are in kendras or in trikonas from each other and lagnesh is powerful, this yoga is formed. The person becomes bold, brave, but stubborn and leader of the community. He may be a head of village / city or MLA. / MP. He may be an army / police officer.

12.Lakshmi yoga

If owner of 9th house in its exalted or in own sign occupies a kendra or trikona house, this yoga is formed. The person will be handsome, virtuous, noble, intelligent, learned, honest, popular and wealthy. He may be a ruler enjoying all comforts in life.

13.Vesi, Vasi and Ubhaichari yogas

When benefics other than Moon occupy 2nd bhava from the Sun, they form Vesi yoga, occupy

12th from the Sun, they form Vasi yoga and if occupy 2nd and 12th both the houses from the Sun, they form Ubhaichari yoga. The person will be fortunate, famous, wealthy and happy. Please note, if malefics occupy they will give adverse / reverse results.

14.Sunpha, Anpha and Durudhara yoga

When planets other than Sun, Rahu and Ketu occupy 2nd house from the Moon, they form Sunpha yoga, when occupy 12th house from the Moon, they form Anpha yoga and when occupy 2nd and 12th both the houses, they form Durudhara yoga, an auspicious yoga. In all the situations the person is skillful, hard working, successful and wealthy. He becomes famous.

15.Kemdrum yoga

If there is no planet in 2nd and 12th houses from the Moon, this inauspicious Kemdruma yoga is formed. It lessens the benefits of other yogas. But it will not affect the person, if Moon is in own sign Cancer in kendras.

16.Chandra-Mangal yoga

If Mars combines with Moon, this yoga is formed. The person earns money through occupations such as selling liquor, black-marketing, keeping brothels etc.

17. Pushkal yoga

If an owner of a sign / house associated with lagnesh and Moon in kendras (1, 4, 7, 10 houses), this yoga is formed. The person is sweet spoken, sympathetic, wealthy and famous. Government honours and respects him.

18.Budhaditaya yoga

When Mercury and Sun both occupy a house, this yoga is formed. The person will be intelligent and knowledgeable. He will get a gazetted post in government. If this yoga is formed in seventh house, it brings dryness in family life and in fourth house person will be unintelligent and foolish.

19.Gajkesri yoga

If Jupiter is in kendras from Moon, this yoga is formed. It makes the person polite, generous, sweet spoken, wealthy and famous in the society or community. He may be head of a village or a city or a state.

20. Sakat yoga

If Jupiter is in 6th or 8th house from Moon, this yoga is formed. The person loses his wealth and honour several times and becomes poor and melancholy.

21.Kusum yoga

When Jupiter is in Lagna, Moon in 7th and Sun in 8th from Chandra Lagna, this yoga is formed. The person is reputed and distinguished. He may head a state or a country.

22. Kalanidhi yoga

If Jupiter occupies 2nd or 5th house in the signs of Mercury or Venus and is aspected by them, this yoga is performed. The person is highly passionate. He enjoys all comforts in life such as house, personal conveyance and other luxury items. He is sweet spoken and good-natured. His officers or authorities respect and regard him.

23.Anshavatar yoga

When the lagna is in movable sign and Venus and Jupiter both are in kendras, this yoga is formed. The person is intelligent, learned, balanced, virtuous, reputed and respected. He gets all luxuries in life and leads a royal life.

24.Sanyas yoga

When Moon or Moon occupied house owner is aspected by Saturn, this yoga is formed. The person is a great saint.

25.Mahabhagya yoga

When a person takes birth in daytime and Lagna, Moon, Sun all these three in odd Signs or when he takes birth in nighttime and Lagna, Moon, Sun are in even signs, this yoga is formed. He is most lucky and fortunate in every sphere of life.

26.Mokshaprapti yoga

If lagna is Sagittarius and Jupiter in Aries in Navansh, Venus in 7th house and strong Moon is in 6th sign, this situation confirms such yoga. The person gets Moksha after Purnau / Parmau or maximum longevity.

27. Nabhas yogas

The word Nabhas means the sky. These yogas are formed in the sky with the help of all the three constituents, namely all the seven planets (except Rahu and Ketu), 12 signs and 12 houses in a particular pattern, order or number. They influence the person through out the life. Maharishi Parashar indicted 32 Nabhas yogas divided in four categories defined as below.

A. Three Ashrya yogas

(i) **Rajju/Musall/Nall yoga:**

If all the planets in a birth chart are in 1,4, 7,10 signs, it is called Rajju yoga. The person tries to reach to his goal at the earliest. For this purpose, although he travels abroad one or two times, yet he is always seen unhappy and jealous. If all the planets are in 2, 5, 8, 11 signs, it is called Musall yoga. Such a person joins high-level gazetted post in Government and becomes famous, respected, prosperous and wealthy. If all the planets are in 3, 6, 9, 12 signs, it is called Nall yoga. Such a person is determined and stubborn but well in riches. He may be prone to accidents after the age of 32 years.

B. Two Dal yogas

(i) **Mala or Shrak and Sarp yoga**

If all the benefis Venus, Mercury and Jupiter except Moon are sitting in Kendra, they form Mala or Shrak yoga. Person gets all happiness in life. If all the malefics Sun, Mars and Saturn are sitting in Kendra they form Sarp yoga. Person always face miseries in life.

C. Twenty Akrati yogas

There are twenty Akraties (Images) such as Gada, Sakat, Pakshi, Shrangatak, Hul, Vagra, Yav, Kamla, Vapi, Yup, Shar, Shakti, Dand, Nauka, Koot, Chatra, Dhanush, Ardhachandra, Chakra and Samudra. Mainly six are defined below.

(i) **Shakti/Dand/Koot yoga:**

If all the planets are in 7th, 8th, 9th, 10th houses, Shakti yoga is formed, the person will be lazy, unhappy, poor and miserable, if all the planets in 10th, 11th, 12th, 1st houses, Dand yoga is formed, he will be neglected by close relatives and if all the planets in 4th, 5th, 6th, 7th, 8th, 9th, 10th houses in a line, Koot yoga is formed, he will be a miser and a terrible liar.

(ii) **Ardhachandra / Chakra / Samudra yoga:**

If all the seven planets except Rahu and Ketu commencing from any house but are in continuity or in a regular line, this Ardhachandra yoga is confirmed. The person will be handsome, magnetic, popular and working in a government office as secretary or minister. If all the planets are in all the odd houses Chakra yoga is formed. The person is like a king. If all the planets commencing from 2nd house are in even house Samudra yoga is formed. The person will be like a king generous, popular and wealthy. His kingdom may limit up to the distant area of seas and oceans.

D. Seven Sankhya yogas

(i) **Kedar / Pash / Dam / Veena yoga:**

If all seven planets are in 4 houses, Kedar yoga appears in mind, the person becomes a successful farmer helping his fellow creatures, if in 5 houses, Pash yoga is formed, person is wealthy, honest and just having devoted friends and faithful servants, if in 6 houses, Damini yoga is verified, the person is generous, kind and liberal always fond of helping others and if in seven houses Veena yoga is formed, the person may be good singer or dancer.

(ii) **Golak/Yuug/Shool yoga:**

If all seven planets except shadowy planets (Rahu and Ketu) are in one house, Golak yoga is confirmed, the person will be poor, illiterate and lazy. If in two houses Yuug yoga is formed, the person will be poor, filthy and an atheist and if in three houses Shool yoga is made, the person becomes a warrior, avaricious, fond of murdering or butchering.

Chapter
9
Life Related Important Aspects

9.1 Longevity - Long or medium or short

Longevity (span of life) of a person may be long or medium or short. It all depends on the location and situation of the placement of the planets in the houses and signs in a birth chart. After casting a birth chart of a male or a female, the most important thing is to know whether he / she has been bestowed with some longevity or not. It will be merely a fun, if we analyze and predict about all his / her facts of life such as health, education, profession, income, marriage, married life, status, dignity and overall personality without knowing his / her survival. Longevity may be short or shorter or shortest and if it is short or shorter or shortest, for a true astrologer, it is not good to predict things about one's future.

Though the 2nd and 7th houses are called the Marak (killer) houses, yet it is not necessary that the owners of these two houses or planets occupying or aspecting these two houses may also be Marak (killer). They may be or may not be. Generally longevity is related to the 1st and 8th houses. Therefore the positions, locations, combinations and connections of the owners of these two houses from Lagna and Chandra Lagna both, are to be viewed carefully.

Ordinarily it is experienced that one's ascendant (Lagna) is enough to know one's logevity of life but all the time it does not appear to be true. However, we can consider everything about it.

1. If Lagna is Taurus or Libra or Capricorn or Aquarius in a birth chart, the person may be short lived.

2. If Lagna is Gemini or Virgo, longevity may be medium or average.

3. And if lagna is Cancer or Leo, the person may be long lived.

As stated above longevity can be divided in the following three divisions

(i) Short span of life

Short span of life (Alpaayu) period is fixed from 0 to 32 years of age. But those, who live only for a few hours, days, months, years up to 8 years of age is treated as shortest span (balaristh). Those, who live more than 8 years and up to 20 years of age are called shorter span and those, who live more than 20 years of age and up to 32 years of age are defined or ascertained as having short span of life (Alpaayu yoga). Some astrologers are of the view that short span of life goes up to 42 years of age.

(ii) Medium span of life

Medium span of life (Madhyaayu) period is fixed between 32 to 64 years of age. Those, who live longer than short span of life up to 64 years of age, surpass a medium span of life. It is known medium longevity (Madhyaayu yoga).

(iii) Long span of life

Long span of life (Dirghaayu) period is ascertained from 64 to 96 years. It is named long longevity (Dirghaayu yoga). Those, who live more than 96 years of age and die in 100 years of age or after, that is named or called maximum longevity (Parmaayu).

While reaching to the above divisions, we need to see the positions of the owners of 1st and 8th houses. Are they powerful or weak? Powerful means exalted / positive / favourable in a sign / house and weak means debilitated / negative / unfavourable in a sign / house. In Vedic Astrology, the planets are to be counted powerful or weak in all the three signs / houses of Purush Trine / Aishwarya Trine / Prakrati Trine / Vairagya Trine.

If the owner planet is in an exalted sign with a strong position or in a powerful / positive / favourable location, it will be treated powerful in all the three signs. For instance if Mars is exalted in Capricorn, then it will be taken in the same manner in Taurus and Venus signs also. That means powerful in all the three 10th, 2nd and 6th signs / houses of Aishwarya Trine (Artha Houses) as already stated. Similarly if Sun is debilitated in

Libra sign i.e. in a weak position or weak / negative / unfavourable location, it will be treated weak in Gemini and Aquarius signs also, means that in all the three 7th, 11th and 3rd signs / houses of Prakrati Trine (Kama Houses). Reasons regarding longevity of life short / medium / long are given below

Reasons for Short span of life

Placements, aspects and combinations of the planets, which indicate short span of life of a person, means a very few chances of long survival, are given as under

1. If the owners of 1st and 8th houses are debilitated or weak.

2. If both 1st and 8th houses are in the aspect of debilitated or weak planets.

3. If owner of 1st and 8th houses being one and the same is placed in 6th or 12th house and is aspected by Saturn, the life may be short. It does in the case of Aries or Libra lagans, where Mars or Venus is one and the same.

4. If the owner of 1st house is debilitated or weak and at the same time, this house subject to strength of 8th house is occupied by a planet in debilitated situation or is aspected by debilitated or weak planet.

5. If the owner of 8th is debilitated or weak and 1st house is aspected by debilitated or weak planet.

6. If both the houses are occupied by the debilitated or weak planets.

7. If the owner of 8th house is debilitated or weak and 8th house is afflicted by two natural malefics by their location or aspect, life may be short lived.

8. If the Moon is in 1st sign in conjunction with or aspected by Saturn, and the owner of 8th house is in 1st house or Sun is debilitated or weak, life is short.

9. If the child is born at the time, when Moon is crossing in the area of a Gand Star i.e. in 1, 9, 10, 18, 19, 27 stars and owner of the Moon sign in 1st house.

10. If both the owners of 8th and 1st houses occupy 1st house.

11. If the Sun and Moon both are debilitated or weak and afflicted by malefics.

12. If the owner of a sign, where 8th house owner is posited, occupies 1st house with its owner, life is short.

13. If Rahu and Ketu are in 9th and 3rd or 5th and 11th Dharma and kama houses in conjunction with the owner of 1st house except Mars, life is short.

14. If the Sun and Moon both are debilitated in 5th and 9th Dharma houses and aspected by Saturn.

15. If malefics are placed in 2nd and 12th houses and not aspected by benefics.

Note Four Kundlis two of shortest, one shorter and one short span of life and two kundlis each one of Medium and long span of life of the natives, who died after their birth within the period of Alpaayu, Madhyaayu and Dirghaayu, with reasons identified, are given below.

1. Kundli No. 40 - Here lagna is Aries. Lagnesh and 8th house owner is one and same Mars located in 6th house with Rahu. Saturn is placed in 12th house and aspects Mars. Debilitated Jupiter is situated in 10th house influences lagna and also aspects Mars in 6th house, hence shortest span of life (Balaristh) almost three hours less than 8 years.

2. Kundli No. 41- Jupiter, the 8th house owner influences lagna and aspects its owner Sun in 4th house is placed with debilitated Moon and Mars, hence shortest span of life (Balaristh) almost three years less than 8 years.

BIRTH CHART   BIRTH CHART

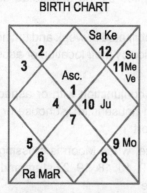

Kundli No. 9.1 (K-40)

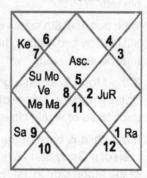

Kundli No. 9.1 (K-41)

3. Kundli No. 42 - Lagnesh Moon is situated in 6th house and is aspected by Saturn, the 8th house owner. Jupiter is placed in 8th house and aspects Saturn. Rahu and Sun both aspect 1st house (lagna). Thus lagna and lagnesh both are weak. Owners of 1st and 12th houses both are in Pap kartari yoga, hence shorter span of life (Yogaristh) i.e. death in teen age.

4. Kundli No. 43 - Debilitated Venus, the 8th house owner aspects lagna and Rahu aspects 1st house owner lagnesh in 6th house. Debilitated Sun with Ketu is situated in 8th house also, hence short span of life i.e. death in young age near about thirty-two years of age.

BIRTH CHART   BIRTH CHART

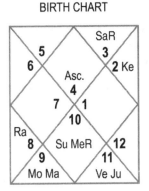

Kundli No. 9.1 (K- 42)   Kundli No. 9.1 (K-43)

Reasons for Medium span of life

Situations and combinations of the planets in sign / house of a birth chart are given below, which point out medium span of life (madhyaayu) of a person.

1. If lagnesh is weak, Jupiter is in one of 1,4,7,10,5,9 houses and malefics are in 6th and 8th and 12th houses, native completes average age.

2. If 8th house owner occupies 1 or 4 or 7 or 10 house, Mars in 1st house and Jupiter in 3 or 6 or 11 house, one completes average age.

3. If Saturn is in lagna, Moon in 8th and other planets in 11th house, one completes medium years of age.

4. If Jupiter is in lagna in its own Sagittarius sign and Mars, Rahu are in 8th house, one beats medium span of life.

5. If Moon is located with malefics in 6th or 8th house and owner of 8th house is in 7th house, he completes medium span of life.

6. If Venus is in 10th house aspected by Mercury, Jupiter and Moon, he completes medium years of age.

7. If Aquarius is lagna and Jupiter is in 8th house and malefics in kendras, he beats medium span of life.

8. If Venus is in lagna, Mercury and Saturn in kendras and other exalted planets in 3rd or 11th house, the person surpasses medium years of age.

9. If Saturn is in Lagna, Moon in 4th, Mars in 7th, Sun in 10th with Jupiter and Mercury with Venus in unfavourable houses, he surpasses medium span of life.

10. If lagnesh is Mercury, the person may complete an average span of life.

11. If Moon is placed in lagna in its own sign Cancer, Sun in 7th house and Saturn in 8th house, he completes medium span of life.

12. If a person is born in daytime and in his birth chart, malefics occupy 8th house from Chandra lagna, he enjoys medium span of life.

13. If Moon sign owner is placed in 8th house with malefics and 1st house owner in 6th house with malefics and is not aspected by benefics, he surpasses medium span of life.

14. If malefics from lagnesh are placed in 6th, 8th, 12th house but not in 8th house of birth chart, native beats medium span of life.

15. If Chandra lagnesh and Hora lagnesh both are placed in 8th house and 8th owner is in kendras, he beats medium span of life.

Note Two kundlis one is medium span of life and second is long span of life are given below:

5. Kundli No. 44 - It is a birth chart of medium or average span of life. The native died in his fifties.It is a Virgo lagna kundli. Owner Mercury is weak and afflicted by two malefics. Saturn is placed in lagna and aspects three benefics one Jupiter in 7th house and two Moon and Venus in 10th house. Ketu also aspects lagnesh Mercury and 8th house owner Mars. Hence lagnesh and owner of 8th both afflicted are responsible for average age.

6. Kundli No.45 - This birth chart belongs to Ex. president USA Late Mr. Richard Milhous Nixon. It indicates long span of life. The native enjoyed more than 80 years of age. Lagna is Leo and lagnesh itself is Sun placed in 5th house a trine house, a friendly house. The owners of 1st, 8th, and 10th houses are in kendra and in trine houses. From lagna Jupiter is in trine. From lagnesh Jupiter is in kendra. Thus four planets are occupying 5 th house. From lagna almost all the benefics are up 6 th house. These above facts gave him a long life.

BIRTH CHART   BIRTH CHART

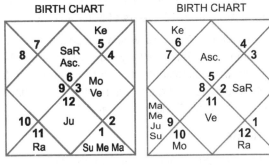

Kundli No. 9.1 (K-44)   Kundli No. 9.1 (K-45)

Reasons for Long span of life

Following locations, conjunctions and aspects on houses of a birth chart of a person indicate long span of life (Dirghaayu) and maximum longevity (Parmaayu).

1. If owner of 8th house and Saturn both are posited in 8th house, the person surpasses long longevity.

2. If owners of 1st, 8th, and 10th houses are placed either in kendras or in trines, he will live long.

3. If Saturn is placed in lagna, Jupiter in 4th and Sun in 10th houses with lagnesh, he completes long span of life.

4. If all benefics are located in 1st six houses from lagna and malefics in next 6th houses in a birth chart, the person is well educated, well behaved; virtuous and long lived (Dirghaayu).

5. If lagnesh is friendly to Sun, the person surpasses a long span of life.

6. From lagnesh, if Jupiter is in kendras, the person surpasses long span of life.

7. If ascendant is a dual sign and its owner is in Kendra or in exalted or in mool trikon or in own sign or in friendly sign, the native enjoys long life.

8. If lagna is Leo and four planets occupy 5th and 9th houses, the person beats100 years of age (Parmaayu).

9. If lagna is Taurus or Cancer occupied by Jupiter and three planets in the chart are in their exalted signs, one may complete 100 years or more than 100 years of age (Maximum longevity).

Note :There are more factors, which lessen the span of life such as death by committing suicides, death by judicial punishments, (sentence for hanging till death), assassinations / murders and also death due to natural calamities such as earthquakes, tornadoes, hurricanes etc. These deaths may be in any age. Read below carefully.

Death by suicide

Below are some placements, aspects and combinations of planets, which create suicidal tendencies in the mind of a person and he suddenly commits suicide. Adolph Hitler and his wife Eva Braun's suicide is an example.

1. If 1st and 7th houses both are occupied by debilitated planets.

2. If one out of 1st and 7th houses is occupied by a debilitated planet and second is receiving an aspect of debilitated planet.

3. If 1st and 7th houses are aspected by debilitated planets.

4. If Moon is aspected by Mars and Sun by Saturn, the person may commit suicide.

5. If the owner of the 1st house is a natural benefic and is located in 11th house with Rahu or Ketu and Sun and Moon both are aspected by Saturn.

6. If the owners of 1st and 7th houses are debilitated and weak.

7. If the owner of 7th house and Sun both are debilitated and Sun is aspected by Mars or Saturn also, the person commits suicide.

Death by punishment / assassination

There are some important situations, locations of the planets, which lead towards unnatural death. These may be because of judicial punishment or personal enmity. He may be hanged till death or assassinated or murdered. Pak. President Julafikhar Ali Bhutto died on account of judicial punishment, Smt. Indira Gandhi Prime-Minister of India and John Fitzgerald Kennedy President of USA because of assassination (murder) are such examples.

1. If 1st sign Aries is aspected by Saturn and Mars occupies 8th house.

2. If Saturn and Mars both occupy 7th house.

3. If the 8th house is afflicted by two natural malefics and Mars either occupies or aspects 8th house.

4. If the 8th house is weak and occupied or aspected by Mars.

5. If the Sun and Moon both are afflicted by themselves or by Saturn and Mars.

6. If Moon is placed in second natural sign Taurus and afflicted by at least two natural malefics.

7. If an exalted planet occupies 8th house and Saturn or Mars conjoins or aspects Moon.

Death by natural calamities

It is the part of Mundane Astrology. Though it pertains to the birth chart of a country or region yet brings loss of people and their resources. When Sun and Moon motions change, eclipses occur, the earthquakes and hurricanes develop, the nature shows her terrible face, many more livings and nonlivings die or destroyed. In last five years Samoa and Sumatra by Tsunami, China by Sichuan earthquakes, American state Louisiana by Katrina, Philippines by Ketsana were destroyed by hurricanes. More than 3,00,000 lives were lost, 10,00,000 were noted missing / homeless and amounting 10 billion US $ personal properties were lost and uncountable nonliving were out of sight. Only seawater was seen far off and no land or island. Every year in one region or the other of this world, this natural phenomenon occurs troubling livings / nonliving. Recently in January 2010 Haiti earthquake destroyed the vast area of island and two lacs people died and many more are still missiing

9.2   Education-General and Technical

The next important aspect after longevity is his / her education, whether he / she will take education in Humanities, Commerce, Science subjects or study technical subjects like Civil, Mechanical, Electrical engineering, or Computer etc. From lagna to fifth and ninth houses indicate the academic field of the person. Lagna indicates primary education, 2nd house further learning, 3rd house mental tendency, 4th house academic qualifications, 5th house the wisdom (the real education) and the achievements and 9th house the higher studies in a particular field. Thus 4th house is most indicative regarding academic qualifications / distinctions. We need to see the 4th house (sign) owner, occupyancy and that occupy planets 4th house / sign in the Birth chart and Navansh chart. For the branch of real education, bhava Madhya (centre) of 4th house in Cuspal Chart may also be examined to know. What type of sign is there, whether it is a fiery or earthy or airy or watery sign?

But Maharishi Parashar calls 5th house as the house of intelligence and knowledge both. Maharishi Jaimini uses 5th house as a house of education only. Therefore 5th house along with 4th house may be taken for college education and to know the talent of the person. However, following points may be studied in the birth chart of a person regarding his life long higher education, if all are found in an auspicious house and sign, he/she may be highly educated and if not, simply be a graduate or Plus two or matriculate or may be illiterate.

1. Lagna and lagnesh for sound body and sound mind

2. Moon's position for fertile mind

3. Venus for artistic abilities in early childhood

4. Mercury for inclination towards studies

5. Jupiter for knowledge

6. Sun for high ideals, spiritual values, success and educational achievements and Satunr for Education in foreign country

7. Ninth house and owner of 9th house for higher studies such as Research and PhD.

Please see four birth charts No. 46, 47, 48, 49 on next page. In two birth charts above seven factors are found fit, hence first two natives got higher education and now working as doctor and computer engineer in a foreign country. Remaining two don't have the above points. Hence one could do only graduation and the last was only illiterate.

(1) Kundli No. 46 - A qualified doctor, who studied medical science for a long period and did MBBS from India, DPM and MRCP from London and now he is a doctor serving in New Zealand.

(2) Kundli No. 47 - A qualified Engineer, who got his B.E. Electronics degree from India and did MBA from USA, now he is working with world fame Multinational Software Company in California (USA).

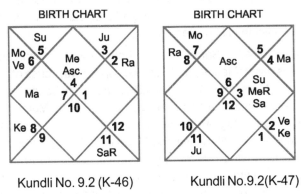

Kundli No. 9.2 (K-46)   Kundli No.9.2(K-47)

(3) Kundli No. 48-Regarding a household lady, who could only complete her Graduation.

(4) Kundli No. 49-An illiterate person, who could hardly know about alphabets.

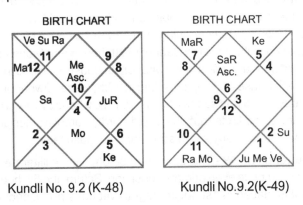

Kundli No. 9.2 (K-48)   Kundli No.9.2(K-49)

Kundli No. 46 - Lagna is Cancer an auspicious sign. Moon is placed in 3rd house of Mercury and Mercury is situated in lagna exchange of signs. Owner of 4th house Venus is sitting in 3rd house in friendly sign with Moon. From 3rd house both Moon and Venus aspect 9th house of higher studies. From lagna, the 5th house owner Mars is placed in 4th house and aspects 7th house its exalted sign, which is 5th from Moon, and its own 10th house of action and 11th house of income. Saturn also aspects 10th and 5th houses. Jupiter is situated in Gemini nearest to lagna and aspects 5th house and its owner Mars. Friendly Ketu is in 5th house increasing its strength. Sun is posited in 2nd house in its own sign. Due to all these aspects, he studied medical science and now he is a good physician in New Zealand.

Kundli No. 47 - Saturn, the 5th house owner is situated in 10th house with its owner Mercury and Sun and aspects 4th house of academic qualifications. Mars from 11th house also aspects 5th house in its exalted sign. Mercury is lagnesh also. From 10th house Saturn, Mercury and Sun influence 1st house (lagna). Jupiter is placed in Aquarius aspects Saturn, Mercury and Sun in 10th house and Moon in 2nd house. Venus, the 9th house owner is situated in its own sign Taurus in 9th house. From Chandra lagna Jupiter is in 5th house of Saturn and aspects Saturn, Mercury and Sun in 9th house of fortune. All these combinations, and aspects are enough to say that he studied Engineering. Actually he did B.E. from BITS India and MBA from USA. Now he is working in a world fame multinational software company in California (USA).

Kundli No. 48 - This birth chart belongs to a household lady. Lagnesh (1st house owner) Saturn is placed in 4th house of Mars and aspects lagna and friendly Mercury sitting there. From 1st house Mercury aspects Moon placed in its own sign Cancer in 7th house and Moon aspects 1st house and Mercury. Mars, the owner of 4th house is placed in 3rd house aspects 9th house and Jupiter sitting in 10th house. Owner of 5th house Venus is combust and sandwiched by malefics, hence weak and afflicted. These are some facts that she could hardly complete her graduation. She is not working anywhere and simply a house lady.

Kundliu No. 49 - This birth chart belongs to an illiterate man, who could not complete even primary education. Saturn, the 5th house owner, though it is placed in 1st house (lagna) yet does not aspect 4th or 5th house or any planet in the birth chart. It is sandwiched by malefics (Mars and Ketu). Lagnesh Mercury, owner of 4th house Jupiter and owner of 9th house Venus all are situated in 8th house giving no strength to the chart. Mars is located in Marak house and aspects 5th house and Sun in 9th house. Therefore these facts are enough to prove his illiteracy.

Note: Fifth house indicates university level education. It denotes talent and wisdom. As per views of Maharishi Parashar and Jaimini, if 5th house is in Shubh Kartari yoga and Jupiter conjoins, the person becomes genius and learned in many branches of education especially pertaining to science subjects. Jupiter in angles or triangles is also good for wisdom. If Mercury and Venus both are in 5th house, they provide success in academic achievements and a bright career. Thus benefics give sharpness in intelligence, while malefics such as Saturn, Rahu make dull and weak in education. We should also note the presence of constellation (nakshatra), where the owner of 5th house is situated and next to it the mahadasha of the planet. Favourable constellations (nakshatras) provide the opportunities for desired education.

Planets and Education

1. **Sun** – If in auspicious (benefic) signs   Political science and if in inauspicious (malefic) signs   Mathematics, Biology and Science of Medicines.   .

   Sun with Mars - Ear, Nose and Throat specialist Doctor or a Dentist;

   Sun with Mercury - Advocate, Accountant and Chartered accountant (types of subjects).

2. **Moon** – Fine arts, Music, Painting, Chemistry

   Moon with Jupiter   Politician, Minister, Administrator.

   Moon with Mercury and Venus   Author, Artist, Poet

   Moon with Venus   Actor, Film director, Architect or Agriculturist

3. **Mars** – Technical or Engineering Trades, Martial arts.

   Mars with Mercury   Mathematics

   Mars with Jupiter   Officer in Army or Police department, Economics, Financial subjects.

4. **Mercury** – with Jupiter   Astrology or Occult Education

   Mercury with Saturn   Industrial Management or Chemical institution related subjects.

Mercury with Rahu   Electronics and Computers related education.

5. **Jupiter** – Literature, History and Classical or Religious subjects, Banker, Manager, Priest or Orator.

6. **Venus** – Fine arts and Interior Decoration subjects. (TV worker, Announcer, Dress designer, Photographer, Painter and Contractor).

7. **Saturn** – Philosophy, Sociology, Labour laws, Politics and Leadership.

8. **Rahu** – Computers Education, Other Electronic Devices education, Researches, Foreign languages.

   Rahu with Moon - Philosopher, Psychologist and Doctor.

9. **Ketu** – Forensic Sciences, Criminology and Devotion to God, Detachment with the worldly fun and pleasures.

So for the university level education, we have to see the strength of the 5th house and its owner. If the owner of the house is powerful and house itself is not aspected by malefics he/she will get good higher education and if weak or aspected by malefics, he/she will be a bit literate. Following points may also be kept in view

1. If Mercury and Jupiter both are in 5th house, the person will be intelligent and knowledgeable. He will get higher education as per connections with others.

2. What type of subjects, he will prefer in education, it depends on the alliances of 5th house and   owner of 5th house with other houses and their house owners. Subjects are already given above.

3. If 5th house owner is in exalted, own or friendly sign / house or creating Rashi Parivartan yoga (exchange of signs / houses) and is not aspected by Saturn, the person will complete graduation in any of the branches / subjects already mentioned above planet wise.

4. If Libra is the ascendant and Saturn is the owner of 5th house located in 1st house in exaltation and not aspected by benefics,, the person will only stand up to 10th Standard (Matriculation).

5. If owner of 5th house neither in exaltation nor in its own sign and Saturn aspects the house or house owner, the person will not get any type of education. He will be illiterate or a bit literate.

Note: You better know this fact that 5th house is also the house of children. Therefore one thing is to keep in mind, if you get nonliving things in maximum numbers, living things goes out. Education is nonliving. If you are most educated, you may be childless. If you are less educated you may have children. Certain exceptions are or may be that one is well educated having children. However this will be mentioned in children's heading of this chapter.

9. 3 Occupation or Profession Business or Service

After getting education, one wants to enter in the field of profession or occupation. Profession can be his own business or in partnership. He may join service also either in a private concern or in a Government office. Astrological observations are as below-

For business

Strong connections and associations among 10th and 7th houses, their owners and Mercury indicate the business. It may be his own or in partnership. If 7th house is powerful than 10th house, person may start his business with a great zeal and if 11th and 2nd houses of gains and financial matters, their owners or planets occupying the houses also make a relationship with strong 7th house and 7th house owner, business may prosper with good earnings. But in no case lagnesh or Chandra lagnesh should be in 6th, 8th and 12th houses. Thus alliance of 10th, 7th and 11th houses is essential for business.

Persons in Business

There are two types of persons in business class (category), who help in starting and running the entire business

(1) Service Providers

First type of persons is service provider. They do not invest money, but they provide their services. They may be skilled and unskilled. Skilled are those, who are intelligent and learned being their 5th house is powerful for education and desired qualification. They may be technical consultants, machinist, skilled workers, lawyers, physicians and so on. Unskilled are those, who are little educated or uneducated as the 5th house is weak in their charts. They may be helpers, packers, weightlifters, drivers, cleaners etc. They all help in production, transportation and further extension.

(2) Investors

Second type of persons is investor. They take risk to invest money. They may be manufacturers and distributors. Manufacturers are those, who invest money in industries being a good combination of strong 7th, 11th and 2nd houses and house owners in their birth charts. They may be such as Tata, Birla, Dalmia, Ambani, Laxmi Mittal, Bill gates and so on. Distributors are those, who also take risk to stock the manufactured goods and help in marketing / selling those goods at the earliest. They may be whole sellers, retailers, petty shopkeepers and so on.

Note: Powerful 7th than 10th along with 11th house and planet Mercury make a person as a first category businessman, service provider and if 2nd house also relates with them, then he may be so called second category businessman, the investor. In such cases 5th house also adds its strength. If it is powerful in their birth charts, they may be skilled and knowledgeable service provider and / or risk taker investors.

For service

If 10th house with its owner is more powerful than 7th house and its owner and have good relations with 11th house, the persons join service. They may be administrator or office worker. They may join service in private concerns or in government. Administrators are those, who are highly qualified being their 5th house is stronger. They may be president, prime minister, governor, chief minister, secretary, commissioner, director, etc. They are highly paid and responsible for their office duties. Office workers are those, who may be qualified but not so powerful. They may be superintendents; clerks, cashiers etc. They serve in low salary paid jobs either in private concerns or in government. But there is a condition that lagnesh and Chandra lagnesh should not be in 6th or 8th or 12th house. These days youths prefer to join Private Concerns because of high salaries and other perks provided to them.

Persons in service

There are two types of job facilities for both the educated and the illiterate persons (1) Private Jobs (2) Government Jobs

1. Private Jobs

If benefics especially Mercury is stronger than Sun along with powerful 10 th house and its owner and have relationship with 11th house of gains and profits and its owner, the person may join service in private concerns. If he is well educated and skilled due to strong 5 th house, he may serve as manager, cashier and clerk in the office or if illiterate or bit literate and unskilled, he may work in labour type jobs.

2   Government Jobs

If significator Sun and 10th house is powerful and have relationship with11th and 6th houses and their owners and also person is qualified due to strong 5th house, he may join government service. He may be a gazetted officer, doctor, lawyer, army or police officer. He may be an IAS or IPS officer. He may be Secretary / Director / Commissioner / Administrator / Head of the state or country.

BIRTH CHART

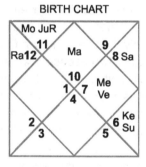

BIRTH CHART

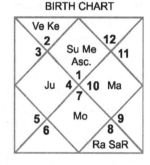

Kundli No. 9.3 (K-50)   Kundli No.9.3 (K-51)

Kundli No. 50 -It is a computer engineer's birth chart, who is working in a multinational company. The lagnesh is Saturn. It is placed in 11th house of gains and profits and aspects lagna and Mars which is placed there in lagna is in its exalted sign. Saturn and Mars both are forming Rashi Parivartan yoga. Mercury is placed in 10th house of vocation in sign Libra with its owner Venus. Both are benefics. Retrograde Jupiter being benefic is strengthening the position of 10th house, its owner and Mercury with its 9th aspect also. Rahu aspects Sun in 9th house placed with Ketu and is afflicting its position. This position of benefics led the native to join service in a private concern.

Kundli No. 51 - This kundli belongs to an IPS police officer working under central government. Its 5th house is powerful. The owner Sun is placed in lagna in its exalted sign Aries with Mercury. Lagnesh Mars is also situated in its exalted sign in 10th house and aspects lagna and friendly Sun and 4th house, where Jupiter the planet of wisdom is placed in its exalted sign and also 5th house. Mercury with Sun is forming Budhaditaya yoga in lagna. Saturn, the owner of 10th and 11th houses sitting in Scorpio sign of lagnesh Mars aspects Mars in 10th house of action. Hence 5th and 11th both the houses are powerful. He is qualified and wealthy.

Note: A weak 5th house but powerful 11th house may give a better life than a powerful 5th house and weak 11th house. Persons, who have the strong position of both the 5th and 11th houses, are the luckiest persons. They get every opportunity of benefits and respect. They lead a luxurious life.

9. 4 Marriages and Married Life or No Marriage

It is a known proverb that the marriages are made in the heaven. It means that the marriage has divine approval and blessings. Still one needs to look for the right mate (companion), only then he / she can find a true partner. Male and female are nothing but two aspects (two sides) of nature. Hence it is natural for them to be united into a holy wedlock.

In India, marriages are considered as a relationship, which may last till eternity. It needs (confers) equality on both the partners in matters of Dharma (Right Conduct), Artha (Financial Position), Kama (Sex Relations) and Moksha (Liberation).

Family is the essence that helps, define our very identity, devotion, sharing, warmth, love, belonging, laughter, smiles, caring, memories. Family means believing, loving and supporting each other. Family is the fundamental unit of society. This unit is facing a great danger today. More or less it is in the state of disintegration with more broken families everywhere. For this purpose, the sad state of affairs can be traced to the increasing fragility of marriages around the country.

Divorce, Separation and Single Parenting are the main problems in the society, which have damaged the happiness of young couples. Stable married life can be achieved through proper analysis of horoscopes of a bride and a bridegroom before marriage.

A marriage is not an invitation for brute sense of gratification, nor it is a civil agreement that affects only the two life partners but it means parents, society and the country as it is the base for creating a healthy future generation. Some times sweet love affairs may culminate in a successful marriage till life. It all depends on the adjustment of both the life partners, whether it is an arranged marriage or a love marriage.

Marriage is concerned with the 7th house from lagna and Chandra lagna. Significator (Karak) in case of male is Venus and in case of female is Jupiter. Both these planets may also be taken in view. Where are they situated in the birth chart? Are they influencing the 7th house or owner of the 7th house? What is the position of sign and owner of the 7th house in Navansh chart? The position of Mars may also be seen, that there is no Mangleek Dosh in the kundli. It means Mars is in 12th, 1st, 4th, 7th and 8th houses in the birth chart of a male or a female.

Types of Marriages

Because of increase in education in cities and countryside, the thoughts and things are changing. Now a days two types of marriages are prevailing in the country and out of country. These are arranged and love marriages. But in big cities love marriages are registered in courts. Astrological factors involved in both the types are as under:

(1). Arranged marriages

Arranged marriages depend on the will of the family and the society. These are arranged and managed by parents after personal meetings of both the parties of boy and girl and also relatives, to make the married life of the couple happy and fruitful. Following are the main points involved arranged marriages.

1. If owner of 7th house whether benefic or malefic is placed in its own house and none associates or aspects.
2. If owner of 7th house aspects 7th house and none else.
3. If owner of 7th house is powerful / positive / favourable and none occupies or aspects 7th house.
4. If 7th house and Venus both are in even signs.
5. If Moon or Venus or both are in 7th house.
6. If we count 7th and 11th houses from the house, where 7th owner is situated, there are benefics.
7. If Venus occupies its own sign or owner of 1st house is in its own house in 1st house or in 7th house.
8. If owner of 1st or 7th house or both are in 2nd house.
9. If owners of 2nd, 7th and 11th houses are in 1,4,7,10,5,9 houses and Jupiter aspects them.

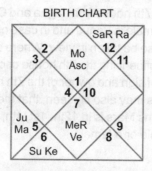

Kundli No. 9.4 (K-52)   Kundli No.9.4 (K-53)

Astrlogical Observations

Please see above kundlis No. 52 and 53 of an arranged marriage. In male birth chart, from lagna and Chandra lagna 7th house owner Venus is situated in its own 7th house with friendly Mercury and aspects lagna. From lagna and Chandra lagna both Moon aspects 7th house and its owner Venus. In female birth chart from lagna 7th house owner Mars aspects 7th house and also 7th house from Chandra lagna sign Taurus. From chandra lagna, 5th house, where the sign pisces is rising also conjoins friendly Mars in lagna and aspects 7th house. It is a successful marriage. They have two children in fifteen years and so far there is no problem in family.

2. Love marriage

There is hardly a human being, who doesn't have feelings of attraction to towards opposite sex. A strong 7th and 2nd houses and Venus indicate successful love affairs and further may culminate into a marriage so it depends on the will / wish of both the partners. If anyone out of the above mentioned planets is debilitated or weak then there will be no commitment of marriage. More about it is given below

1. If owners of 7th and 5th houses and Venus conjoin or aspect each other, Love marriage may be fixed.
2. If owners of 5th and 7th houses exchange their signs and form Rashi Parivartan yoga, love marriage may be fixed.
3. If Mars aspects Venus, love marriage may be fixed.
4. If Venus and owner of 7th house both occupy 5th house, love marriage may be fixed.
5. If Sun occupies 5th or 7th house, love marriage may be settled.

BIRTH CHART

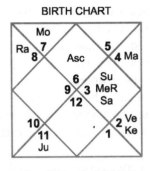

BIRTH CHART

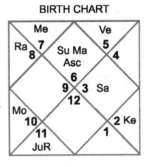

Kundli No. 9.4 (K-54)   Kundli No.9.4 (K-55)

Astrological Observations

Please see above two kundlis No. 54 and 55 of a love mariage. In male birth chart from Chandra lagna Jupiter is placed in 5th house and aspects 5th house owner Saturn and Moon. Owner of 5th house Saturn aspects 7th house of Jupiter in birth chart. From 11th house Mars aspects Moon, its own exalted sign Capricorn in 5th house and Jupiter in 6th house. In female birth chart Jupiter is placed in the sign of 5th house owner Saturn and aspects it. Owner of 5th house Saturn aspects 7th house of Jupiter in birth chart and also Venus, the owner of 5th house from Chandra lagna. Owner of 7th house Jupiter also aspects Venus. Moreover Sun and Mars both aspects 7th house. Therefore these are the main points of love marriage. This marriage is a happy marriage. So far thirteen years passed. They have two sons and are leading a comfortable, peaceful and luxurious family life in a foreign country. It looks that the future of the couple may be better, brighter and more successful.

Life after marriage

It is believed that after marriage, life may be happy and comfortable. Both the partners may respect each other and there may be no mishappening. But we feel in many cases unhappiness is seen that leads the partners towards separation (divorce). Both happy and unhappy life related astrological reasons might be noted as below

For Happy married life

Following placements, aspects and combinations are essential for happy married life. Therefore these are to be viewed carefully.

1. If Mars is placed in the same house or sign in both the male and female birth charts, their married life may be happy.
2. If Mars in the female horoscope occupies the same sign as Venus in the male horoscope or vice versa, it may give good physical attraction to both the life partners.
3. If Mars and Venus occupy the same house in both male and female birth charts, there may be better physical attraction between both the life partners and they may enjoy good conjugal happy life.
4. If the owner or ascendant or lagnesh is posited in a Kendra in male or female birth chart, and aspected by benefics, it may produce good marital happiness.
5. If there is an exchange of houses between the owners of 5th and 7th houses or close conjunction of both, he / she may get a devoted and lovely life partner.
6. If owner of 7th house is powerful and placed in its own house and aspected by benefics, the couple may lead a peaceful and happy married life.
7. If owners of 5th, 7th and 9th houses are occupying 1, 4, 7, 10 houses, the married life may be happy.
8. If the longitude of Sun in the male birth chart is equal to the longitude of the Moon in the female birth chart, it shows pleasant marital life.
9. If the longitude of Venus in both the male and female birth charts is similar, it also gives good marital happiness.
10. If Venus in male birth chart and Jupiter in female birth chart are situated in the houses other than 6th, 8th and 12th houses, their married life may be far better.
11. If Sun / Moon / Venus and 5th house or owner of 5th house are not aspected by Saturn, the married life of both the husband and wife may be happy.

For Unhappy married life

Following placements, aspects and combinations regarding unhappy arranged/love marriages may be as below

1. A weak 7th house leads to late marriage. The partnership may be quarrelsome, unhappy and after sometimes break / divorce / death may occur to one of the life partners.

2. Natural malefics play a very big role in disturbing happy married life, if afflicts 7th house or its owner.
3. A single malefic does not harm but two / three malefics harm and affect married life. It becomes painful.
4. Jupiter being a natural benefic may produce worst results, if it occupies 7th house or 10th, 2nd and 6th signs in a birth chart. Married life may be hell.
5. If 7th house owner is located in its exalted sign and Saturn aspects it, the married life is disturbed.
6. If the natural 12th sign Pisces is in 7th house and Sun, Mercury both occupy 7th house, the married life may be hard   hit and troublesome.
7. If a debilitated or weak planet occupies 7th house, it may show worst results after marriage.
8. If 7th house is in Paap Kartari Yoga or sandwiched by two / three malefics, the married life may be disturbed.
9. A weak 7th house and a debilitated Venus both may give a poor, unhappy, and disturbed married life.

Time of marriage

It is a general question. When will the boy / girl marry? Now normal age of marriages is 22 years to 25 years. Late or delayed marriages may take five years more i.e. 27 years to 30 years of age. Seventy percent marriages happen in dasha period of the owners of 1st, 5th, 7th houses. Sometimes marriages are also made in Rahu and Venus dasha period. Mostly the owner of 7th house helps in getting marriages done. Planets occupying or aspecting these houses also affect the time of marriage.

Following is the result of birth charts of a couple with longitudes of planets and mathematical formula to know the time of marriage. Please see Kundlis No. 52 and 53 on the previous page under heading arranged marriage. See table 9.4 (T-17) and calculated time of marriage on next page.

Note : Jupiter is powerful in both the charts, placed with 1st house owner. In Male chart it is in 5th house and aspects 1st house and Moon. In Female Chart it is in 1st house and aspects 5th and 7th houses.

Table 9. 4 (T-12) Knowing Time of Marriage

Longitude of planets	Male Born on Oct. 08 / 1968	Female Born on Nov.30 / 1970
Longitude of 1st house owner	04 – 17 – 04	06 – 16 – 21
Longitude of 7th house owner	06 – 21 – 06	06 – 02 – 15
Longitude of Moon	00 – 15 - 24	07 - 26 - 57
Total	11 – 23 – 34	08 – 15 – 33

In this case, we got the resultant as Pisces sign in male chart and Sagittarius in female chart hence both the charts are showing Jupiter's dasha. This dasha may be the time of marriage. Pisces is the 12th natural sign and relates to 12th house of Vairagya Trine or Moksha houses, covering Cancer and Scorpio signs in male chart, therefore, marriage may take place in dasha period of the owner of Pisces or Cancer or Scorpio sign. In case of female chart Sagittarius sign appears. It is 9th natural sign, comes in the category of Purush Trine (Dharma houses) covering Aries, and Leo signs. Hence marriage may take place in any one of these signs Sagittarius or Aries or Leo owner's dasha. Indeed marriage took place on 27 / 02 / 1994 in male and female charts in dasha periods of Moon and Jupiter.

No marriage

If we carefully see one's birth chart, following situations/locations apply to stop one's marriage or marriage does not take place.

1. If owner of 7th house is debilitated or combust or in 6th, 8th and 12th houses.
2. If owner of 7th house is located in 12th house and lagnesh and Chandra lagnesh both occupy 7th house, this situation stops marriage.
3. If Mars and Venus are placed in 7th or 5th or 9th house, there will be no marriage.
4. If Moon places in 5th house and two malefics in 7th and 12th houses, marriage is denied.
5. If Saturn and Moon occupy 7th house, they stop marriage of a person, either male or female.
6. If 5th house, its owner, Sun and Venus are aspected by Saturn directly or indirectly, there will be no marriage.

7. If Venus, Mercury, Saturn are in debilitated sign either in birth chart or in navansh chart, it stops marriage.

For this we can take Birth Chart of our respected Ex. P. M. Atal Behari Bajpai, who is unmarried because of the following locations of planets. See his birth chart No. 56 on page 274.

1. Owner of 7th house and Chandra lagnesh Mars both is in 6th house and in a weak position being in 12th sign (one out of Cancer, Scorpio, and Pisces signs).

2. Exalted Saturn from lagna aspects Sun in 3rd house and being adjoining to 2nd house, affecting Venus and Moon, where both are placed.

3. Saturn is powerful in lagna and aspects 7th house also.

4. Mars also aspects lagna.

5. Moon is placed in its debilitated sign.

9.5 Children, Male or Female and No children

After marriage, the next imperative and emotional need of the family is the children (living ones). This word (term) Children is concerned with the 5th house from lagna and Chandra lagna. Jupiter is the significator (karak) for children. The position of Jupiter is to be seen. The strength of the house is also to be viewed from Chandra lagna. The Cusp of the 5th house may be noted, where does it stand? It will be better that woman's birth chart is to be taken in consideration for children. Results may likely be more correct in comparison to the man's birth chart. If both the birth charts are available and considered, very good results may be achieved regarding children. Higher Education now changed the trends of the couples. They do not want more than two issues. They may be male or female. In some cases, children take birth at a later age. Sometimes it does that there is no issue and couple is childless. Such couples may adopt a child. Therefore there are three situations regarding children.

(1) Children and delayed children

(2) Male and female children and

(3) No children / adopt a child.

Children born earlier or later

After marriage children may take birth earlier or later. Born in later stage are called delayed children. Following are the astrological observations regarding birth of children.

A. Children may be earlier

1. From Lagna (ascendant) or Chandra lagna (Moon sign), if natural benefics are in 5th house or natural benefics aspect 5th house.
2. If a benefic being the owner of 5th house is in 5th house or aspects 5th house.
3. If owner of 1st house alone is placed in 5th house.
4. If Owners of 1st and 5th houses are in a positive / favourable house.
5. If Owner of 1st house is in 5th house and owner of 5th house in 1st house.
6. If both the owners 1st and 5th houses aspect each other.
7. If Jupiter is fortified and lagnesh is in 5th house.
8. If strong Jupiter is in 5th house and lagnesh aspects it.
9. If both the owners of 1st and 5th houses conjoin and place in their own or exalted or friendly signs.
10. If owner of 2nd house is strong and owners of 1st and 5th houses in conjunction with benefics are placed in 1,4,7,10 houses.
11. If owners of 1st and 9th houses are placed together in 7th house.
12. If Ketu is placed in 5th house only in Aries, Taurus and Cancer signs.

B. Children may be later in later age

1. If owners of 1st, 5th, 9th houses together are placed in 6th, 8th, 12th houses.
2. If benefics are in 10th house and malefics in 5th house.
3. If a malefic or Jupiter is placed in 4th or 5th house and Moon in 8th house.
4. If lagna sign is malefic with a malefic planet situated there and Sun is weak and Mars in an even sign.
5. If Jupiter in 5th house and owner of 5th house is in conjunction with Venus.

6. If owner of 5th house and Jupiter are in Kendra.

7. If Jupiter is in 9th house and owner of 5th house with Venus is sitting in 5th house.

8. If Moon is placed in own sign Cancer with a malefic or aspected by a malefic and Saturn aspects Sun.

9. If Rahu is situated in 11th house.

Male or female children

A. First born child may be a Male

1. If a male benefic is placed in 5th house and is also aspected by a male benefic.

2. If a male benefic being the owner of 5th house is situated in 5th house or aspects 5th house.

3. From Chandra lagna the owner of 5th is a benefic or aspected by a benefic and owner of 5th house is situated there.

4. If lagnesh is located in 5th house and Jupiter is strong or a strong Jupiter is placed in 5th house and lagnesh aspects it.

B. First born child may be a Female

1. If owner of 5th house being female benefic i.e. Mercury / Venus / Moon is weak or is aspected by a female.

2. If owner of 5th house is in 2nd or 8th house.

3. If even signs are there in 5th house and in navansh and Saturn or Mercury or Venus or Moon is located in these signs.

No children

A. The person may be childless

1. If Jupiter is situated in 5th house in debilitated or weak signs i.e. in Capricorn / Taurus / Virgo signs or aspects 5th house placed in these signs.

2. If owner of 5th house is in 6th / 8th / 12th house and aspects 5th house or owner of 6th/8th/12th house is in 5th house and aspects one of these houses.

3. If Moon and 3rd house owner or lagnesh and Mercury are situated in 1, 4, 7, 10, 5, 9 houses.

4. If Mars in 5th house, 5th house owner in 6th house and Saturn in Leo sign.

5. If Moon is in 5th house and all malefics in 8th and 12th houses.

6. If Jupiter is in 5th house, Venus with Mercury is in 7th house and malefics are in 4th house.

7. If owner of 5th house is debilitated or combust.

8. If Sun is in lagna and Saturn in 7th house there will be no child.

9. If Sun and Saturn aspect 7th house and Jupiter and Moon aspects 10th house.

10. If Sun, Saturn and 6th house owner are located in 6th house and Moon in 7th house not aspected by Mercury.

11. If Saturn, Mars, Sun and Jupiter are debilitated or weak.

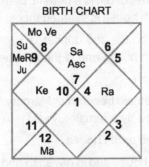

Kundli No. 9.4 (K-56)   Kundli No. 9.5 (K-57)

The above kundli No. 57 belongs to a retired bank manager, who has no issue. The factors regarding astrological observations are below:

1. Owner of 5th house Jupiter is placed in 12th house with Mars, the owner of 6th house and Mercury, the owner of 8th house.

2. From lagna Moon is situated in 6th house and from Chandra lagna Sun is also placed in 6th house. Thus both Sun and Moon are placed in malefic signs / houses.

3. Owner of 3rd house, Saturn is located in 9th house and aspects both the planets Sun and Moon from 9th house.

On the basis of above locations and situations of the planets, we can conclude that the native is childless on being medically fit along with his wife after passing more than forty years period of his marriage.

9.6 Financial Position - Wealthy, Mediocre, Poor

There are three types of people in the world. Firstly are those, who are very aristocratic and commanding immense wealth. Secondly are those, who are middle class people. They have enough to eat, but not much to spare. Thirdly are those, who are the poor and have only one meal a day. They are hard pressed for money. They have no house, no conveyance and no comforts for their existence. They haroiy earn money for one time meal. So far Middle class people or mediocre can hardly meet extra expenses having good salary. Therefore to know about the financial differences among the people, we can calculate it through following mathematical formula

Our great astrologers have fixed some Root Numbers for the seven planets to calculate Dhanu lagna. Planet root numbers are Sun 30, Moon 16, Mars 06, Mercury 08, Jupiter 10, Venus 12, and Saturn 01.

We take three Birth Charts given earlier for calculating Dhanu lagna. First we have to find out the Bhagyesh (owner of 9th house) from lagna and Chandra lagna both. How many planets occupying or aspecting those 9th houses? Are they benefics or malefics? Are they in angles or in trines? We have to note these things to possess a correct analysis. First we have to add Root Numbers of the owners of both the 9th houses and divide the total by 12 because there are 12 signs/houses in a birth chart. Then take the remainder and count up to the remainder number from the sign, where Moon is placed. That sign will be the real Dhanu lagna. See birth chart No. 52 on page 266 of this book.

When we see the birth chart No. 52 on page 266 , from Janam Lagna, owner of 9th house is Jupiter and from Chandra Lagna; owner of 9th house is also Jupiter i.e. one and the same, because Moon is placed in lagna hence

From lagna Jupiter Root Number	= 10
From Chandra lagna Jupiter Root Number	= 10
Total	= 20

After dividing the total 20 by 12, we get remainder 8. Now from Chandra lagna Aries (Mesh) in the birth chart, we have to count up to remainder numbers 8 to know special Dhanu Lagna. After counting from Aries (Mesh) 1 to 8, it comes Scorpio (Vrishchik). None out of seven planets is here. Owner of Scorpio (Vrishchik) Mars aspects it and none else. It is pure Malefic but Scorpio (Vrishchik) is its own sign and Mars is lagnesh also. Therefore we can conclude, he will be moderately wealthy (mediocre). Mars being in trines will give him wealth in its mahadasha / anterdasha.

Note - If any malefic planet is situated in any one of 3,6,8,12 houses from special Dhanu lagna, it may destroy the native's wealth in its mahadasha / anterdasha through unnecessary expenses and he may be poor. Following are some main astrological points, which brings poverty.

More Points of poverty

1. If the owners of 1st, 4th and 9th houses occupy 8th house, person suffers poverty.

2. If the owner of 2nd house is in 12th and owner of 12th house is in 2nd, the person is poor.

3. If owner of 2nd house is in 12th and owner of 12th is in lagna aspected by Marak planets, person is poor.

4. If the owner of 5th house is in 6th house and owner of 9th house is in 8th house aspected by a marak planet, the person suffers poverty.

The kundli No. 49 on page 257 belongs to a poor man, who remained poor. He passed a hard life. We see that from lagna the owners of 1st, 4th and 9th houses are located in 8th house. It shows poverty. Indeed, this person remained hand to mouth in his whole life and died.

More Points of Being Wealthy

1. If owner of 2nd is in 5th and owner of 5th house in 2nd or owner of 2nd is in 11th and owner of 11th in 2nd house, the person is wealthy.

2. If owners of 5th and 9th occupy their own houses, the person earns much wealth.

3. If owners of 2nd and 11th houses conjoin the owners of 5th and 9th houses, the person is wealthy.

4. If owners of 2nd and 11th occupy lagna the 1st house, the person becomes wealthy.

5. If owners of 1st, 2nd and 11th houses are placed in their own houses, the person is wealthy.

6. If Jupiter combines the owner of 2nd house and Mercury, the person will earn immense wealth.

On the basis of year 2009 report of annual ranking of wealthiest persons of the world compiled and published by Forbes Magazine dated March 11, 2009 William Gates is the first wealthiest person of the world this year 2009. Therefore we can take his example

When we see his birth chart (Kundli No. 6 on page 78) of this book. We find that from Janam lagna owner of 9th house is Saturn and from Chandra lagna owner of 9th is Mars, hence:

From lagna Owner of 9th Saturn Root no.	= 01
From Chandra lagna owner of 9th Mars Root no.	= 06
Total	= 07

The total 7 is less than 12; therefore it is not needed to divide by 12. Now counting from Moon sign Pisces up to 7 numbers, Dhanu lagna comes 6th i.e. Virgo sign, which is in 4th house of William Gates' birth chart. Mercury the owner of 4th and lagnesh both is placed here. It is in its exalted sign also. Moreover Mercury is in conjunction with Mars, the owner of 11th house of gains and profits and Moon the owner of 2nd house of financial matters aspects Mercury and Mars in 4th house from 10th house of action. This is the best equation to be the wealthiest. You may see his birth chart No. 6 on page 78 of the book.

Now we take a poor man's birth chart No. 49 given on page 259. We find that from Janam lagna owner of 9th house is Venus and from Chandra lagna owner of 9th house is also Venus, hence

From lagna owner of 9th Venus root no.	= 12
From Chandra lagna owner of 9th Venus root no.	= 12
Grand Total	= 24

The above grand total is 24. Now we have to divide it by 12 and after dividing it, remainder is zero (0). Further add this remainder zero (0) in the Moon sign Aquarius No. 11, and it will be the same 11. Therefore Moon sign Aquarius will be Dhanu lagna. It is in 6th house, where Rahu is also placed. Such Rahu gives illness and makes lazy and idle. Moreover as per astrological observations, this is a Virgo lagan kundli (birth chart). Such persons are often fond of changes moving here and there for livelihood. They work even in unfavourable situations to earn money to fulfill the daily needs of the family. See Astrological observation ahead

1. Lagna considerations

Lagnesh and Surya lagnesh both are placed in an inauspicious 8th house. Only Chandra lagnesh, the owner of a malefic house is occupying lagna bhava and that too between malefics (Pap kartari yoga). Thus lagna and Chandra lagna both are not in activation.

2. Placements, aspects and combinations

The owners of 1st house of body (health) Mercury, 4th house of comforts Jupiter and 9th house of fortune and religion Venus all together are placed in 8th house. This combination brings poverty since birth. This is not a good position.

3. Conclusion

From the early childhood, he had been poor. His parents were also poor. His 9th owner Venus is Marak (Killer) also being the owner of 2nd house. Hence he led a poor and miserable life till his death in 2007.

9.7 Foreign Travels

Nowadays foreign travels (Visits) have been very common. Air services made it most easy. We can reach from one corner to another within a day. Worldwide business facilities, higher studies and service needs are the factors for foreign travels (tours) for the benefit of new generation. Wealthy persons visit foreign countries only for fun and pleasure. You better know that 8th house indicates oceans and next to 8th i.e. 9th house shows traveling across the ocean in foreign lands. Thus foreign travels may be studied from 9th house. The 4th from 9th house is 12th house. It indicates houses / groups of houses (cities) of the foreign countries. If we want to reside in a foreign country, we have to consider it from 12th house. Lagna (1st house) and placement of lagnesh (the 1st house owner) are also important to be taken, while analyzing foreign travels in a birth chart.

The following are the important combinations (yogas), which interpret the foreign trips or residence of a person in a foreign country.

1. If malefics aspect 8th house or 8th house owner, the person travels to a foreign land.
2. If Sun or 1st house owner (lagnesh) occupies 8th house, person tours out of his country.
3. If signs in 9th and 12th houses are moveable or owners of 9th and 12th houses are in moveable signs, the person takes trips to a foreign land.

4. The owners of 9th and 1st houses are placed in their houses or exchanging their houses, the person travels abroad.
5. If Saturn is placed in its exalted or in its own sign and occupies 9th house, person travels to a foreign land.
6. If owners of 9th and 12th houses are situated in signs of those owners, which are seated in moveable signs, the person takes foreign tours.
7. If the owner of 12th house is in its exalted or in its own sign with a benefic, it shows foreign trips.
8. If the owner of 12th is placed in lagna and lagnesh is in 9th house, he travels abroad.
9. If owner of 12th is placed in a moveable sign in 8th house, the person takes foreign tours.
10. If owner of 9th or 12th house with owner of 4th house occupies 12th house, he visits foreign countries.
11. If owner of 12th house is in conjunction with or aspect by malefics, he takes foreign trips.
12. From 1st house owner or lagnesh, if 12th house owner is placed in 1st, or 4th, or 7th, or 10th house of a birth chart, the native travels abroad.
13. If the owners of 12th, 9th and 1st houses are placed in 3, 4, 7, 8, 11, 12 signs, the person visits abroad
14. If lagna and lagnesh both are in moveable sign and are aspected by a planet sitting in moveable sign, he travels abroad.
15. If owners of 1st and 9th houses both occupy 9th house, the person travels foreign countries.
16. From lagnesh the owner of 12th house is weak, debilitated and inimical to lagnesh, he takes foreign tours.
17. From Chandra lagna, if lagnesh occupies only 9th house, the person travels to foreign countries.
18. If Sun is situated with Moon or in 12th house from Moon sign, he travels abroad.
19. If Rahu or Ketu is placed in 3rd or 4th or 9th or 12th house, the person takes trips to foreign countries.
20. If owner of 12th house or 3rd house has an exchange with 9th house or owner of 9th house, he enjoys foreign trips.
21. If the owners of 12th, 7th and 3rd houses occupy their own houses or aspect their houses, the person takes foreign tours for his livelihood.

9. 8 Male / Female Diseases

Good and sound health is the foundation of a happy and prosperous life. Lagna bhava (1st house) indicates an individual's health. The sign in lagna, its owner, planets occupying or aspecting lagna and karak Sun are the main functionaries, which counts one's health. If lagna is powerful and its owner is in lagna or placed in an auspicious house in conjunction with or aspected by benefics, his health will be sound. He will be bold, active and hard working. If lagna and lagnesh both are weak and afflicted, the person may be idle and sick. He would not be successful in life.

An individual's structure depends on five elements. They are earth, water, fire, air and ether. Accordingly, he or she may become tall and short, lean and thin, fat or corpulent, solid and bold, active and hard working. Lack or loss of any one of the above five elements in one's body creates troubles and the person falls a prey to some disease.

Types of diseases

There are two types of diseases (ailments) ever seen in one's body, may be a male or a female.

1. Common diseases - These are seen for a short period such as fever, cough, cold, stomach pain, body pain, headache etc.

2. Chronic diseases - They take long time to recover such as heart problems, tuberculosis, cancer, leprosy, sugar, lunacy, eyes and teeth diseases, fits (hysteria) and gynecological diseases of females only.

Note: Gynecological diseases means disorders of female reproductive system. These are long lasting diseases.

It has already been mentioned in 1st chapter of the book that astrology is the science (knowledge) of time. Time is known as kaal in Vedic terminology. The time (kaal) is most valuable and powerful factor in casting birth chart of a person. Kaal is also personified as Kallpurush and twelve houses / signs of a birth chart are its limbs. Taking this recognition, we can easily interpret the limbs of human body, which are ruled by 12 houses and 12 signs and their owners. Limbs (parts), its rulers and the concerned diseases table 9.8 (T-13) is given ahead.

Limbs (Parts) of Body and their Rulers Table 9.8 (T-13)

Sr. No.	Limbs (parts) of Body	Rulers of Limbs	Diseases
1	Head, brain and body as a whole	1st house, 1st sign and their owners	Headache, Brain Tumor
2	Face, mouth, Right eye, throat and neck	2nd house, 2nd sign and their owners	Throat cancer, eye trouble
3	Arms, Right ear, hand and respiratory canal	3rd house, 3rd sign and their owners	Arms injury, Asthma
4	Lungs, Chest / breast and nipples	4th house, sign and their owners	Tuberculosis, breast cancer
5	Heart and the upper part of abdomen	5th house, 5th sign and their owners	Heart attack, Belly ulcer
6	Intestines, and lower part of abdomen	6th house, 6th sign and their owners	Intestine narrowness
7	Sexual organs, kidney, Uterus, Vagina and bladder	7th house, 7th sign and their owners	Kidney problem, Genitals
8	Scrotum or Testicles	8th house, 8th sign and their owners	Disease of sex related parts
9	Backbone, waist, hip and thighs	9th house, 9th sign and their owners	Backache, Hips jam,
10	Parts of the legs up to knees	10th house, 10th sign and their owners	Fracture and Pain
11	Left ear, Parts of the legs from knees to feet	11th house, 11th sign and their owners	Knee cancer, Elephantiasis
12	Left eye, Feet, sole, anklebone and heels	12th house, 12th sign and their owners	Feet injury, Bone fracture

Principles and rules

It is noticed, that malefics generally cause diseases, but sometimes benefics also give rise to diseases according to their physical properties in different parts of one's body. Following are the principles and rules regarding diseases.

1. All malefics / benefics cause troubles in the parts of the body according to their physical properties.

2. Fast moving planets Moon, Mercury, Venus, Sun and Mars give temporary diseases for a short period.

3. Slow moving planets Jupiter, Saturn, Rahu and Ketu give long time chronically diseases.

4. As per the elements, Fiery planets 1st, 5th, 9th sign owners Mars, Sun, Jupiter bring burns, pimples, boils, wounds, migraine, Severe headache, insomnia, fits (hysteria), etc. Earthy planets 2nd, 6th, 10th sign owners Venus, Mercury, Saturn give rise to paralysis, pains in joints, arthritis, rheumatism etc. Airy planets 3rd, 7th, 11th sign owners Mercury, Venus, Saturn cause mental tensions, despondency, deficiency, brainlessness etc., and Watery planets 4th, 8th, 12th sign owners Moon, Mars, Jupiter create tumor, cancer, cough, hysteria, perturbation, phobia etc. and very slow moving far off planets bring Ether related diseases. Thus, except Sun and Moon, remaining planets give two or more types of diseases. In giving rise to physical ailments, Rahu follows Saturn and Ketu pursues Mars.

5. When a fiery planet occupies earthy or airy or watery sign, its properties change. In the same way, if earthy places in airy or watery or fiery signs and airy locates in watery or fiery or earthy signs and watery sits in fiery or earthy or airy signs, they change their properties and give rise to different diseases.

6. These diseases start, when the owners, occupying and aspecting planets are weak and afflicted. We are to see, which are the weak and afflicted planets and where are they posited, the house and sign both.

Reasons of weak and afflicted planets

1. If a natural malefic aspects a house, may it be its own house, the house will be treated as weak and afflicted.

2. If an owner occupies its own house / sign and a malefic aspects, it will be treated as most weak and afflicted.

3. If a house / sign and its owner both are sandwiched by malefics, the house / sign will be taken as weak and afflicted.

4. If Rahu and Ketu, the malefic planets aspect 5th and 9th houses / signs from the house / sign, where they are situated, then that house / sign will be taken as weak and afflicted.

5. All the debilitated / combust planets are treated as weak and afflicted.

6. The planets, which are not the owners but occupy trio (6, 8, 12) houses, are always weak and afflicted.

7. A house or planet is heavily afflicted, when it is in 5th or 9th from Saturn and Mars combined placement.

8. Moon is treated weak, if it is nearer to the Sun or in the range of 72* degree or up to 3rd house from the Sun.

9. Natural benefics Jupiter, Venus and Mercury, if occupy 3rd and 6th houses and natural malefics Sun, Mars and Saturn, if occupy 4th, 5th, 9th houses lose their 50 percent strength.

Example Kundlis No. 58, 59, 60, 61, 62, 63

Kundli No. 58 The boy is mentally retarded since infancy, when Moon mahadashha and Rahu anterdasha was in operation. He was simply 2 ½ years old. Now he is 10 years old. He can neither talk nor eat food. His mother feeds him. Facts are that debilitated Saturn from 7th house aspects 1st house (lagna) and the sign Libra and its owner Venus is in 9th house. Saturn situated in 1st sign Aries aspects its owner Mars in 1st house and Moon in 4th house. Sun and Mercury associate it. Rahu also influences lagna and aspects Moon and Jupiter from 10th house. Therefore these facts show this disease.

Kundli No.59 The girl is a patient of knee cancer since June 2008. Now she is 15 years old. This problem diagnosed, when in Mars mahadasha, Jupiter anterdasha started. Here in 11th house debilitated Mercury is sandwiched by Mars and Sun. Mars is also weak in 12th sign and the owner of 11th house Pisces is aspected by Mars, Sun and lagnesh Venus. From 7th house Rahu aspects 11th house and planets Mars and Mercury sitting there and also lagna and Moon placed in lagna. From 10 th house Saturn, the 11th sign owner, aspects both lagnesh and Chandra lagnesh Venus. These are the real facts for the knee cancer. Her life is in danger. She is always on bed and unable to move.

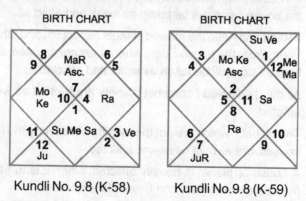

Kundli No. 9.8 (K-58)   Kundli No.9.8 (K-59)

Kundli No. 48   Please see this kundli on page 257. The native is now almost 40 years old. Debilitated Saturn is placed in the 4th house and 4th house owner Mars is in 3rd house. Saturn and Mars both aspect 6th house of disease. Saturn alone aspects 10th house and Jupiter, the owner of 12th and 3rd houses sitting there. Mercury owner of 6th and 9th houses is placed in lagna. Ketu aspects debilitated Saturn. Thus weak malefic Saturn made her a tuberculosis patient, during Venus mahadasha and Mars anterdasha period. After Mars anterdasha, she became quite well. But now after a month or two she suffers from severe headache. It may be due to Saturn's aspects or because of side effects of medicines she took for a long period.

Kundli No. 60   Here is a case of Kidney failure. The person is 40 years old. In his birth chart lagna is Leo occupied by Ketu and Mars. From 9th house debilitated Saturn, the 6th and 7th house owner aspects 7th sign and its owner Venus is in 3rd house and Jupiter is sitting there in that house. From lagna Mars, the owner of 9th house aspects 7th house and Rahu (sitting there) and from 7th house Rahu aspects 3rd house that belongs to Venus sitting with Jupiter. Moon has no planet on both the sides and Ketu aspects it. All these factors afflicted his kidney. He has been operated and new kidney is planted, given by one of his family members.

BIRTH CHART   BIRTH CHART

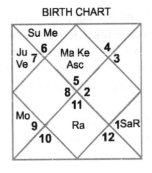

Kundli No. 9.8 (K-60)   Kundli No.9.8 (K-61)

Kundli No. 61 It is a case of brain hemorrhage. While getting down from a bus far away his own city, he suddenly fell and died this year at the age of almost 64 years. Here Ketu is occupying lagna by its 5th aspect on Moon, and sign Aries and also aspects the Sun, the natural owner of 5th house and sitting in its own 5th sign Leo. Sign Aries owner Mars is in 6th house of disease and aspects Sun sitting in 9th house. From 7th house Saturn also aspects Sun in 9th house. All the above facts and aspects gave him a setback or fatal blow giving brain hemorrhage in Rahu mahadasha and Moon anterdasha.

Kundli No. 62 It is a case of jammed hips joints. Here 9th house is weak being Jupiter the owner itself in debilitated position gripped by Mars and Ketu. From 7th house Saturn the owner of 10th sign aspects 9th house and planets occupying the house and also Moon in 4th house. From 3rd house, Rahu also aspects 9th house and planets occupying there. Mars aspects Moon in 4th house. These facts are enough to prove the disease of Jammed Hips joints. He could not move after this disease always lying on bed. It continued till death.

BIRTH CHART   BIRTH CHART

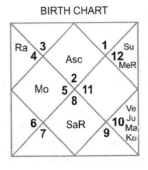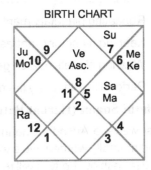

Kundli No. 9.8 (K-62)   Kundli No.9.8 (K-63)

Kundli No. 63   It is a case of lost eyesight. The owner of 2nd house Jupiter is debilitated and Ketu aspects it, Moon is sitting there, hence 2nd house is weak. From 3rd house Jupiter, the owner of 2nd house aspects 7th house. Saturn from 10th house insluences the owner of 2nd sign Venus in lagna and aspcts 2nd sign Taurus in 7th house. Mars and Rahu both malefics also aspect the owner of 2nd sign Venus sitting in lagna. Sun is also debilitated and malefic. Saturn aspects it. Because of all these facts, the person lost his one eye in his childhood.

9.9 Remedial Measures

Vedic astrology is such a complete system that it shows not only the possibilities of certain events, but also provides us ways to enhance the positive events and deflect the negative or challenging ones. But it is the subject of devotion with full faith and belief. Devotion with full faith and belief gives us remarkable results and relief. Faith and belief makes us healthy and mentally strong to meditate and to fill the vacuum in the universe. By aushdhi snaan (Herbal bath) we refresh our body and by chanting planetary mantras, we allow and remind the universe to fill the missing areas. It is an easy but a powerful source to defeat the challenges. They help us in changing our views and actions. Keeping planetary yantras at home or in wallet are next to mantras. They encourage one's energy, happiness and faith. They weaken the disease. Gemstones are after yantras to enhance the power of planets, which are weak in one's birth chart. In the same way, performing planetary fire rituals such as Grahpuja (worshiping planets), Hawan, Yagya etc. also create the atmosphere of positivity and favour us. Therefore we will now discuss five.most common remedies or therapies as below-

1. Aushdhi Snaan (Herbal bath)
2. Repeating planetary mantras
3. Keeping planetary yantras
4. Wearing planets related gemstones
5. Performing planetary fire rituals Grahpuja, Hawan, Yagya etc.

(1) Aushdhi Snaan (Herbal Bath)

First we take Aushdhi Snaan (Herbal Bath). If we are unhealthy (sick) and mentally worried, we can take herbal bath for a week or so to clean and refresh our body. It will recharge our energy to go ahead. It will lessen our weakness and disease. What type of herbs we need for favour of weak and afflicted planet? Herbs are available at a grocery shop. While purchasing herbs, quality of the herbs may be maintained with the help of capable herbal chemist.

Before taking herbal bath, we have to see and note the time of planetary nakshatras and one day earlier put all the herbs in the Ganges water (clean river water) for 24 hours. And the next day after putting out the herbal waste mix this river water with more clean water and take bath to refresh the body.

Planetary Time and Herbs for Herbal Bath Table 9.9 (T-14)

Sr. No.	Planets	Nakshatras	Herbs
1	Sun	Kritika, Uttra Phalguni, Uttra Ashadha	Manshila, Elaichi, Deodar, Kesar, Khas, Mulethi, Swetpushpa, Laal Kaner, Madhu, Amaltas, Kamal, Kumkum. Saathi Chawal
2	Moon	Rohini, Hasta, Shrawan	Doodh, Dahi, Ghee, Cow Dung, Cow Urine, Gaj Madh, Sankh, Seepi, Sweth Chandan. Sfatic. Chaandi. Moti. Kamal
3	Mars	Mrigshira, Chitra, Dhanishtha	Vilb Chaal, Laal Chandan, Dhamni, Laal Pushpa, Singruf, Maal Kaangni, Molsiri, Belphal, Jatamaansi, Hinglu Saunth, Saunf
4	Mercury	Ashlesha, Jyeshtha, Revti	Cow Dung, Akshat, Phal, Gorochan, Madhu, Moti, Swarn, Swet Sarson, Harar, Anvlaa, Jaayphal
5	Jupiter	Punarvasu, Vishakha, Poorva Bhadrapad	Malti, Pushpa, Swet Sarson, Mulethi, Madhu, Sweth Pushpa, Damyanti Patra, Gular
6	Venus	Bharni, Poorva Phalguni, Uttra Ashadha	Elaichi, Manshila, Suvraksh Mool, Kesar, Kum kum, Kathal, Jaayphal, Mooli Ke Beej
7	Saturn	Pushya, Anuradha, Uttra Bhadrapad	Kale Til, Surma, Loh Baan, Dhamni, Saunf, Muthra, Khilni, Satpushpi, Lodh, Nagar Motha, Khas
8	Rahu	Ardra, Swati, Shatbhisha	Loh Baan, Til Patra, Mutthra, Gaj Dant, Kasturi
9	Ketu.	Aswani, Magha, Moola,	Loh Baan, Til Patra, Mutthra, Gaj Dant, Chaag Mutra

One time all planetary aushdhi snaan

If we want to take one time all planetary aushdhi snaan (herbal bath), we can use Lajvanti, Deodar, Koot, Kangani, Khilla, Jav Sarson, Haldi, Sarvopdhi, Lodh, Nagar Motha, Sarpankh herbs for taking bath.

(2) Repeating Planetary Mantras

Secondly we take planetary mantras, which are a part of the traditions of Vedic astrology. Mantras are based on simple physics. By mantras we remind our universe to fill the vacuum or missing areas. If we want to enhance the energy of a planet to make it more positive and favourable to us, we will have to repeat relevant planetary mantra daily to the extent of numbers given in the table considering it as a regular (routine) duty of an ideal life. We are not to spend money on it. We are to set our mind to meditate for facing our challenges. Definitely, we will win in strengthening the power of a planet and then receive the energy from it. It is most essential in case of weak and afflicted planets. We are to continue incantation of mantras to make the weak planets powerful so that they may further transfer energy to us. Surely we will get success, wealth, prosperity and popularity. Mantras related to each planet with numbers and timings are given in the table. Some items planet-wise, which can be donated to the helpless old and disabled people to get blessings from them with a view, that it will also add a kind of energy to the planet and back to us, are also given. Mantras in Sanskrit Language Given below. English Version See table 9.9 (T-15) on next page.

Mantras in Sanskrit Language

Surya Mantra	ऊँ हां हीं हौं स: सूर्याय नम:
Moon Mantra	ऊँ श्रां श्रीं श्रौं स: चन्द्रमसे नम:
Mars Mantra	ऊँ क्रां क्रीं क्रौं स: भौमाय नम:
Mercury Mantra	ऊँ ब्रां ब्रीं ब्रौं स: बुधाय नम:
Jupiter Mantra	ऊँ ग्रां ग्रीं ग्रौं स: गुरुवे नम:
Venus Mantra	ऊँ द्रां द्रीं द्रौं स: शुक्राय नम:
Saturn Mantra	ऊँ प्रां प्रीं प्रौं स: शनये नम:
Rahu Mantra	ऊँ भ्रां भ्रीं भ्रौं स: राहवे नम:
Ketu Mantra	ऊँ स्रां स्रीं स्रौं स: केतवे नम:

Planetary Mantras Table 9. 9 (T-15)

Sr. No.	Planets	Mantras	Numbers and Timings	Items to be donated
1	Sun	Om Hram Hreem Hraum SA Suryay Namah	7000 at Sunrise	Wheat, Red cloth, copper
2	Moon	Om Shram Shreem Shraum SA Chandramase Namah	11000 at Sunset	Rice, white cloth, silver
3	Mars	Om Kram Kreem Kraum SA Bhaumay Namah	10000 at Sunrise	Wheat, red cloth, copper
4	Mercury	Om Bram Breem Braum SA Budhay Namah	9000 before Sunset	Moong, Green cloth, gold
5	Jupiter	Om Gram Greem Graum SA Guruve Namah	19000 at Sunset	Grams, yellow cloth, salt
6	Venus	Om Dram Dreem Draum SA Shukraya Namah	16000 at Sunrise	Rice, white cloth, silver
7	Saturn	Om Pram Preem Praum SA Shanye Namah	23000 at Noon	Oil, black cloth, Iron coin
8	Rahu	Om Bhram Bhreem Bhraum Sa Rahve Namah	18000 at Midnight	Coconut, blanket, Sesame seeds
9	Ketu.	Om Sram Sreem Sraum SA Ketve Namah	17000 Before Sunrise	Coconut, Blanket, Sesame seeds

(3) Keeping Planetary Yantras

Planetary yantras are also a source of energy and mental peace. They change our minds and give good thoughts. If we are scary, they make us strong and powerful. Every planet has its own yantra given in almanacs. We can prepare it at home on a square piece of paper sheet or a metal sheet with the help of kesar (safforn) colour pen, if not, we can purchase from a religious items selling shop. We may keep it every time with us for better results.

Table - 9.9 (T-16) Tables of Planetary Yantra

MERCURY YANTRA

7	12	5
6	8	10
11	4	9

VENUS YANTRA

9	14	7
8	10	12
13	6	11

MOON YANTRA

5	10	3
4	6	8
9	2	7

JUPITER YANTRA

8	13	6
7	9	11
12	5	10

SUN YANTRA

4	9	2
3	5	7
8	1	6

MARS YANTRA

6	11	4
5	7	9
10	3	8

KETU YANTRA

12	17	10
11	13	15
16	9	14

SATURN YANTRA

10	15	8
9	11	13
14	7	12

RAHU YANTRA

11	16	9
10	12	14
15	8	13

(4)Wearing Planetary Gemstones

Wearing planets related gemstones is next easy Vedic therapy. I have personally seen and experienced the remarkable results of the gem of a particular planet. Once my son's friend, who was not getting his promotion and also losing his lended money came to me and asked, "Uncle, what should I do now?" I advised him to put on Blue Sapphire ring. He put on a ring of Blue Sapphire and soon he got his promotion and recovered lost money. One more client was advised to put on a ring of Yellow sapphire and he was happy to see the desired results in no time. In case of gemstones one thing is most notable, that stones used should be natural in order to assure their molecular integrity and they should not be dyed, heat-treated and colour enhanced. Gemstones sold in jewellery stores are not the type of stones, which you want to use for Vedic purposes. These days prescribing a gemstone has been tricky type of business, hence better to take advice from a nearest capable astrologer and experience the stone for a few days or weeks and see if you are gaining benefits. Gemstones can be set in rings for both gents and ladies. Ladies, if they so desire or like pendants, they can get the gemstones set in their pendants. But mind it pendants should be uncovered from backside so that it may touch a part of body. Pendants can only be worn in the neck. Two to six carats weight gemstone is enough for a young or adult. Planetary gemstones rings or pendants when and where should we put on is given in the table 9.9 (T-17) below-

Planetary Gemstones Table 9.9 (T-17)

Sr.No.	Planets	Gemstones		Day	In
		High price	Low price		Finger
1	Sun	Ruby	Red Spinal	Sunday	Ring
2	Moon	Pearl	Moonstone	Monday	Index
3	Mars	Red Coral	Carnelian	Tuesday	Index
4	Mercury	Emerald	Green Tourmaline	Wednesday	Pinkie
5	Jupiter	Yellow Sapphire	Yellow Topaz	Thursday	Index
6	Venus	Diamond	White Sapphire	Friday	Middle
7	Saturn	Blue Sapphire	Tanzanite	Saturday	Middle
8	Rahu	Hessonite	Orange Zircon	Saturday	Middle
9	Ketu	Chrysoberyl	Cat's Eye	Saturday	Middle

Diseases cured by Gemstones

Planets have their own physical properties, whether they are malefics or benefics. They influence one's body every time. Slow motion planets are more troublesome than fast moving. As per remedial measures, we can use gems of good quality to lessen the problem of disease. Certain diseases and curable gems are listed below. See table 9.9 (T-18) given below-

Some Diseases and Gemstones Table 9. 9 (T-18)

Sr.No.	Disease	Gems
1	Joints Pain	Red Coral 9 Carat and Yellow Sapphire 5 Carat
2	Asthma	Emerald 6 Carat, Yellow Sapphire 5 Carat White Pearl 6 Carat
3	Pleurisy	Red Coral 6 Carat, Yellow Sapphire 5 Carat
4	Myopia	Red Coral 6 Carat, White Pearl 6 Carat
5	Blindness	Ruby 6 Carat, White pearl 6 Carat
6	Blood Pressure,	Acidity White Pearl 6 Carat
7	Tuberculosis, Sugar	Ruby 6 Carat, White Pearl 6 Carat
8	Epilepsy or Fits or Hysteria	White Pearl 6 Carat
9	Skin Diseases	Red Coral 9 Carat, Cat's eyes 6 Carat
10	Indigestion	Emerald 5 Carat, Hessonite 6 Carat
11	Heart problem	Red Coral 6 Carat, Ruby 6 Carat
12	Cancer	Yellow Sapphire 5 Carat
13	Genitals problems	Diamond 1/2 Carat or Blue Sapphire 3 Carat
14	Mentally Retarded	Emerald 5 Carat, White Pearl 6 Carat
15	Kidney Problem, Diabetes, Liver, Tumor	Yellow Sapphire 6 Carat
16	Pimples, Boils, Piles	Red Coral 6 Carat
17	Failure of Nervous System	Emerald 5 Carat
18	Liprosy or Leucoderma	Diamond 1 / 2 Carat
19	Jaundice or Diarrhea or Leucoria	Cat's eyes 6 Carat
20	Insomnia	Hessonite 6 Carat
21	Bone Fracture	Ruby 6 Carat

(5) Performing Fire Rites and Rituals

To perform planetary fire rites and rituals is the fifth important common remedial measure for domestic happiness. A capable priest well versed in this practice should perform the above performances such as Grah Puja, Sarvdev Puja, Hawan, and Yagya etc. By offering scents, seasonings, fruits, and flowers with wide range of Sanskrit shloks, the priest tries his best to appease a weak and unfavourable planet on your behalf. Sometimes your presence is necessary and sometimes not. Fire rituals can also be performed to enhance the wealth and prosperity and to remove the obstacles of the way of your progress. Marriage ceremony, Child's Birth ceremony and many more other ceremonies for health, happiness, charity, success and wealth are also performed from time to time in the family.

In very olden days king Dashrath of Ayodhya performed Putreshthi Yagya and after a year, his queens gave birth to four sons. After Dashrath his eldest son Shri Ram the then king of Ayodhya performed Rajsuya yagya to be a Chakravarti king all over the world. Therefore yagya power is remarkable, if it is performed with devotion and belief. You may argue that these are myths but in the opinion of the author, if we will act honestly, the benefits definitely come to our doorstep.

Glossary
Vedic words and English words

Author used several Vedic words in the book. Mostly English words are given with the Vedic words in Brackets. Some Vedic words are used frequently such as lagna, lagnesh, bhava, bhavesh, navansh on several pages of this book. Please see below, the glossary of Vedic words with English words and their meanings, where it is necessary:

Vedic Words	English Words	Vedic Words	English Words
Aishwarya	Riches	Hawan	Fire Rites
Aishwarya Trine	A Tringle of 2-6-10 Houses	Janam Kundli	Birth Chart
		Janam	Birth
Asuras	Demons	Jyotish	Astrology
Anterdasha	Sub Period	Kaal	Time
Artha	Wealth	Kaal Purush	Time Personified
Artha Houses	2-6-10 Houses	Kama	Fun & Pleasures
Astangat	Combust	Kama Houses	3-7-11 Houses
Aushdhi Snaan	Herbal Bath	Kanya	Virgo
Badhak	Opposite	Kapha	Phelgm
Bhava	House	Karak	Significator
Bhava Kundli	House Chart	Karan	Total Longitudes
Bhumiputra	Mars		Moon Minus Sun
Carat	A Measurement of Gemstones	Kark	Cancer
		Karmas	Actions
Chakra	Chart	Kendras	1-4-7-10 Houses
Chakravarti	Emperor	Kumbh	Aquarius
Chandra Langn	Moon Sign	Kundli	Chart
Chandra Lagnesh	Moon Sign owner	Lagna	Ascendant
Charan	Segment	Lagnesh	Onwer of
Dainik	Daily		Ascedant Sign
Dasha	Period	Lok Shabha	Lower House
Dharma	Religion	Maharishi	Saint
Dharma House	1-5-9 Houses	Makar	Capricorn
Dhanu	Sagittarius	Mangleekdosh	Mars in 12-1-2-4
Duskarma	Bad deeds		7-8 Houses
Grahas	Planets	Marak	Killer
Guru	Teacher	Maya Moh	Worldly Affairs

Vedic Words	English Words	Vedic Words	English Words
Mesh	Aries	Sarini	Table
Meen	Pisces	Sarvdev	All Gods
Mritsanjeevani	Knowledge of	Shubh Kartari	Between
Vidhya	reanimating a	Yoga	Benefic Planets
	dead	Shubh Varga	Planet aspected
Mithun	Gemini		by Benefic
Moksha	Salvation	Simha	Leo
Moksha House	4-8-12 Houses	Suras	Deity
Nakshatra	Constellation	Surya Lagna	Sun Sign
Navansh	A Divisional	Surya Lagnesh	Sun Sign Owner
	Chart	Trikona	Trine
Nivrati	Complete	Tula	Libra
	Surrender	Upnishad	Hindu Holy
Pap kartari Yoga	Between Malefic		Books
	Planets	Vairagya	Far from Worldly
Pandit	Priest		Affairs
Parivartan	Conversion	Vairagya Trine	4-8-12 Houses
Pitta	Windy	Vaar	Day
Prakrati	Temperament	Vatta	Airy
Prakrati trine	3-7-11 Houses	Vedas	Hindu Holy
Pravrati	Nature		Books
Puja	Worship	Vedant	Holi Book
Purush	Person	Vedic	Pertaing to
Purush Trine	1-5-9 Houses		Vedas
Puranas	Hindu Holy	Vimshotri Dasha	A Period of
	Books		120 Years
Putreshthi -	Hawan for	Vrishbha	Taurus
Yagya	a Birth of Son	Vrishchik	Scorpio
Rajsuya Yagya	Hawan to be	Yama	God of death
	a Famous King	Yog	Total Longitudes
Rajya Sabha	Upper House		Moon Plus Sun
Rashi	Sign	Yoga	Combination of
Sanskar	Conversion		Plenets
Sanyasi	Saint	Yoni	Birth